Chus Martínez

Transient Global Amnesia

I. The Mind as Method

I have been always fascinated by reports of dramatic changes in human behavior caused by banal activities: swimming, immersion in cold water, intercourse, coughing, straining to defecate (I found this in several medical reports), heavy lifting, sawing, and pumping. Imagine emerging from a swim in cold water totally unable to lay down new memories. You remain conscious, aware of who you are, able to talk, able to maintain a coherent stream of thought but unable to remember. These attacks, which last for about eight hours, are called Transient Global Amnesia, and the syndrome was first described in 1956. My idea is simple: try to think about the working method of Mario García Torres not as "another way of telling" but as one of these transient global amnesia attacks—in other words, as a conscious fabrication of perceptual conditions that actively affect the way we read images in relationship to text but, more important, with the memories that all these materials carry with them.

For more than a decade now, García Torres has been developing a conceptual method that, on the one hand, is continuously informed by and refers to the conceptual art practices of the 1960s and 1970s and, on the other, tries to free historical legacy and individual cases and references from memory so that we can situate the works and ourselves in a new present.

García Torres's works address the fact that being aware of the world is a result not of the existence of the mind but rather of the mind in action. Intellect is not an eye that observes us from some vague place within but rather the very fact of thinking. If, as Ludwig Wittgenstein argued, the mind-matter duality does not in any way reflect reality and is instead a metaphor that serves to foster belief in the notion that thought, will, and imagination are not made of the same substance as the world, objects, and things, then we must search for a new logic by which to understand the relationship between the world and ideas. Nothing can happen beyond the real, and the real can be grasped only through language. This means a revolution: since we cannot expect to find correlations between the world of ideas and the world of matter, our questions cannot hope to find answers and instead become sense-making operations. Like untangling a knot, solving a problem involves changing the order of the known.

In the work of García Torres, there is a constant concern with understanding how we access knowledge through perception and how art relates to knowledge. His work reflects on ways of going beyond modernist concerns with the relationship between man, word/image, and world. He finds in conceptual art practices and visual memory a method toward the production of new relationships with space and time and with images and words. Therefore, I think it is not accurate to position his work in the line of those who try to expand our ideas of these practices and produce "new narratives." The work is not—or not primarily—about the possibility of telling a different story but is instead a deep research into how what is linguistically articulable relates to the nonlinguistic aspects of the pieces, images, and imaginations that take place in them.

Art becomes, then, a complex site through which we locate our relations of intelligibility with others and with the world. Art becomes the mode by which our assumptions about aesthetics and politics undergo a radical transformation. In García Torres's practice art is situated in that whirlpool of change in paradigm; the work asks how, through artistic practice, we can approach problems related to the interpretation of the world, on the one hand, and to the interpretation of the modern subject, on the other. How do we address the world in a time that could be described as post-word and even post-image?

II. It Is Not Storytelling

Often García Torres's videos and installations are described as visual essays. In his work we have become familiar with the complex interplay between fictional elements, a trip he did not take to Afghanistan to follow the path of the Italian artist Alighiero Boetti (1940–1994) in the country, with work and materials that were the result of an actual search for Boetti's traces in Kabul. I am referring here to *Shar-e Naw Wonderings (A Film Treatment)*, 2006. All through his different works we sense a trust in the possibilities offered by speculative exercises created from the entanglement between research and imagined material. But I would propose to read the result not as a story or an artist's tale but as the manufacturing—almost as an artisan would craft something—of an experience that is very common in the work of García Torres: heterogenesis.

The word refers to abnormal organic development, but I use the notion here to name a continuous effect created by the fact that García Torres does not follow the logic of language, the logic of the sentence. He mimics it all the time but just to remind us of the dependency between conceptual art practices and the linguistic turn and, much more important for today's situation, that we cannot reduce conceptualism to the substitution of textual material for visual content or vice versa. His works do not present us with new or alternative readings or fictional readings of visual materials. What he is always stressing is the radical and complex disparities that different codes produce among materials. Like an expert botanist, García Torres exercises heterogenesis in his particular way of cultivating text, image, sound, and—fundamentally—the displays he uses in each and every carefully calculated presentation of his works. His interest in form responds to the need to find radical, post-avant-garde, after-modernist ways of creating a new grammar of relations among elements and text, images and space.

García Torres's work follows very strictly the rules of the period of the dominance of formalist understandings of art in order to create an appearance of communicability. But distinct from historical conceptualism or modernism, art today is not a place to produce theoretical statements again or to formulate ethical and political attitudes without turning ideological or dangerously simplistic. However, it seems crucial to García Torres's way of understanding the role of art and artists to rehearse the use of concepts, projects, ideas, and political messages in order to inquire into the role thought has played and will play in the way experience is being reformulated. His works possess the language of affirmative aesthetics so characteristic of the modern trust in language and progress to very soon produce a sense of amnesia that empties them of any utopian vision, leaving them alone as material to reflect on the way knowledge evolves today. They reflect on the particular trust that form nourishes among an "aesthetically" educated urban class. This is the same social class that for some centuries has aspired to have its values reflected in the institutional milieu that art and artists should enhance and protect.

García Torres's working method sheds light on the particular cultural environment that privileges an idea of historical transmission based on steady centers, institutions, and human centrality. The way he deals with all

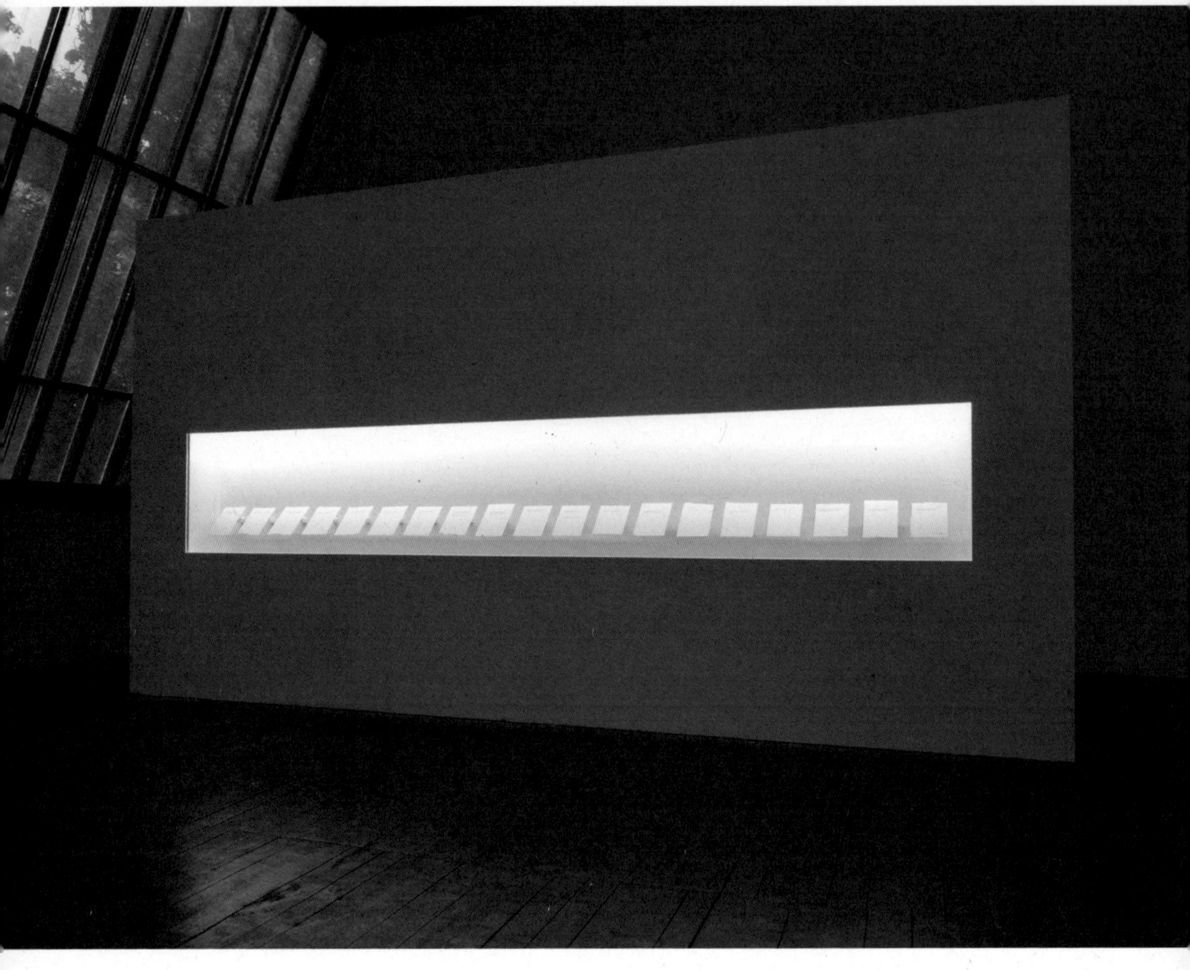

Shar-e Naw Wanderings (A Film Treatment)
2006, nineteen sheets of thermal paper, dimensions variable
Thyssen-Bornemisza Art Contemporary Collection, Vienna

the questions of late modernity and conceptual art, however, implies a deep interest in what this project does not know how to deal with, all the detours that lead not to the museum but to the fields, to the community, to the materials... in other words, to the possibility of a different type of intelligence. The work seems to insinuate many times a need to observe the hinterlands of conceptualism. It is possible to think about the work of García Torres as a proposition to reconsider the role of certain discourses, certain ideas of form and art that do not play any role outside a certain urban context. What if all this incredible rehearsal of the formal, aesthetic, conceptual, institutional, and linguistic attitudes that certain art presupposes establishes a corpus, an enormous collection, in order to investigate the subordination of certain acquired ideas of art and thinking to the urban environment?

This is a hypothesis of mine based on his radical, if you will, insistence on us looking from a certain perspective. It is this insistence on studying the sensibility a certain way of looking back to face the now that seems to pose questions: How should art address all that is left out of this universe? How does historical transmission work outside the cities and institutions, outside the archives and the disciplines that collect and remember art for the citizens?

III. Universes Are Made of Worlds: Singularity

It is very difficult to answer the questions above. But I will invite you to keep them in mind, since I believe the work explores the controversies and sociopolitical aspirations of an art that is mutating and now is moving not only toward language and storytelling but also toward nature and the structure of life outside the cities. How to argue this through specific works is still unclear, but García Torres's interest in media sparks an interest in art and all the contexts in which art functions, but it also sparks a fascination, to say the least, with all those other places where art seems not to function.

García Torres's work pays special attention to the important moment when a new media identity is being formed. A time defined not by "media" or by the preeminence of the image but by a new understanding of the strange coexistence of technology with culture. Technology is part of a new natural and social order in which we are active participants but also designers, in an unprecedented dialogue with instances of the technological but also of the natural order. This new order—call it the condition of technological singularity—marks an order where intelligence is not the realm of the human but a circumstance of the machine and organic life. Once intelligence is not exclusive to humans, the "eye" also gains a dimension beyond the organ we use to see with to name the possibility of feeling images not only to distinguish them. Experience has been transformed in ways that we are unaware of because we do not share a common verbal language with animals and computers. We know that they sense, however, and that their sensing involves organs we do not even know about. The nature of our participation in a project is epistemological but also political—since it implies that the reordering of the relations we establish with many types of otherness, natural and technological, is pressing. In this new status quo, art, and an art aware of this new real, is essential to interpreting our way of being in the world and what the term agency (our capacity to interpret reality and to act accordingly) means to each of us.

In this context, Alain Badiou made a fundamental distinction— one that Giorgio Agamben later referred to. In political terms, we need to differentiate between being members of and being included in a project. Being members of a project, party, and so on has to do with the order of presentation. Inclusion in a project or party, in contrast, takes place at the level of representation. For Badiou, a term (an individual) is "normal" (in the epistemological sense, clearly) when he or she is present and represented in a situation. That is, when he/she is both represented in the structure of the political system (state, party) and present in that structure. An anomaly appears when this second function does not occur, when an individual is represented without being present. This complex question of presence versus representation is key to understanding the logic of the entire oeuvre of García Torres. The works embody the search for balance between the different levels on which an individual can define herself or himself within a system but also involves the question of, on the one hand, how to strike a balance within a given political, social, or economic system and, on the other, how to create exceptions within this system to make it possible for other systems, other logics of social organization, to appear.

The notion that several worlds coexist is fundamental to the discursive opening that contemporary philosophy formulates. The question lies in determining on what basis we can say that many worlds exist while investigating the role that different systems of symbols play in each of those worlds. The often repeated call for a pluralistic world is not at all related to the coexistence of systems that articulate reality in completely different ways. In a world capable of encompassing multiplicity and contrast, there is the possibility that together many similar worlds form a sort of unit. This difference is key when considering what Derrida postulates. The possibility of a new logic resides in the conception not of a single world, as it were, but of several worlds and in being able to think of and interpret them. As we become used to the idea that apparently antagonistic logics cannot be reduced to a single logic and can, feasibly, coexist, we must not seek the unit in a certain thing, but in a new global organization that can take the shape of the types and functions of images and of the systems of knowledge that these images create.

This is the task of García Torres's work: universes are made of worlds, and the worlds themselves can be constructed in many ways. Through a very personal and specific method of interpreting image, function, repetition, and excess, his work constitutes a critical act, in both the most trivial and the most complex sense of the word: it is a critique of life. At the point where vision and speculative organization converge, the possibility of things being different arises. But the critical dimension of the work also has a more specific, practical sense. It represents an exhibitive reflection both on our cultural heritage and on the context from which the work originates. From within the profane, the trivial, and the domestic, an interest in the meaning of being can be discerned. The potential of the work lies in turning the backdrop of irrationality—which always borders the world as we know it—into something productive. Mistakes are pure potentiality; without them, without this opening up to the unknown, thought would not be possible.

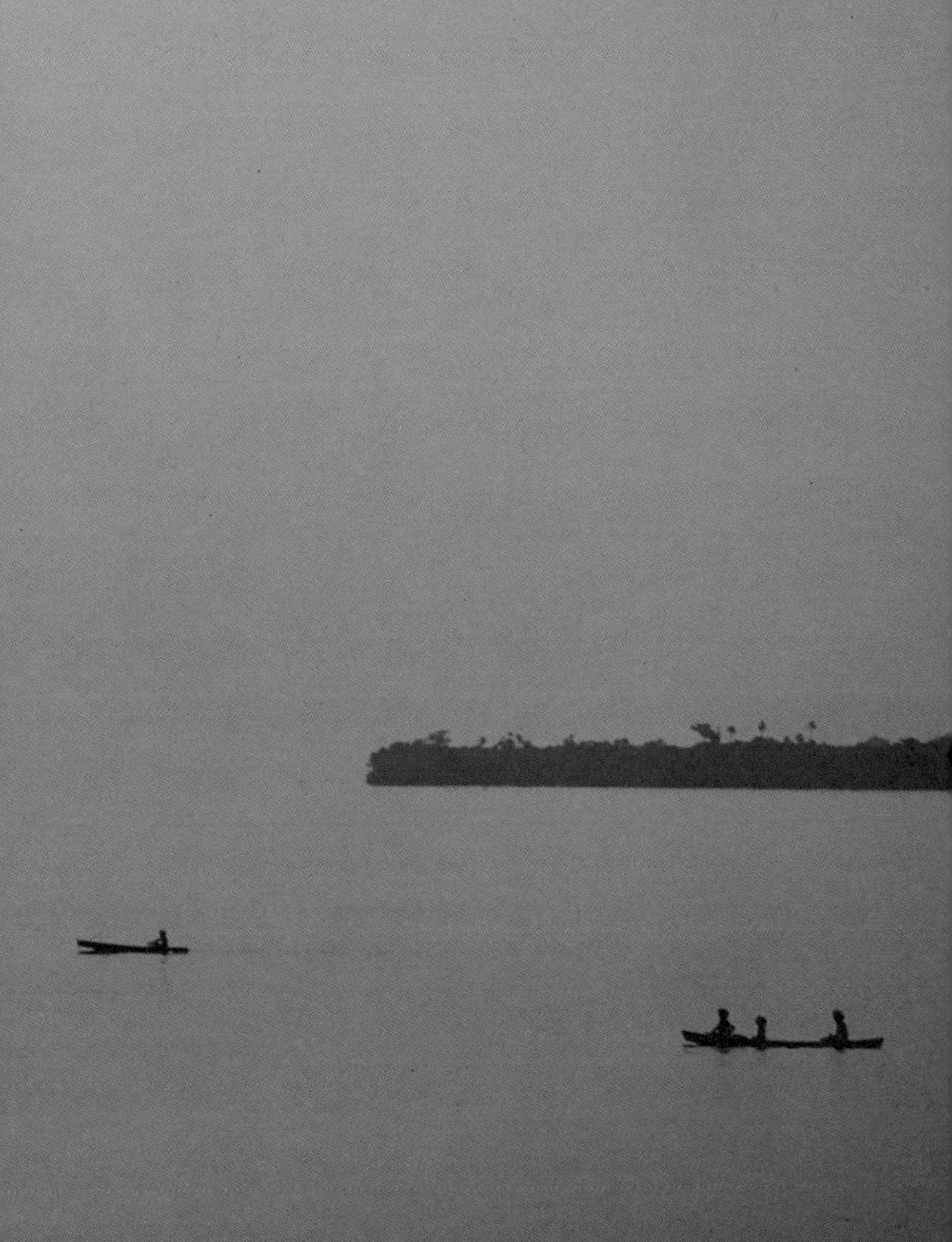

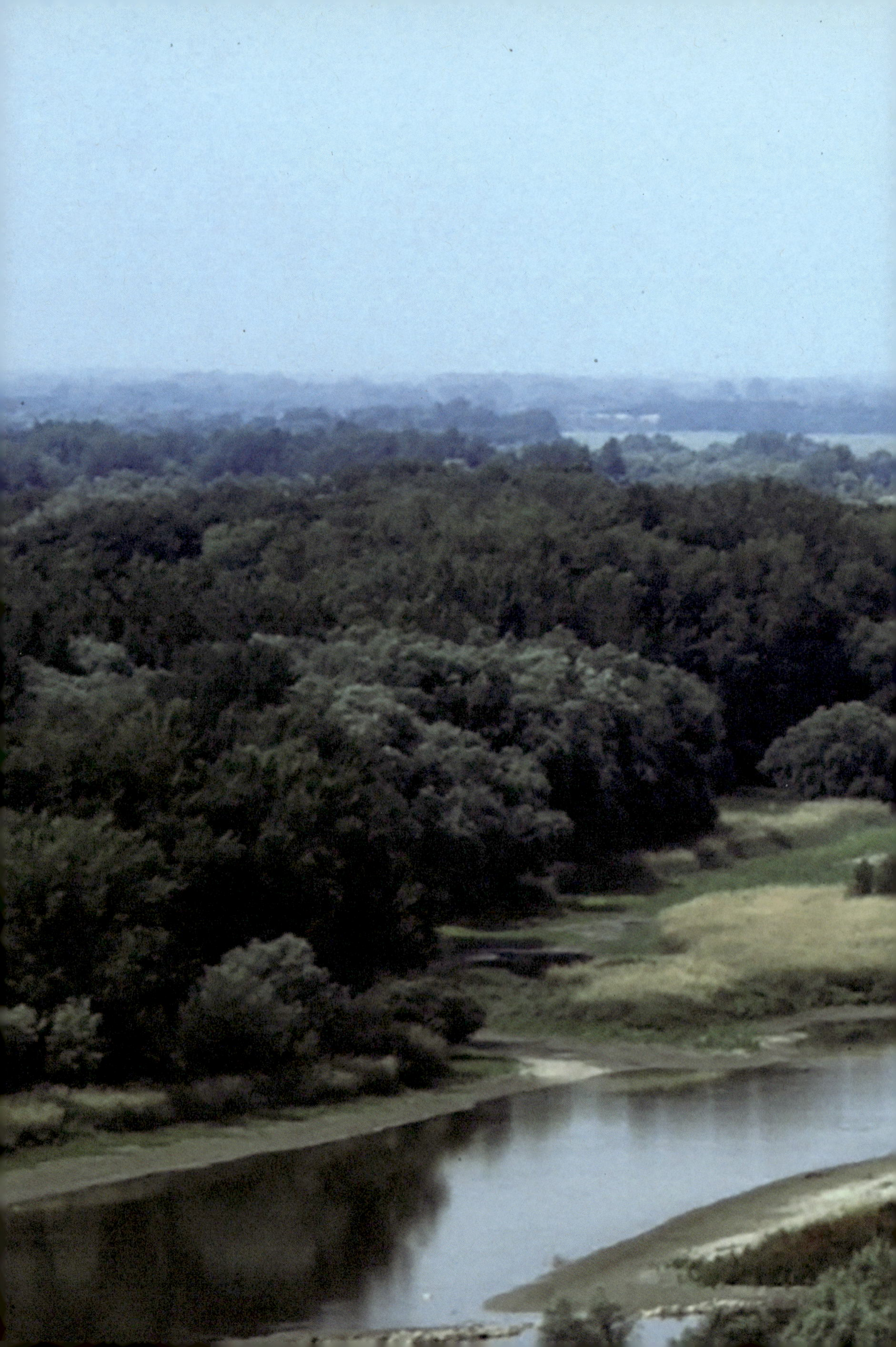

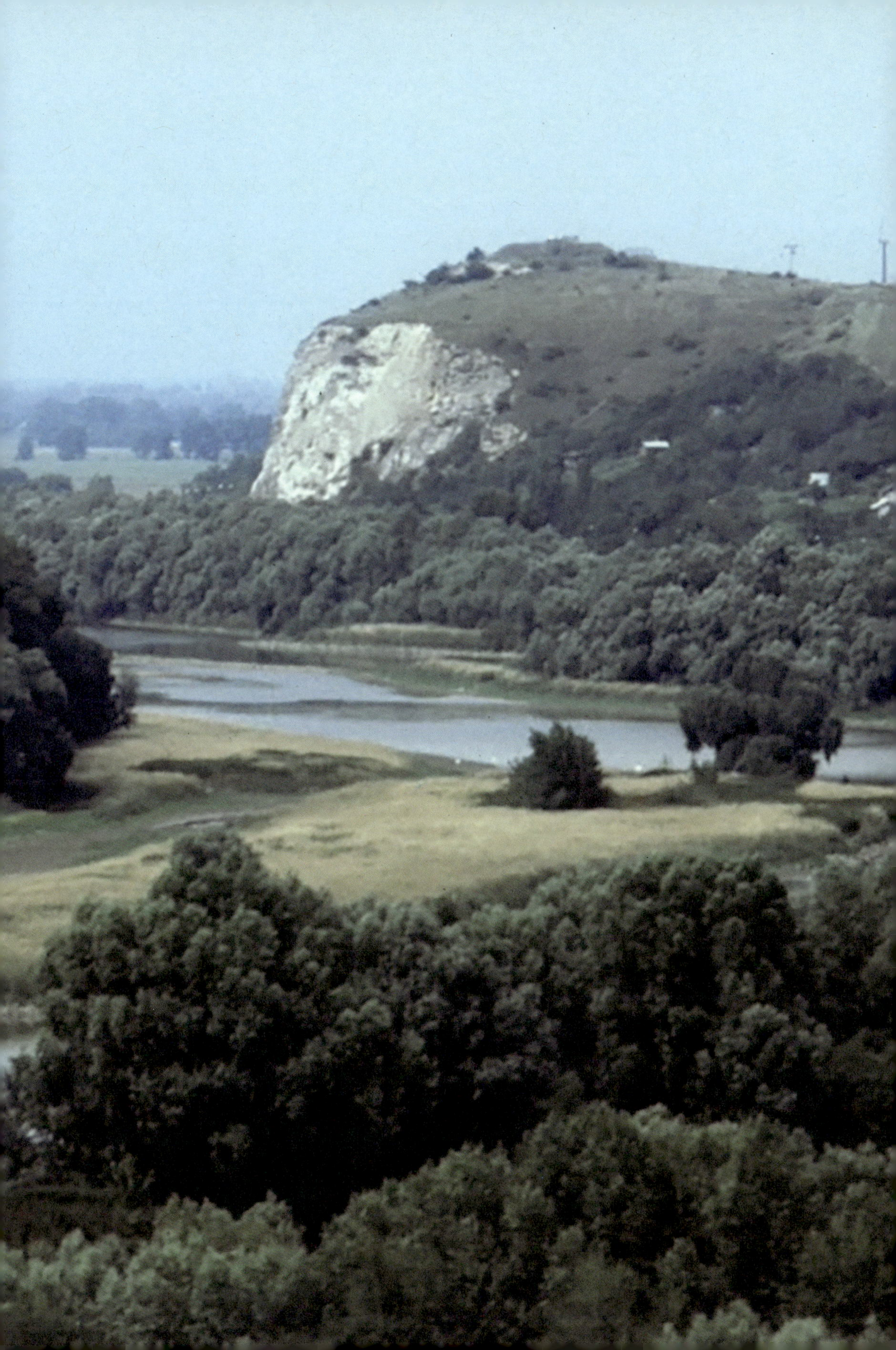

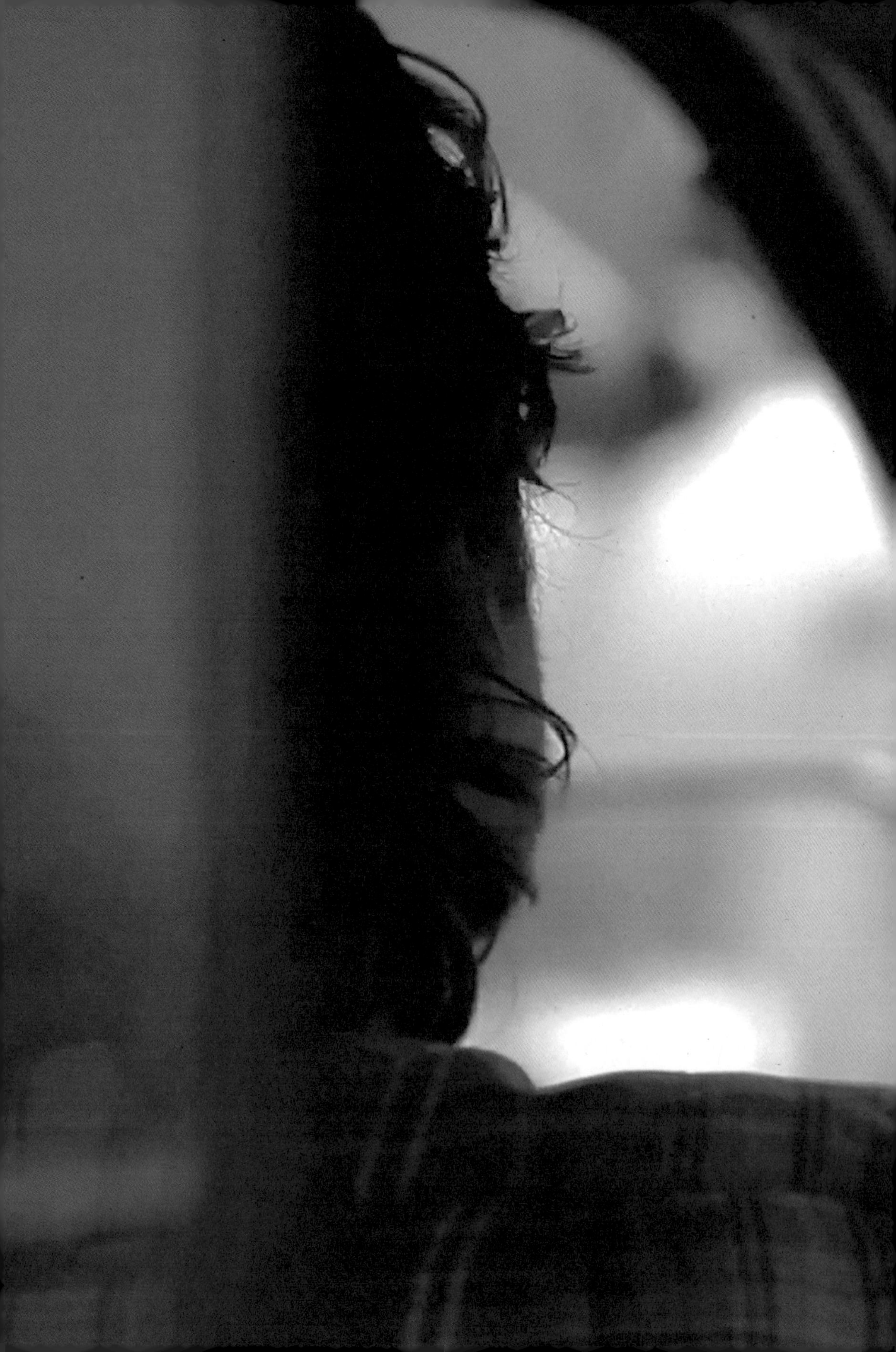

Mario García Torres
An Arrival Tale

Edited by
Daniela Zyman
Cory Scozzari

T² B A Thyssen Bornemisza Art Contemporary

Sternberg Press

Table of Contents

Carta Abierta a Dr. Atl (Open Letter to Dr. Atl)

2005, single-channel Super 8 transferred to video,
color, silent, 06' 26" looped, Thyssen-Bornemisza
Art Contemporary Collection, Vienna

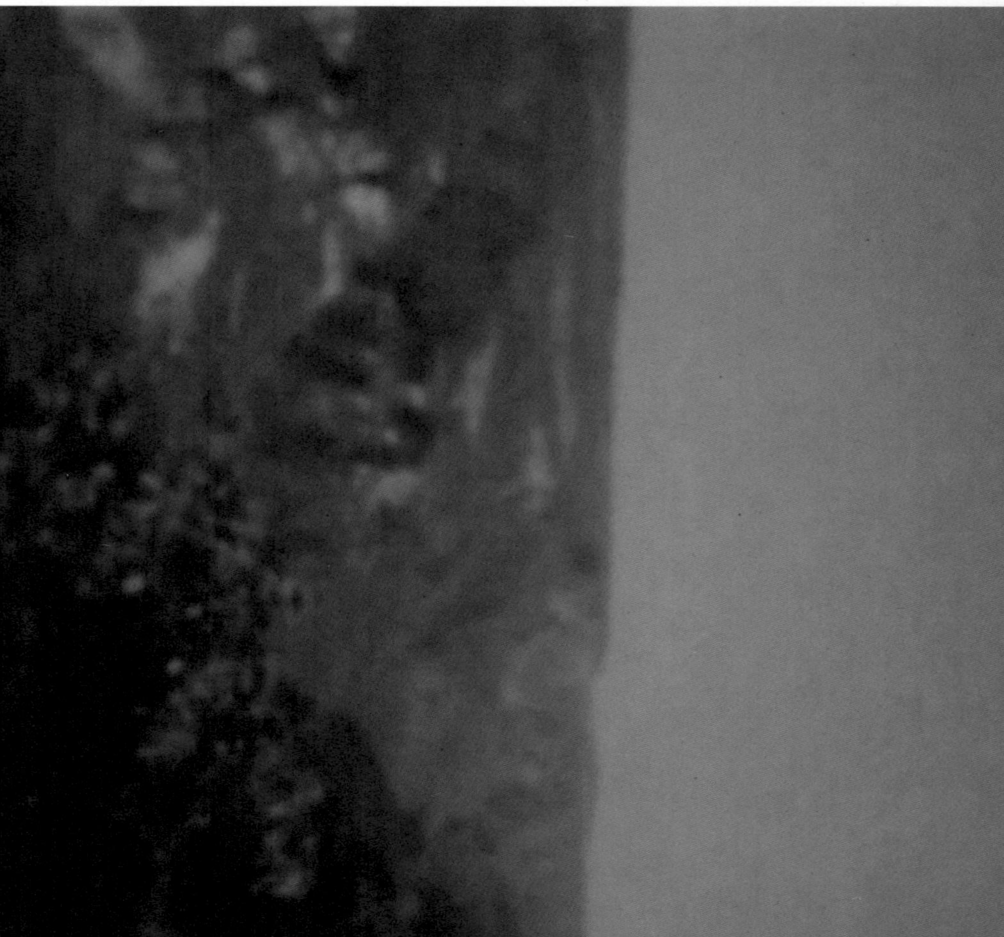

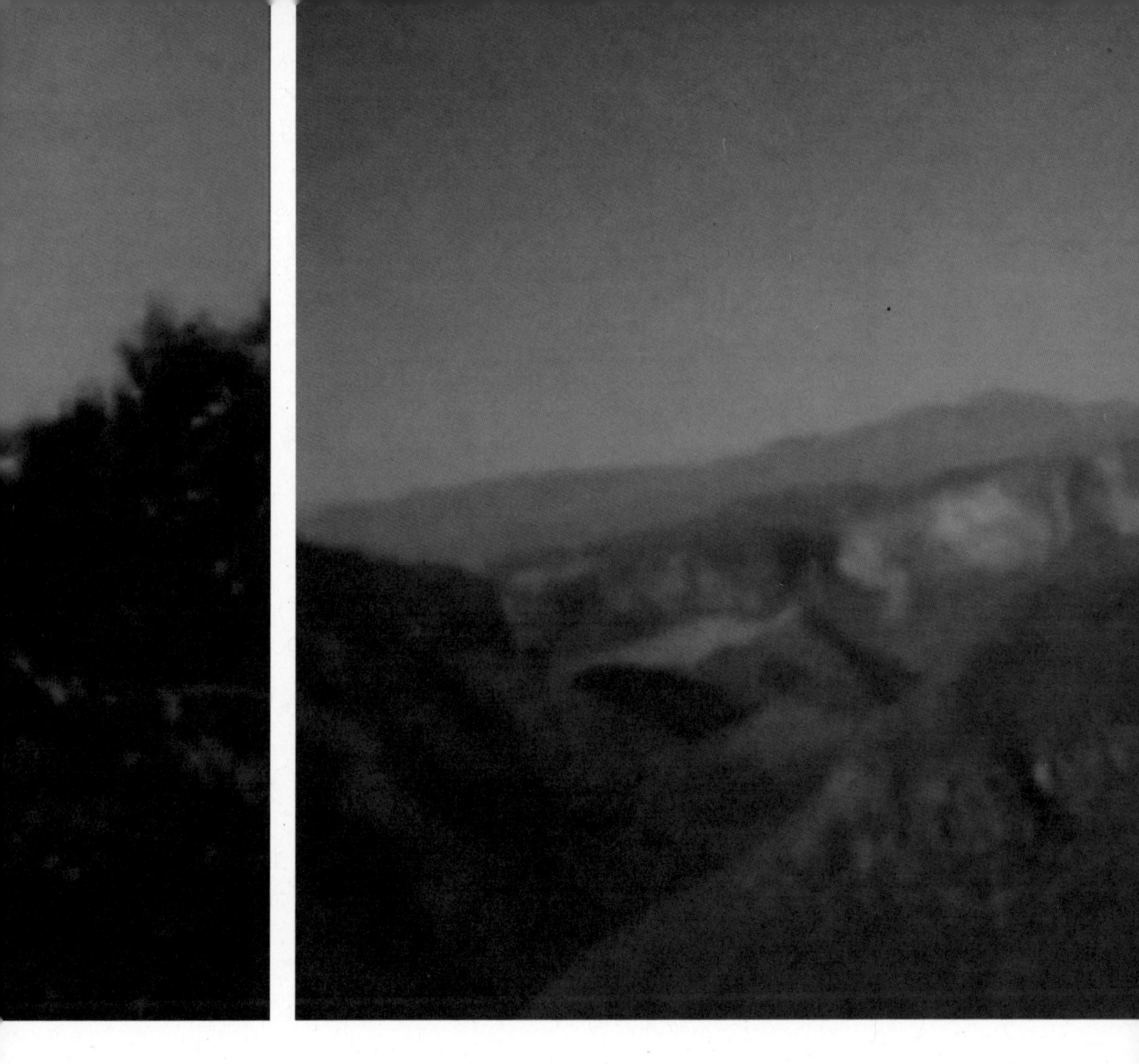

Dear Dr. Atl,
I wanted to drop you a line since I have been
thinking about your paintings lately.

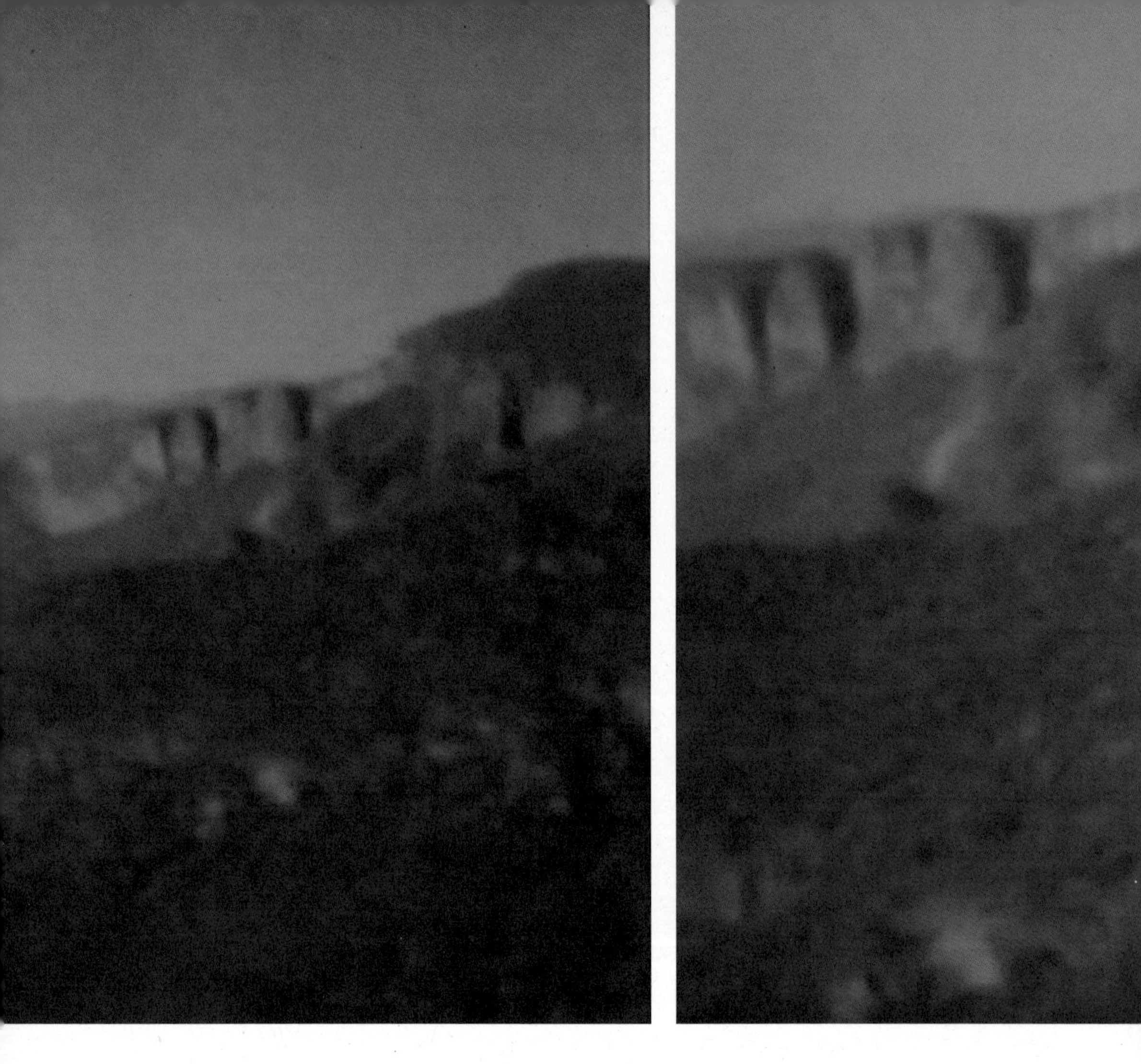

On the surface, everything sounds terrific,
but once you start digging in, some more
specific problems arise.

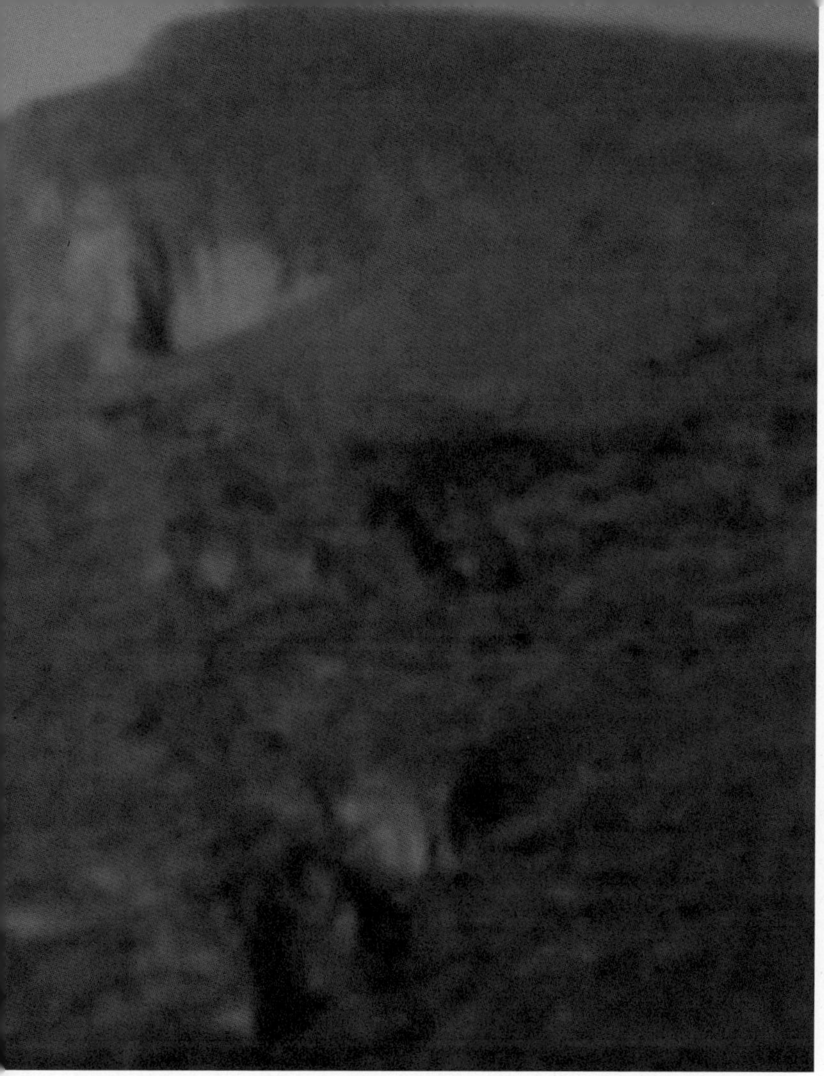

The establishment of an institution as powerful
as this in our country could necessitate
economic and intellectual compromises.

06' 26"

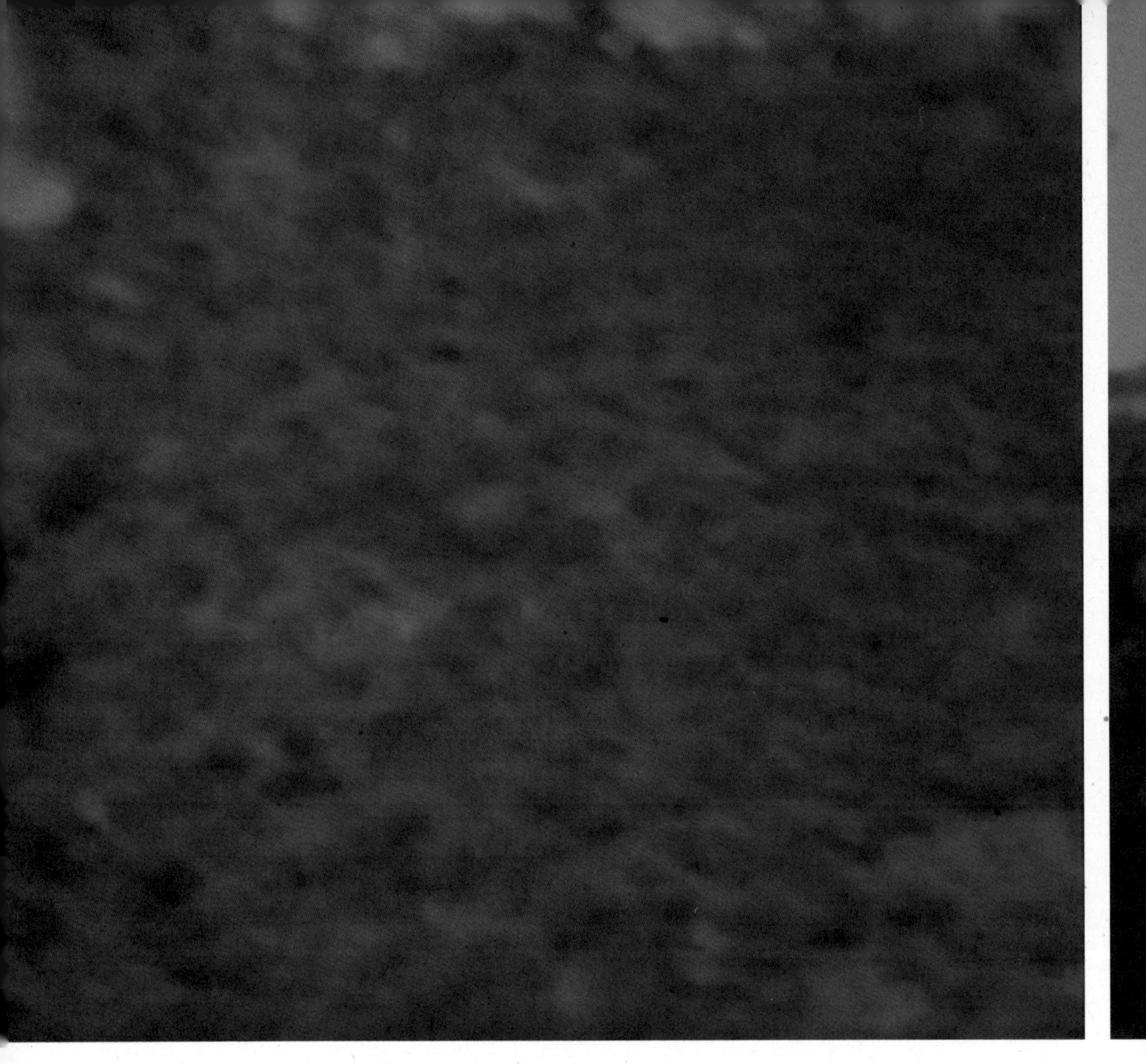

It is not difficult to determine if the opening
of a Guggenheim Guadalajara intends to play an
active role in the country's cultural discussion
or if it only pretends to work as a new
destination on the cultural tourism catalogue.

00' 00"

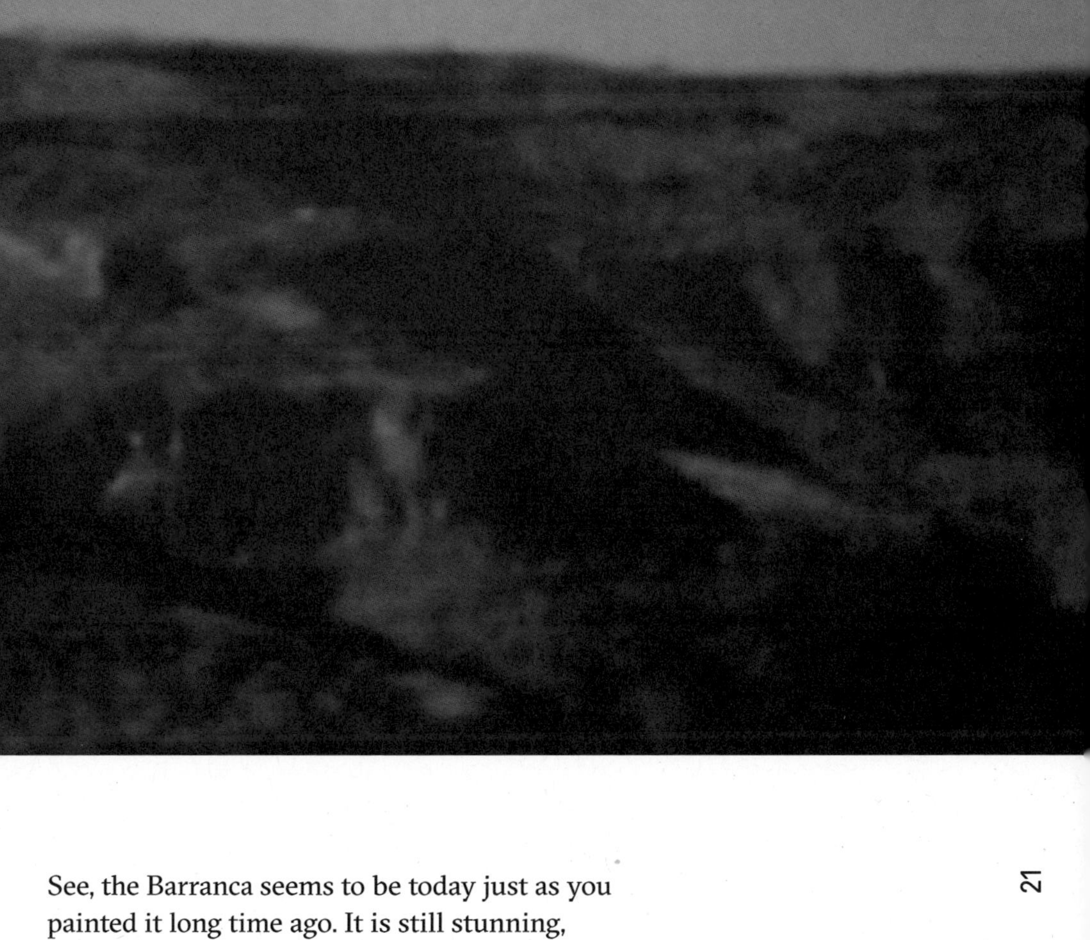

See, the Barranca seems to be today just as you
painted it long time ago. It is still stunning,
and that is precisely what has created so much
speculation.

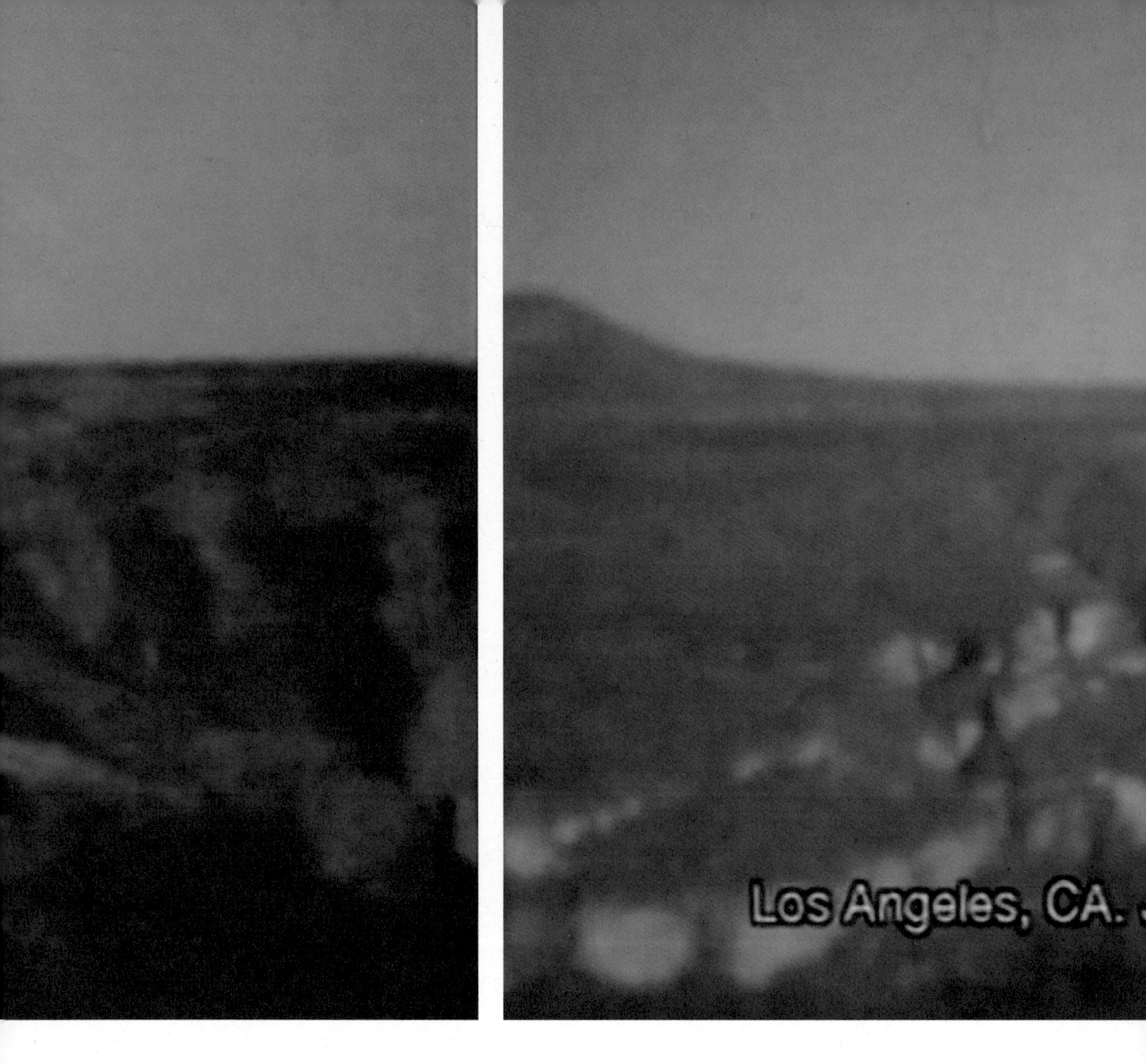

You know, I keep asking myself, what could
be the real motivation behind visiting the same
collection but this time superimposed on the
image of a faraway landscape...

00' 00"

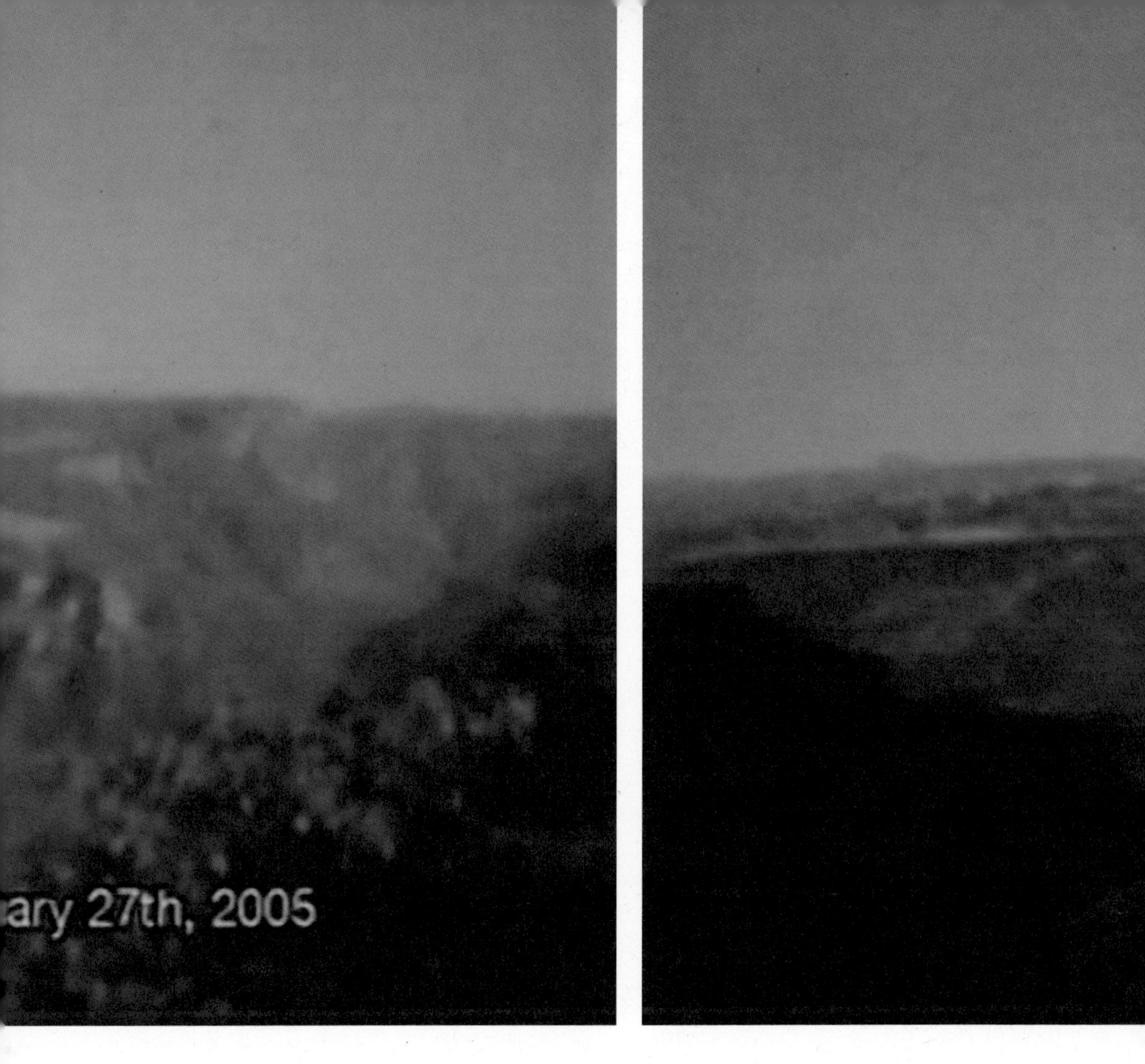

06' 26"

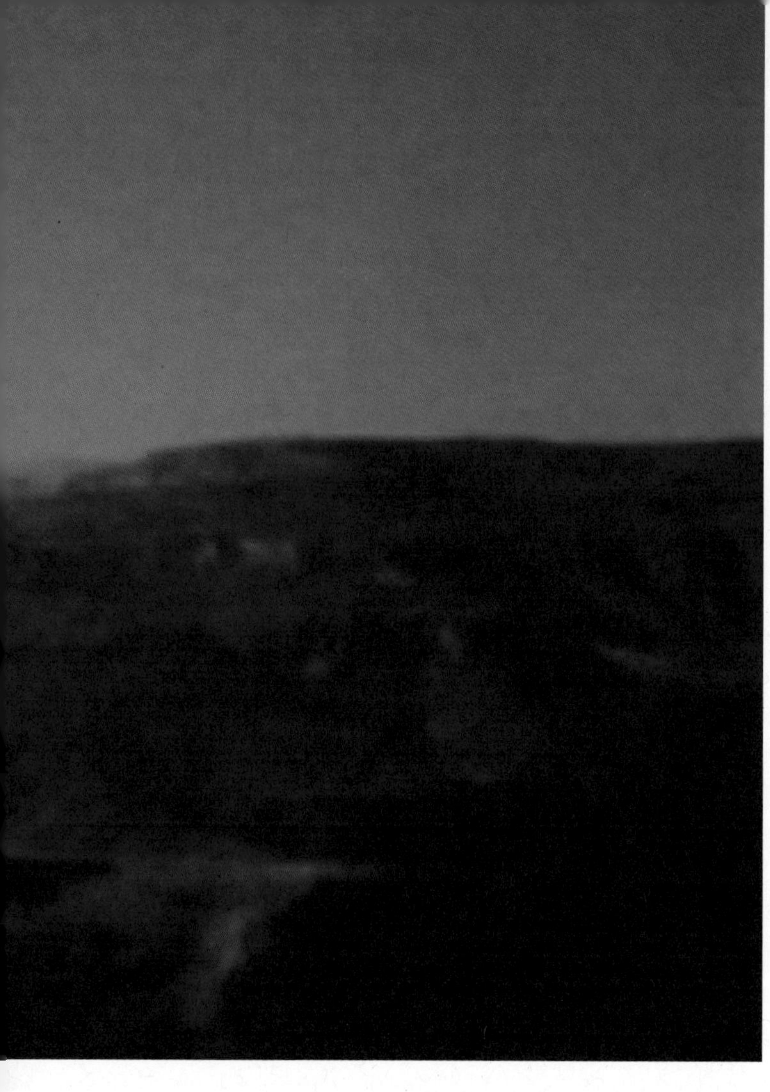

The Agencies of Death

A conversation between
Carl Michael von Hausswolff and Mario García Torres

This conversation was conducted over email between March and July 2016.

CARL MICHAEL VON HAUSSWOLFF
The first time we met, I didn't know what your profession was or what you
were interested in, but you immediately agreed to drive around Mexico City
with me to try to find the houses where the writer William S. Burroughs had
lived. Were you, at this time, already interested in working with and around
other artists' personas and/or materials?

MARIO GARCÍA TORRES
I guess that idea had intrigued me for some time. It was guided by a different
approach than the way I work today. Around that time I made a piece—with
an artist friend, Stefan Brüggemann—"repositioning" a work that David
Lamelas had sketched in the late 1960s but had never actually realized, a
film to be made in Berlin along with Marcel Broodthaers.[1] In this unrealized
work they would walk together and approach the camera and then disappear
behind it. Broodthaers's work had been a reference for me, and Lamelas was
in a way a threshold to conceptually-oriented practices, as seen from south
of the Rio Bravo. When we found out that *Study for a Film Project with Marcel
Broodthaers* (1973) had never been realized, we couldn't help but want to
repair that misconnection and jump into that conversation in some way.

CMVH
So in the case of Lamelas/Broodthaers, is it the thrill of the unfinished piece that
needs to be finalized, or is it the artists themselves, their perhaps "unfinished"
lives that need to be mended? (Lamelas is still alive but not Broodthaers.)

---

1   Mario García Torres and Stefan Brüggemann, *Historic Reposition (Lamelas-Broodthaers)*, 2002.

I just found a sixteen-channel magnetic tape, recorded in 1987 by the Swedish rock band Cortex. It has drums, guitars, bass, but most importantly, singing. The singer passed away a few months ago. He was a very good friend, and half of me is hesitant to listen to it at all or to mix it for a release, and the other half of me is eager to put together that last bit of his biographical puzzle. This is why I ask about the work or the story!

MGT

Is it the close relationship you had that makes it difficult to act?

CMVH

It's the feeling of great uncertainty and ambivalence that makes it difficult to act—the right and wrong—entering a territorial safe house or trespassing a private threshold. Either you get a nice hot meal or you get a bullet in your head. What matters is the movement. I agree that unrealized concepts should be carried on by someone else—someone who happened to cross the path of the idea. The unrealized work cries out for assistance, and I guess the artist in waiting falls into this pit.

MGT

I want to believe that ideas, unfinished ideas, should live and be part of someone's work. In the case of the Lamelas/Broodthaers film, the project had been published as a sketch by Lamelas, so there was a certain insistence on making the piece exist, even if only as a sketch. It was as if we were redoing the piece, but in a way it was like repeating a conversation that was just overheard. Inserting myself in that story through my own artistic gesture was a way to belong, to be part of their milieu and their way of thinking. Maybe this and what you describe are both related to the impulse to search for a place you longed for.

The process of looking for places, like Burroughs's houses, has been a constant component of my practice. I think every time I have managed to arrive at a place, a split similar to the one you outline happens. Partly I am intrigued by the place and keep looking into every detail, trusting that you can grab a certain old story, but at the same time for my more pragmatic side it becomes a disappointment to see the actual bricks, with a life of their own.

CMVH

How do you look upon the matter of choice? How do you choose work? Or is it vice versa: does the work choose you? Looking at the

Lamelas/Broodthaers—or maybe the Alighiero Boetti work—where do your points of entry lie?

MGT

I wrote a text for documenta in preparation for my film *Tea*, in which I talk precisely about arriving late to a place and about the many layers at play when one decides to accept an invitation. I argue that I had actually been invited to stay at Boetti's One Hotel in Kabul. The problem was that I arrived more than thirty years too late.[2] The question then became how do you behave: do you still come with a bouquet of flowers, or do you come in through the back door, the kitchen door, and are you even obliged to take care of the place, reactivate it? I guess, to answer your question, I have not been shy about these choices, and most of the time I have gone for it. What is wrong? What is politically wrong? Is trespassing on somebody else's story morally wrong? I would argue that it's not. If anything, it would be the context that could seem to bring about complications.

When we started to consider that part of documenta could take place in Kabul, a long list of politically complicated questions came about. I decided, in a very personal way, that it was worth the effort, even if the context was debatable. After the experience I was convinced that the initiative made a real impact on the ground and a very different one than it ever could have had in Kassel. In Kabul it was not an unrealized project but just one that had an abrupt ending.

CMVH

It seems that there is an unfinished line, or perhaps even several lines, running through major works of almost every artist's project cycles and perhaps even throughout their entire lives. When I look at artists with whom I have worked while they were alive, like the musical pioneers Else Marie Pade and Rune Lindblad, they have all stagnated at some point but then happily (I hope) were driven forward until the very end. And when that end is near, there are still myriad paths to finding an ending—to concluding. This is also how I see your work that engages the oeuvre of the composer Conlon Nancarrow, *Sounds Like Isolation to Me*. Your installation is fulfilling something in his music and his character. Can you tell me more about it?

2   Mario García Torres, *A Few Questions regarding the Hesitance at Choosing between Bringing a Bottle of Wine or a Bouquet of Flowers*, 2011.

The Nancarrow story is a long one, but maybe I should start by addressing the sound component. Well, the sound actually transcends the spatial configuration of the installation, so it's a discrete element, but at the same time it is the one you notice even before you enter the piece. It consists of four large metal panels from which cassette tapes are being played. Originally that part of the piece was considered to be the whole work. Early on in the process I wanted to invite different piano composers to Mexico to compose a piece on Nancarrow's piano and record it there. When I visited his studio for the first time, I was very impressed. It was designed by a very interesting Mexican modernist architect, Juan O'Gorman, and was the place where practically all of Nancarrow's oeuvre was composed. No one else had ever worked there.

I was very keen on inviting Nils Frahm, but he couldn't make it. As we were trying to figure out if he could come, we discovered some dusty rolls of magnetic tape. Soon my suspicion was confirmed that those tapes were percussion stock sounds that Nancarrow had recorded in his studio and had planned to cut and edit and turn into a concrete music composition. There is one track that we know of that was made in that fashion.[3] So we cleaned and restored the recordings as much as we could. I sent the recordings to Nils, and he immediately came up with a concrete proposal: to make a composition using the rescued tapes that would play throughout the exhibition. Although it is a whole new composition by Nils, many elements in the piece try to keep as much as possible the spirit of Nancarrow: I feel that it's an extension of his work, a way to keep the legacy alive.

The piece is very well embedded in the exhibition at Augarten, and even if it is audible throughout the exhibition area, it takes some time before you encounter it. It seems like this is a well-chosen strategy: to engulf the audience with the Nancarrow spirit and surround them with the audio piece.

But let's stick with the dead! Another person who was rather famous in the 1970s was Rosemary Brown. She claimed to be in direct contact with deceased composers like Chopin, Beethoven, Liszt, Debussy, and others. The composers "revealed unknown musical works" to Mrs. Brown, and she was able to perform these pieces on the piano.[4] Does this work have

---

3   See Conlon Nancarrow, "Untitled Musique Concrete Piece" (1950–60), aka "Piece for Tape (Untitled)" (ca. 1952).

4   There are several recordings, and Rosemary Brown's LP *A Musical Séance* was released in 1970.

something in common with yours? Apparently Mrs. Brown was more
of a medium than a conceptual artist but still...

MGT

Wow, never heard that story. Sounds really intriguing.

CMVH

If we dissolve the physicalities and the meta-physicalities and just pretend
that there are no factual problems at stake: how would you like to look
upon the relation between "us" and, for instance, artists like Nancarrow
or Friedrich Jürgenson, who operate from "the other side"? We are using
words like possessed and occupied (by genius, ghosts, influences, etc.).
If we consider dead people as still being somehow alive, would that make
this engagement more serious?

MGT

Oh, it would be great to have Mr. Jürgenson around or Mrs. Brown.
Although I don't feel I have really exercised any of those types of sensibilities, I would say more so that I pretend to be some kind of medium. I pretend
to have discussions with these artists I have been interested in. I make a
new space for their work to speak to us, make visible their materiality and
their politics of construction and of being, but I am also really interested
in their stories and their behavior, what separates them from others. That
is the reason why one can say we are having a "conversation," regardless
of geography or time.

A couple of years ago I made a song that took as its starting point an idea
that the Greek artist Takis [Panayiotis Vassilakis], put forward in the late 1950s.
It came from a conversation between him and David Medalla.[5] There Takis
argued that people could communicate through the sun, regardless of their
location, as long as they were under the same sun. I think it's a very intriguing
idea but also a metaphor for our practices. In the end art is that, a space for
searching into those other types of knowledge and different realities, to expand
our ideas, to go back and forth, to make a message return from somewhere
else, maybe a bit distorted but still carrying intentions and hopes.

---

5   Mario García Torres, *Um cabo lá, um porto cá*, 2013, https://umcabola.bandcamp.com/.

CMVH

It brings us to the point of the agency of death. Some people apparently got very upset when Mrs. Brown stated that she was the transition medium for those iconic composers' posthumous pieces. They said it was heresy to use famous names for the sake of personal musical work and certainly almost blasphemy for her to align herself with these giant god-sent artists. In our world, yours and mine, we use the remnants of the deceased in accordance with our profound principles and heritage, affirming the obvious need for completion—but other agencies of death might have other ideas about it, and you can really sense their need to erase. Have you encountered this when working and exhibiting with other artists' work?

MGT

Hmmm... how do we define what death can or will do? When I have gone back to citing or using, definitely "daringly," as you said, somebody's work or legacy, it is because I believe the works or their stories can still have an impact on our lives today, even if they come from the past, even if their creators are no longer physically with us. I hope to see my work reversed, used, and reused as a body of material, even tweaked now. Maybe one day people will straighten it out again, or not. What I mean is that there is a point when the work becomes a scratch on time, and it might get out of sync. One can only hope that the work will travel at its own pace and at some point, for somebody, it syncs again. What do you feel the future of your work should be? What does the work do when we are no longer here?

CMVH

One point of departure is the physical artwork, and another is the effect of the artwork. The physical piece hopefully generates a prime energy, inserting its contents into the receptor. If it has a prime effect, it will produce several generations of activity. And if it does, there's an imaginary eternity created, an eternity that coexists, intervenes, reacts, and mutates together with a multitude of other eternities. Perhaps this will shape a better world!

But I also have often wondered about the negative effects of the artwork. There's an old story about the modernists' aesthetic being used during the Spanish Civil War to construct horrible prison cells—in which the prisoners could hardly sit or lie down. Have you ever had any thoughts about this?

MGT

I think we need to ask how long our thoughts and work will have relevance. Even if we make sure that the work is politically very clear, it will still be distorted. We cannot predict what the context of the future will be, can we? I definitely believe in what you say, of course, about the power that a work can have and that of course its intentions are always for a better world, at least from my point of view. I guess lately, looking at our world, I am just less optimistic. Or maybe it's actually about a lack of trust; it's about not trusting the future.

CMVH

Not trusting the future also means not trusting the past. Can we trust that the past has been any good?

MGT

You never know what the past will bring. I feel like the past is always being reshaped. The past and the future can be moved, can be rethought. So far the past has been generous. It's been for sure full of great surprises and discoveries. My pessimism comes more from the devastating situations we have now. To talk about death in Mexico is an everyday matter. But more than numbers and the political problems we have here, it's the way people conceive of other peoples' lives as so easily disposable.

CMVH

It has been exactly one hundred years since Dada appeared in Zurich, and most art that I find interesting leans somehow on the Dada fundament, Duchamp in particular. Where do we stand? We are collaborators in the Duchampian world for sure, but do we want that? Are you, with your work, trying to break off from the past by distrusting the future? Did the uprising of 1916 fail?

MGT

The Duchampian modes of operation are somewhat normalized. There isn't the slightest feeling of a revolution when we use them today. They have become a sensibility that sets the language in which one chooses to communicate and the type of subjectivities that we want to communicate with. I think the important question now is how to rediscover those modes of operation and make them work in different ways. I am fascinated by how the same gesture made in different times and geographies can trigger different implications and complications. The 1916 revolution has certainly paved the way, not only by being radical but also by offering a new set of tools that can still be used today but in a different fashion. I don't think the rhetoric of breaking away today is the way to go. We need a subtler and more discursive revolution, one that brings a different sensibility to the discussion. Here, from Mexico, it feels like going out to the streets just doesn't work anymore; it just brings frustration. We need not to be radical in that sense but also to be convincing, to speak the language of the other in order to change things.

CMVH

When we read about what has happened and happens in Mexico, in the Middle East, or even way back in Rwanda, Bosnia, Nazi Germany, and so on, there is a formality around these "faraway" realities that tends to be treated as something abstract and filmic. The reshaping of the past sets this static historical fiction–like past in motion and it becomes more "real." My work around the Majdanek concentration camp showed me this.[6]

Moving over to your piece that takes place in Iraq: can we fit this into the present time—the Arab spring… the Gulf War… the scared face of Saddam when caught by the US military… Palmyra, Aleppo, Tahrir Square, the Egyptian Museum, etc.? How does it fluently stick to the past as we know it or, rather, should know it?

MGT

There is definitely an intention of thinking always from the present. Where else are we to think from anyway? I am not interested in becoming a seer, some kind of oracle whose thoughts make sense only in the latter day. I am interested in thinking about those past strategies to make a better world today.

In *The Way They Looked at Each Other*, one could argue, nothing is done in the work. The gesture was already made. The work is the analysis of such gesture. The interest that made me start thinking about it was precisely to find out that a judge had used the tools of conceptually oriented practices to enhance a point in a legal discussion. This brings about the idea that those symbolic gestures actually have a potential to change the world, the real world!

I am interested in the discussion that this brings. Now that is just the beginning of the story. The context—Iraq and the war and the shifting of time, visiting an event eight years later—become the real frame for that gesture to become meaningful.

6   Carl Michael von Hausswolff's *Majdanek* (1989) and *I–XI* (2010) consists of a series of watercolors using ashes collected and safeguarded for more than twenty years originating from the concentration camp of Majdanek, Poland. The display of the work in the artists' exhibition *Memory Works* at the Martin Bryder Gallery in Lund, Sweden, in 2012 caused public controversy.

But, Carl Michael, I think your point about things perceived as taking place in a fictional or filmic space is quite important. I assume that the sometimes unbelievable character of history makes it that way, as happens with your Majdanek piece or as things are happening today with Trump's at some point unbelievable triumph in the US election and the hate it has unearthed. I think that is precisely what the role of artist is, to measure and negotiate those spaces of perception through our practices.

CMVH

For me and a couple of other people the Majdanek works connected the past with the present. It activated time in a very specific space; a continuity of suffering instead of an intellectual stasis of a past probability. A future was suddenly installed but a very uncertain future.

When I noticed that Nancarrow was in the same prison camp in Gurs, in southwest France, as Hannah Arendt (he in 1939 and she in 1940), it became a present link for me, and the past became vital. Three of the artists you have been working with have more or less been resistance fighters: Nancarrow fighting in the Spanish Civil War, Boetti supporting the Afghan resistance against the Russians, and Dr. Atl engaged in the Mexican Revolution. Has this been a trigger for you to work with them? Are you a potential guerrilla fighter, or rather are you in some way allied with an invisible one-man guerrilla faction linking up with former artist-revolutionaries?

MGT

Wow. Never thought about all those relationships! But of course when one reads that Nancarrow fought in the civil war, one identifies. You cannot have a discussion with someone if there isn't a shared space. When Nancarrow came to Mexico, it was a real moment of hope, a haven for political asylum seekers that gave the country possibly its most exciting intellectual moment in modern history. This is when hopes, ideas, and ideals from somewhere else are again brought in to change a real situation. Then came neoliberalism, globalization, and the rest. As in many other places in this world today, we should all be guerrilla fighters. To fight this battle we need many more people than the ones living. We need to fight together with the ones far away and along with the army of the dead! With Boetti and Burroughs, with Atl and Arendt!

Dear Alighiero
could have bee
Yesterday I dic
On my way bac

keep comparing photos.
the One Hotel's and then
t walk as much. I just we
I stared for a long time at

More later, M

Nov 18, 2001

Dear Alighiero: I keep comparing photos. Sometimes I think any building could have been the One Hotel's and then I think precisely the opposite. Yesterday I didn't walk as much. I just went to get a haircut , by the park. On my way back I stared for a long time at some kids playing stickball.

More later, M

18 نوامبر 2001

Alighiero عزیز: من به مقایسه عکس ها ادامه میدهم. بعضی اوقات فکر میکنم که
هر ساختمان One Hotel مورد نظر باشد و بعد دقیقا برعکس فکر میکنم. دیروز به
ان اندازه قدم نزدم. من فقط برای اصلاح مو ، به نزدیکی پارک رفتم. در راه برگشت
برای مدت طولانی به اطفالی که چوب دنده بازی میکردند خیره شده بودم.

بعدتر، M

                                    + 93 70 27 60 21

Nov 20, 2001

Dear Alighiero: After a few days in the city I haven't managed to find the location yet, although being in Kabul and heaving found the stationary sheets from the hotel encourages me to keep looking. It seems almost as if I were looking for something I had lived myself.

More later, Mario

20 نوامبر 2001
Alighiero عزیز: بعد از چند روز در شهر من تا به هنوز مکان One Hotel را
پیدا نتوانستم، اگرچه با بودن در کابل و پیدا کردن اوراق قرطاسیه ای این هوتل
مرا تشویق به تجسس میدارد. این طور به نظر میرسد که به دنبال چیزی میگردم
به مثل اینکه در ان زندگی کرده ام.

بعدتر، ماریو

Nov 22, 2001

Dear Alighiero: As I look, I keep filling in the spaces of this reality-based fiction. Sometimes I don't really know if it's worth it. So much important stuff is happening around here every day. I don't know if attempting to make art succeeds in raising thoughts or the other way around. By the way, how did you end up coming here in the first place? Yours, Mario

22 نوامبر 2001

Alighiero عزیز: همانطور که برای ساختمان One Hotel جستجو میکنم، من به احساس در فضای تخیل براساس واقعیت ادامه میدهم. بعضی اوقات واقعا نمی دانم که ایا ارزشش را دارد. هر روز در اطراف اینجا اتفاقات بسیار مهمی رخ میدهد. من نمیدانم که ایا تلاش برای پیروزی هنر در رشد فکری است یا بلعکس. بعدتر احساست چطور بود؟ محترمه ماریو

+ 93 70 27 60 21

+ 93 70 27 60 21

Nov 25, 2001

Dear Alighiero: One of the main topics these days is that Zahir Shah is planning to come back as soon as the Taliban regime finally fades away. If I had written this in a few months from now, I would have said that he did, but that he did not make any claim for the throne. Yours, Mario

25 نوامبر 2001

Alighiero عزیز: یکی از مقالات داغ این روزها پلان بازگشت ظاهر شاه بعد از ازبین رفتن کامل رژیم طالبان است. اگر این را چند ماه قبل از امروز مینوشتم، میگفتم که او ادعایی رای تخت پادشاهی دارد اما امروز او هیچ ادعای ندارد. ایا تلاش برای برقراری تماس با او کرده ای؟ در جریان سه دهه گذشته او در رم زندگی کرده است. محترمه ماریو

+ 93 70 27 60 21   + 93 70 27 60 21

Nov 28, 2001

Dear Alighiero: The word is that the US has secretly been airlifting people
from Kunduz –some of them Al Qaeda fighters- to drop them off in
Pakistan. Some of the stuff happening around here could be really
confusing.

      Yours, Mario

28 نوامبر 2001

Alighiero عزیز: گپ اینکه امریکایی ها به طور مخفیانه مردمی را از قندوز که
بعضی شان جنگجویان القاعده بوده اند با هواپیما گرفته و به پاکستان انتقال
میدهند. بعضی اتفاقاتی که در اینجا رخ میدهد واقعا گیج کننده است.

محترمه ماریو

+ 93 70 27 60 21

Nov 28, 2001

Today I walk outside the city. They guy who sometimes help me with translations told me about all the works that have disappeared from the museum… I will try to take a look at its destroyed building on the following days.

PS: You know hotels, like museums, are one of those interesting spaces to rethink what you are doing…

28 نوامبر 2001

امروز خارج از شهر قدم زدم قدم کسی برایم از تمام کارهای که از موزیم ناپدید
شده اند گفت... من تلاش میکنم تا دیداری از ساختمان تخریب شده در
چند روز اینده داشته باشم.

پی نوشت: همانطور که میدانید هوتل ها مانند موزیم از جمله جاهای جالبی
میباشند که اجازه اندیشیدن دوباره به انچه که انجام میدهی را میدهند.

+ 93 70 27 60 21

Nov 30, 2001

Dear Alighiero: The One Hotel building is definitely not around. I can't find any trace of it. Also, Kabul is getting really cold. The mountains are now totally covered by snow. It snows at least two hours every day.
Yours, Mario

30 نوامبر 2001

Alighiero عزیز: ساختمان One Hotel یقینا در این اطرف نیست. من هیچ گونه
نشانه ای از ان پیدا نکردم. همچنین، کابل در حال بسیار سرد شدن است. کوه ها
با برف پوشیده شده اند. هر روز تقریبا برای دو ساعت برف میبارد.
محترمه ماریو

+ 93 70 27 60 21

Dec 2, 2001

Alighiero: Things tend to get lost -disappearing between movements and
changes. Maybe that is the case of the hotel building. In 2004, an Ariana
plane will disappear from the local airport radar for a few days. It will then
be found having crashed in the mountains, almost covered by the snow.
There will be no survivors. Mario

I found an amazing construction near Share-Nau. Maybe you remember it
from the time? It's a house with a polygonal shape, apparently covered
with clay. It's really great. I could maybe use it to film some other part of
the story.

2 دسامبر 2001

Alighiero: چیزها در جریان نقل وانتقالات و تغییرات به نظر گم میشوند. شاید که مربوط به ساختمان هوتل باشد. در 2004، یک هواپیمای اریانا برای چندین روز از رادار محلی میدان هوایی ناپدید شد. که بعدا معلوم شد که به کوه برخورد کرده که با برف پوشیده شده است. باز مانده ای نخواهد داشت. Mario.

                                        + 93 70 27 60 21

Dec 3, 2001

Dear Alighiero: Every day I leave the hostel and go drop my last night notes so they are faxed to you, then I start walking again the same few streets, full of people, looking back at the photos I have, looking for small details I can match. Nothing new… When I get tired, I go for some kebab and rice. Today I went to see the sunset by the river, quite an early sunset. In the evening I try to write some notes. Maybe that is why they are getting shorter and shorter.

M

3 دسامبر 2001

Alighiero عزیز: هر روز بعد از گذاشتن نوت هایم در هتل، انجا را ترک میکنم،
بعد دوباره به قدم زدن در چند جاده همیشگی پر از مردم ، شروع میکنم، به
عکس های داشته ام نگاه میکنم، و به دنبال جزییات کوچکی برای مشابهت دادن
میگردم. چیز جدیدی نیست... وقتی که خسته میشوم، برای خوردن کباب وبرنج
میروم. امروز برای دیدن غروب افتاب به کنار رودخانه رفتم، کاملا یه غروب
زودهنگام بود. در شامگاه تلاش برای نوشتن چند نوت کردم. شاید دلیل اینکه انها
کوتاهتر میشوند این باشد. محترمه ماریو

M

+ 93 70 27 60 21

+ 93 70 27 60 21

Dec 5, 2001

Dear Alighiero: I wish you were here. Afghans have decided for an interim government on a reunion they had in Bonn. If I succeed in finding the One Hotel spot, it could be reconstructed and re-open, just as everything else around here… Can you imagine that? More later, Mario

5 دسامبر 2001
Alighiero عزیز: ارزو میکردم تو اینجا بودی. افغانها در جریان گردهمایی شان
در بن تصمیم بر ساخت یک دولت موقت نمودند. اگر که من موفق به پیدا کردن
مکان One Hotel شدم، ممکن است که دوباره بازسازی و باز گردد، دقیقا مثل
هرچیز اطرف اینجا... باور میتانی؟ بعدتر، ماریو

  + 93 70 27 60 21

Dec 6, 2001

Dear Alighiero: As you might know, the US troops are still around. Less than before they say. Apparently Osama bin Laden has been hiding in the Tora Bora Mountains caves for quite some time now, so they are more concentrated in that region. People say they could have seized Osama from the start, but somehow they didn't.

More later, Mario

PS. I like going to the bicycle repair shop around the corner from time to time. The best gossip is shared there. Someone said they are thinking on using the Gulf Club for demining training. Eventually they will open the course again.

6 دسامبر 2001

Alighiero عزیز: همانطور که ممکن است بدانی،نیروهای امریکایی هنوز هستند. کمتر از چیزی که پیشتر گفته بودند. ظاهرا اسامه بن لادن در غارهای کوه تورابورا برای مدت زیادی شده است که مخفی شده ، که انها تمرکز بیشتر در ان منطقه دارند. مردم میگویند که انها میتوانستند اسامه را در همان ابتدا دستگیر کنند اما به دلیلی نکردند.

بعدتر، ماریو

پی نوشت. من رفتن به دکان بایسکل سازی در همین گوشه را به طور تکرار دوست دارم. بهترین شایعات در انجا پخش میشود.

+ 93 70 27 60 21

Dec 7, 2001

Dear Alighiero: If I am right, only one of the mulberries trees has
survived on the hotel site. The tree is actually gorgeous!

Yours, Mario

7 دسامبر 2001

Alighiero عزیز: اگر که من درست باشم تنها یک درخت شاه توت در ساحه
هوتل باقی مانده است. این درخت واقعا زیباست!
محترمه ماریو

+ 93 70 27 60 21

+ 93 70 27 60 21

Dec 8, 2001

Dear Alighiero: I went back to the spot. Some things do not match. What maps did you give the Afghan people to make the embroideries? I have been thinking about them lately. The world today is certainly different from the last one depicted in 1991. I will let you know more. Mario

8 دسامبر 2001

Alighiero عزیز: من به ان مکان باز گشتم. بعضی چیزها تطابق نمیکن. کدام نقشه ها را به افغان ها برای ساختن گلدوزی ها داده ای؟ در این اواخر درموردشان فکر میکنم. دنیای امروز مطمینا متفاوت از اخرین چیزی است که در سال 1991 به تصویر کشیده شده است. بعدا بیشتر برایت خواهم گفت ماریو

+ 93 70 27 60 21

+ 93 70 27 60 21

Dec 9, 2001

Dear Alighiero: Not much to tell tonight. M

9 دسامبر 2001 .

Alighiero عزیز: امشب چیز زیادی برای گفتن نیست. M.

+ 93 70 27 60 21   + 93 70 27 60 21

                                                    Dec 11, 2001

Dear Alighiero: The papers say the US troops believe heaving heard Bin
Laden's voice on a radio signal yesterday. If so, he is alive and no longer
in Afghanistan.

Yours, Mario

11 دسامبر 2001

Alighiero عزیز: روزنامه ها میگویند که دیروز امریکایی ها صدای بن لادن را در یکی از سیگنال های مخابره شنیده اند. که اگر چنین باشد، او زنده است و دیگر در افغانستان نیست.

محترمه ماریو

+ 93 70 27 60 21

Dec 12, 2001

Dear Alighiero: From above Kabul looks busy. It made me think it keeps reconstructing itself, endlessly.

Soon, Mario

۱۲ دسامبر ۲۰۰۱

Alighiero عزیز: از بالا، کابل شلوغ به نظر می اید. مرا به این باور میدارد که خود را باسازی میکند، بی وقفه.

به زودی، ماریو

+ 93 70 27 60 21

+ 93 70 27 60 2

Dec 14, 2001

Dear Alighiero: I am gone. On December 22, Prime Minister Hamid Karzai will assume power, but the struggle continues. They found satellite spotting maps in the Tora Bora caves. Who knows for how long the US satellites have been taking pictures of the region, and for what? This seems far from over.

Yours, Mario

14 دسامبر 2001

Alighiero عزیز: من رفتم. در دسامبر 22، نخست وزیر حامد کرزی قدرت را
به دست میگیرد، اما کشمکش ادامه دارد. انها در غارهای کوه تورابورا نقشه های
ماهواره ای تعیین موقعیت را پیدا کردند. چه کسی میداند که ماهواره های ایالت
متحده برای چه مدت و برای چه مشغول عکسبرداری از منطقه بوده است؟ این
دور از اختتام به نظر می اید.

محترمه ماریو

+ 93 70 27 60 21

+ 93 70 27 60 21

Dec 16, 2001

Alighiero: I found a recording of the wind running through the Afghan
mountains, from 1985. They say the Russians liked to listen to those
sounds. Yours, Mario

16 دسامبر 2001

Alighiero: من یک ریکورد از اله های موسیقی بادی در کوه های افغانستان مربوط 1985 پیدا کردم. انها میگویند که روس ها علاقه مند به شنیدن ان صداها بودند.   محترمه ماریو

Dec 16, 2001

Dear Alighiero. It seems I will be finally able to take off tomorrow. On April 2002 a CIA executive director will state "The goal has never been to get bin Laden". I hope to write a longer account of my days in Kabul. My film will never be shot. Soon, Mario

16 دسامبر 2001

Alighiero عزیز: به نظر میرسد که بلاخره فردا قادر به پرواز به اینجا خواهم بود. در اپریل 2002 یک مدیر اجرایی سی آی ای گفته « هدف هرگز دستگیری بن لادن نبوده است». امیدوارم که گزارش بلند تری از روز هایم در کابل بنویسم. فیلم من هرگز شوت نخواهد شد. به زودی، ماریو

Armen Avanessian, Anke Hennig, Mario García Torres

The Present Is a Place
We Can Always Come Back to:
Toward a Speculative
Temporality of Images

Let me start with a statement.
Images might have more than one tense.
Their present is changeable, today, and every day.

Like images, the present is a place we can always come back to.
Like images, our present is split, asynchronous, and tense.

An image is plastic; moldable, pliable, malleable.
An image is movable; transferable, variable, alterable.
An image is not a solitary entity; it hides endless copies of itself.

An image it's not a stable statement; it's a past and it's a future. It's just
past, and is an about-to-be-future. Every time the image is reproduced,
                                        seen,
                                            exhibited,
                                                presented,
it becomes a new one.

            (#becomes #anew #later).

Sometimes a vision is brought from the future, and other times it is forwarded to the past. The same image can be different in time; it comes with a different spatiality and geography.

There is always more than one side to it; the one you saw yesterday, the one she came back to today; the one I will get to only tomorrow.

1.

The tenses in language have the capacity to shift our point of view in time. Linguists call the past tense a genuine tense because one can shift one's point of view into the past, describing an event from within the spatial horizon present within the past. Some linguists—for instance, Gustave Guillaume—have gone so far as to claim that it is language alone that makes for our experience of time (#temps #et #verbe). Certainly one can say so for the concept of chronology that is built by the tense system of language. Indeed we can form sentences about a coherent flow of time. "This moment has been future, is present now, and will be past." Arranging three tenses makes the idea of chronology graspable. The moment in the future can't be seen though; neither can the moment in the past. We acquire the concept of chronology through the learning of language. Reading and writing are technologies for the stabilization of a coherent or "chronological" image of time. On these grounds altermodern novels developed a great variety of devices that allow for a complex navigation of time. One can imagine reading in a novel: "He closed the door to the bathroom. Looking into the bright sun, it occurred to him that just a few weeks ago he had been playing ice hockey with his son. He heard José saying something and went to the balcony to see what he wanted. Possibly the camera needs to be taken out of the heat." The tenses allow us to imagine going back in time to such an unspecified moment. We can imagine the character's current thoughts and his memories of the weather at home. We can even imagine seeing what the character saw as he looked out the window, as if we had been there.

Now, let me try to envision that. Think digital montage software for image coupling, for example. Beyond their collage capabilities, they surprisingly use hashtags to couple and recouple images. Doesn't the reframing of images become entirely a game of language with such software? Hashtags are simple words; more precisely, they are nouns. They immediately limit what you can get from an image to what you have a noun for.

It is as worrisome to think of this procedure from the point of view of language, since hashtagging messes around with a poorly understood language. If you think of language as a storeroom of nouns, there is not much you can do with it. What would be the hashtags of the scene from the imagined novel? #man, #bathroom, #door, #hotelroom, #sunlight, #son, #icehockey, #house, #balcony, #camera? Nouns have no tenses. All you can do then is use one noun for another one, which brings you no further than the basic rhetoric of metaphor and metonymy. You couple images of bathrooms with images of the ocean to have a metaphor, images of cameras with images of other devices to get a metonymy. You couple a balcony with a terrace and so on. But both language and the image lose a lot if they are subjected to the crude operation of hashtagging. What they lose is their specific geography and temporality. Instead they become timeless. They can easily navigate in time.

Now how do we bring images back to us? In order to do that, it is worth thinking about who defines an image, who gives it a time. A first quick answer might be: the photographer who takes the shot. The image presents his way of seeing to us. But as feminist theorists like Laura Mulvey (#visual #pleasure #narrative #cinema) and cultural historians like John Berger (#ways #seeing) have argued, we also have to take the gaze of the beholder into account. The beholder's gaze can be sexist, like the one that is implied in Hollywood cinema. The beholder's gaze can be racist, like the one that is implied in lots of colonial imaginary. The beholder's gaze can be a capitalist-realist gaze, as with lovers of minimalism. The beholder's gaze can be militarist and sensational, like the one we can feel in the media coverage of the Iraq war. Every time an image is reproduced, moved, presented, exhibited, or repeated, it becomes a new; and this happens as a result of the beholder's gaze. On rare occasions the beholder's gaze acts passively and does not change the image at all. Lately the hashtagger's response reframes the image too. He turns the image into an abstract noun. Maybe he does not know that all the nouns he is using are abstract. And maybe he does not even know about his blindness toward the concrete thing, desirable surface, singular shape, appalling carnality, compelling brutality, or touching event of the image. If the event of the image happens and if the image becomes a new one, acquires another meaning, comes closer and speaks to our desire, it is because of an active beholder, a beholder who desires to see something, something he doesn't know or doesn't have a noun for. I'd like to think that the gaze of the beholder comes with a critical capacity, at least potentially. But when the beholder's gaze is at stake, what is the tense of the image then? Is there a way to trust images? Is it worth trying to make them stop in time? Who does that and for what reason?

2.

When the Spanish National Court judge Santiago Pedraz went to Baghdad in January 2011, his intention was to make two images in relation to an open court case. Two images that might have helped him solidify his case.

Now let's first look at the roles of images as evidence. At first glance making images for a court case seems surprising as a trial in itself is based entirely on language and speaking. The essential purpose of a trial is to compare spoken evidence of an absent event. The ritual of swearing "to tell the truth" minimizes the danger of fiction coming into play that would deconstruct the idea of evidence given. The use of images as evidence on the other side is very limited due to the fact that images, especially digital images, can be manipulated on various levels and, we would argue, because of their dubious emotional charge too. In a second step the evidence given is considered in relation to the legal code in order to decide if the event is deviant and to be classified as a crime. The judgment addresses both of these moments. What happened and to what extent is it a crime?

Two stories are on trial.

Story One: On April 8, 2003, US troops entered the Iraqi capital. From their position on the Al Jumhuriya Bridge, soldiers inside a tank saw two people on the balcony of the Palestine Hotel. Their way of seeing had been predetermined by military training; their view had been framed by the hashtag "unlawful combatants." The military personnel made a decision that claimed a certain future. In the image they saw, they saw the future. They fired.

Story Two: There is another story that happens at the same time. Two cameramen, Taras Protsyuk from Ukraine and José Couso from Spain, were killed standing on the balcony of their hotel, the Palestine Hotel, while covering the day's events. This happened. In the past. But the judgment about what happened, how things happened, was trapped in two stories, two images; it was caught between two memories or two visions.

The question Judge Pedraz pretended to answer by going there and making those two images was whether the soldiers who killed the photographers could actually—that is, from within a tank from their position on the Al Jumhuriya Bridge—see whether the people they killed were "unlawful combatants." Could they see #unlawful #combatants? Could they see their hashtag? Can anybody see his #? Can you see my #?

The judge went back to the scene and made two photographs to contribute to the procedure of establishing an event and of classifying this event—in this case, as a war crime. These two images, however, cannot serve as evidence. Made eight years later, they were taken too late to be able to prove anything. Instead they go on a journey in #space and #time. But what do they contribute? And what as beholders do we contribute to it?

It is unclear whether Judge Pedraz's critical intention and the critical potential of these photographs can be grasped fully if we see only the relationship between the image of the photographer and the image of the beholder. The critical potential of the image is instead related to a third viewer. He is the one seen, the one who is "shot," the one who sometimes looks into the camera and sometimes doesn't. For Jean-Luc Nancy photography establishes a relationship between an "I" and an "other" at the exact moment the shutter is pressed (#we #others). On one side of the camera there is Gisèle Freund's finger clicking the shutter, which establishes the relationship. Her finger creates a subjectivity that expresses both a "we" and an otherness. On the other side of the camera it is the gaze of the one shot that has reached the finger clicking. The "we" is formed by the otherness of the person in the shot. We see a portrait of James Joyce. The questions asked by Pedraz's photographs then were probably: Did they actually look at each other? Did they at any given moment form a "we"? How did they do that? And what did that communion entail?

One of Pedraz's photographs shows the Palestine Hotel as shot from the Al Jumhuriya Bridge (#baghdad #tank #aljumhuriya #troops #palestinehotel #shoot #later—may we say #2003?). In terms of the open trial, only this photograph seems sufficient; this is the view of those who fired, and the decision is to be taken concerning the view of those soldiers. In the photograph there is a small figure on the balcony, who maybe does look into the camera. Why did he put this figure there? Why did he ask somebody to pose in the roles of Taras Protsyuk and José Couso? Let's imagine that by pressing the shutter he was establishing a relationship between him and the dead cameramen. So was he focusing on the figure on the balcony in order to avoid repeating the gesture of shooting. Did he mean that "we" are not soldiers?

The second photograph is taken from Protsyuk and Couso's balcony at the Palestine Hotel (#baghdad #war #aljumhuriya #palestinehotel #photographers #view #later #2011 #we #other #visual #pleasure #ways

#seeing). It shows a view over Baghdad. Why was this image taken? This image is not a matter of evidence. Was it because they were innocent? Was it because the victims were cameramen? This image shows most likely what they saw last, their last view. Pedraz was clicking the shutter of the camera at the place where Protsyuk and Couso were most likely standing with their cameras. Did he mean, "we are witnesses"?

3.

This brings to mind a common idea, so brilliantly expressed by Roland Barthes (#camera #lucida). A photograph captures a present moment only to preserve it as a past image. The mystery of the photograph consists in this shifting of time. Something present turns past by becoming an image. That is what gives the image a poetic aura. What goes on in these images of Baghdad, however, is a reversal of the temporal relation that Barthes had in mind: the images were taken at one point in 2011 in order to imagine what was seen on April 8, 2003. It reminds me of what tenses do in language. Pedraz's image shows us what we can imagine that Protsyuk saw when he stepped out onto the balcony. This image is a memorial to an imagined sight. This image is an epigraph. It is speculative, and it is poetic. Though we find a kind of counter-Barthes here, we should stay with his intuition that photography is a temporal technology. Images shift time. These two images shift my perspective. It certainly has to do with the third viewer, whose position we are invited to take by Pedraz's photographs. Is it the soldier's or the cameramen's? We might also think that the ethics of this decision have to do with suspended judgment.

It might be exactly the temporal complexity that enables the images to make us think in a deeper way. It looks like the images contain a strange promise. When we come back to the present later, this allows us to make a better judgment.

So what do we base our judgment on? Is it the image that Pedraz captured? Is it the same image but at a later moment, when we see it printed in a newspaper? Or yet again the same image we can log into when we review the case from yet another time, for example, right now?

To a certain degree it doesn't matter which image we look at when we want to establish its temporality. All of these images are past. They have been taken. These images have been taken in 2011. Even if we click (on) them again, they will have been taken, in the mode of the past. But the moment we see them is present, even if they are different presents. What has been seen

on April 8, 2003, claims to have been present. What was seen in 2011 claims
to have been present then. What we see now is present now.

Therefore the image does not transport time by itself; it doesn't
push the past by itself. What it establishes and what becomes visible at
any moment of looking at a picture is this time shift: whenever I look at an
image, I am in the present, yet what I see in the image is past.

    As beholders
              of an image,
we look at a past sight.

Something past
              can be seen nowhere else.
Something past
              can be seen only in an image.

This time shift
              is the image.
This time shift
              takes place in my perception.

I can see something past now.
              I see an image.

It doesn't require much imagination to feel captured by the past sight,
to imagine it as your own and feel your eyes rapidly aging. But it requires
even less imagination to recognize the mechanism of fiction at work here.
Because that's what novels usually do; they present their readers with past
events in a mode "as if" one has been there. And exactly so do these images.
They bring our thoughts into the past. So is the past (also) something we can
always come back to?

But what is this trust grounded in? How come we think that
going back in time and revisiting a present as a past present allows us to
think better? Is this paradigm a click between philosophical and aesthetic
concerns? It is exactly the opposite of what philosophy tells us about the
role of time in the formation of a judgment or the formation of a concept.
Ideally, in the world of (philosophical) ideas, a concept or a judgment should
be timeless. But what if that's not the case, as we saw—as we saw with our
other eyes—above? Maybe we can argue against the idea of a judgment as
timeless. This is not an aesthetic argument. It is not that the present and the

vanishing of any present devalue historical transcendence. On the contrary: if we follow the aesthetic point of view, we see how it creates a tyranny of the present. Aesthetics have restricted our capacity to navigate time. Instead, the usual aesthetic premises let us follow our poetic intuition. It is an intuition that rests on language's temporal mechanics and at the same time on contemporary photography's devices of opening up asynchronous presents and unpredictable pasts.

To project ourselves in time is a basic gesture of emancipation. Feeling closer to some pasts than to others is not just a matter of a short biography in relation to the vast extent of documented times. It allows for a certain autonomy that is dictated by an individual. To project ourselves in time also allows for a capacity to choose which pasts we want to bring closer to us and which ones we'd like to distance ourselves from. It is the tense tense of images. When, where, and under what circumstances do we bring a specific image? Maybe we can argue for a construction of a poetics of time via the image. It might not be exactly an autonomy that it would offer but rather a "poetonomy" to create.

Like our present, asynchronous and tense, that poetonomy might lead us back to multiplicity. It may be through two images—as with two presents, each asynchronous with the other and with themselves—that we reach (again) an asynchronous present, that moldable place. It may well be that we cannot return to the past. But the present is a place we can always come back to.

Tea

1391, single-channel 35mm film transferred to HD,
color, sound, English with Dari subtitles, 64' 00"
Thyssen-Bornemisza Art Contemporary Collection, Vienna

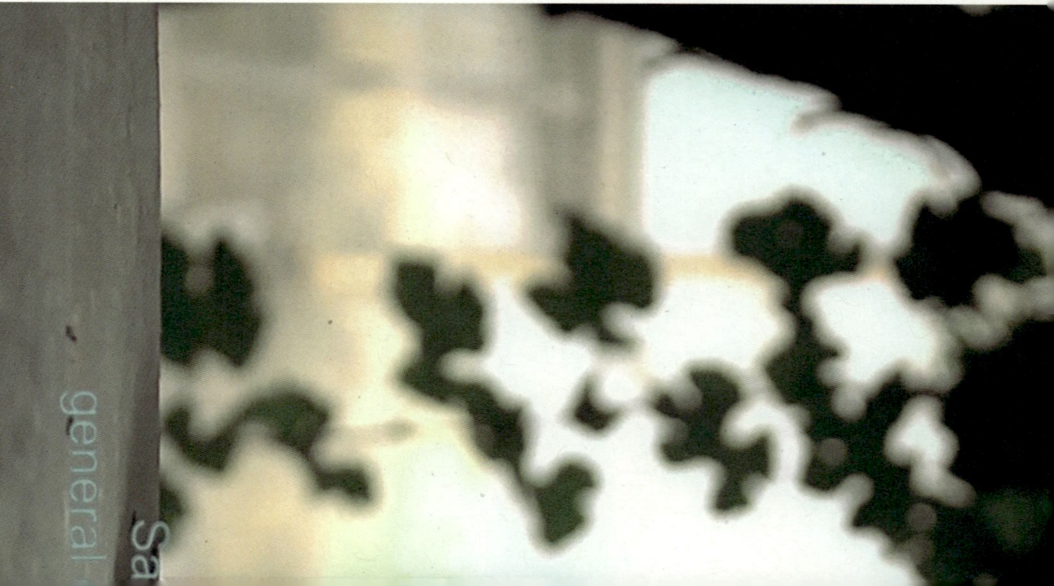

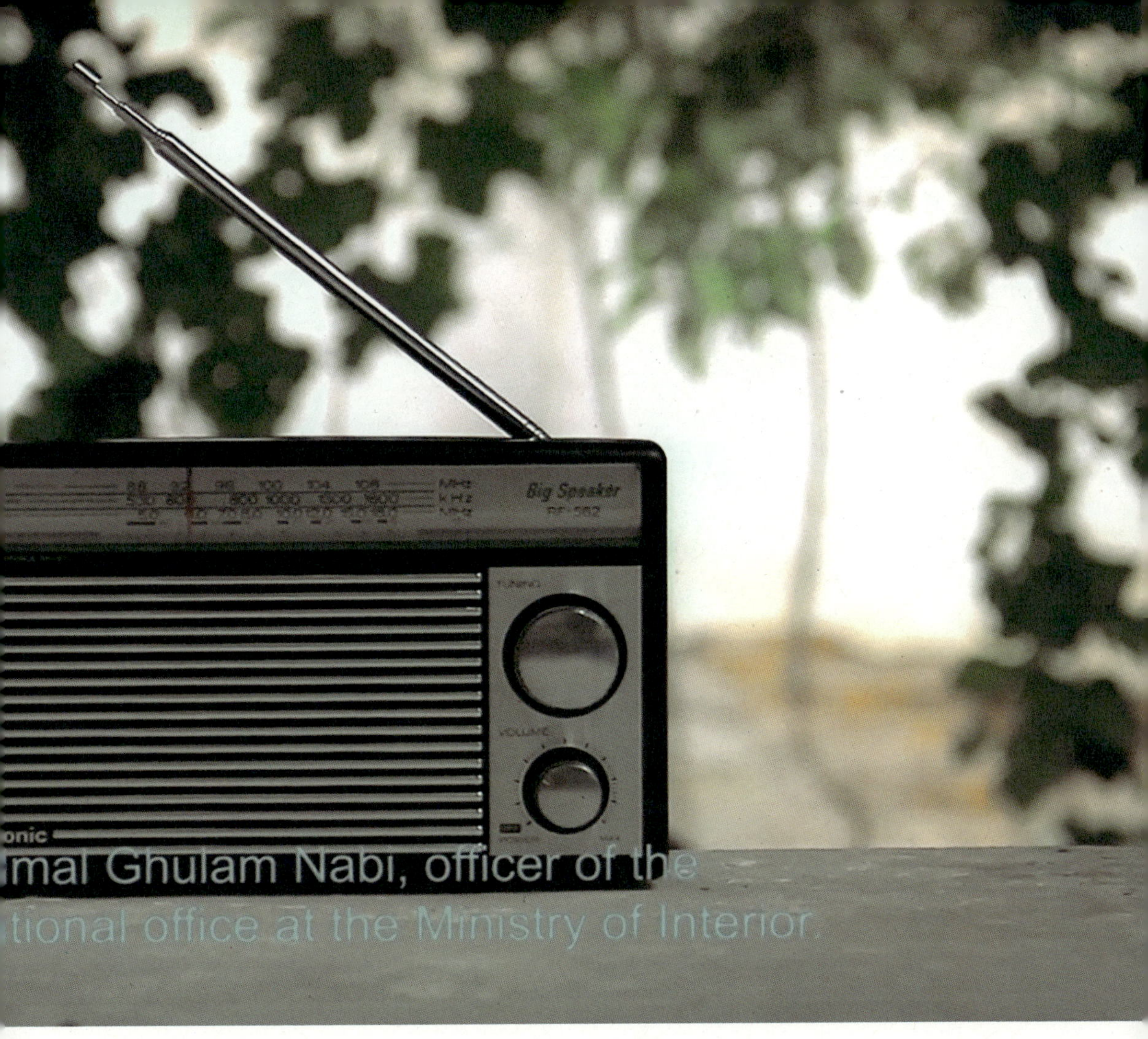
Big Speaker
mal Ghulam Nabi, officer of the
tional office at the Ministry of Interior

64' 00"

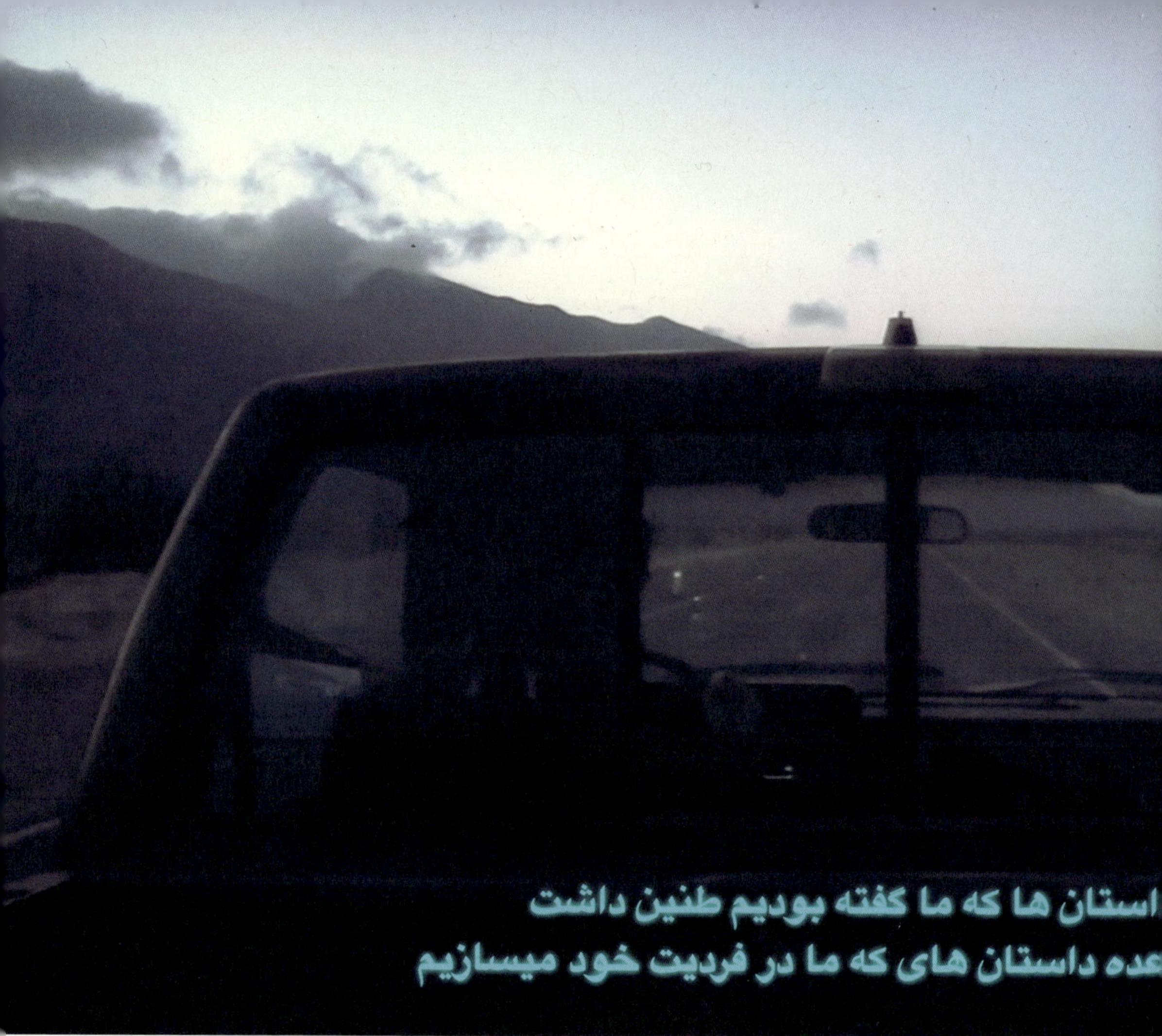

84

There, I got a glimpse of the artist's role.
I started to make connections between
the objects on display and the people
who brought them in.

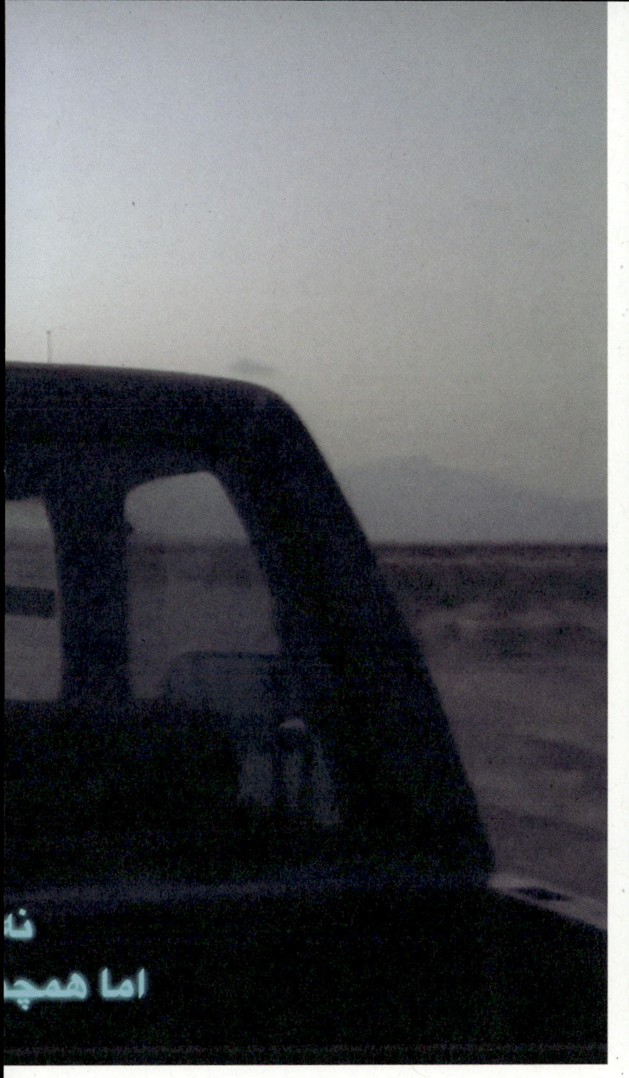

64' 00"

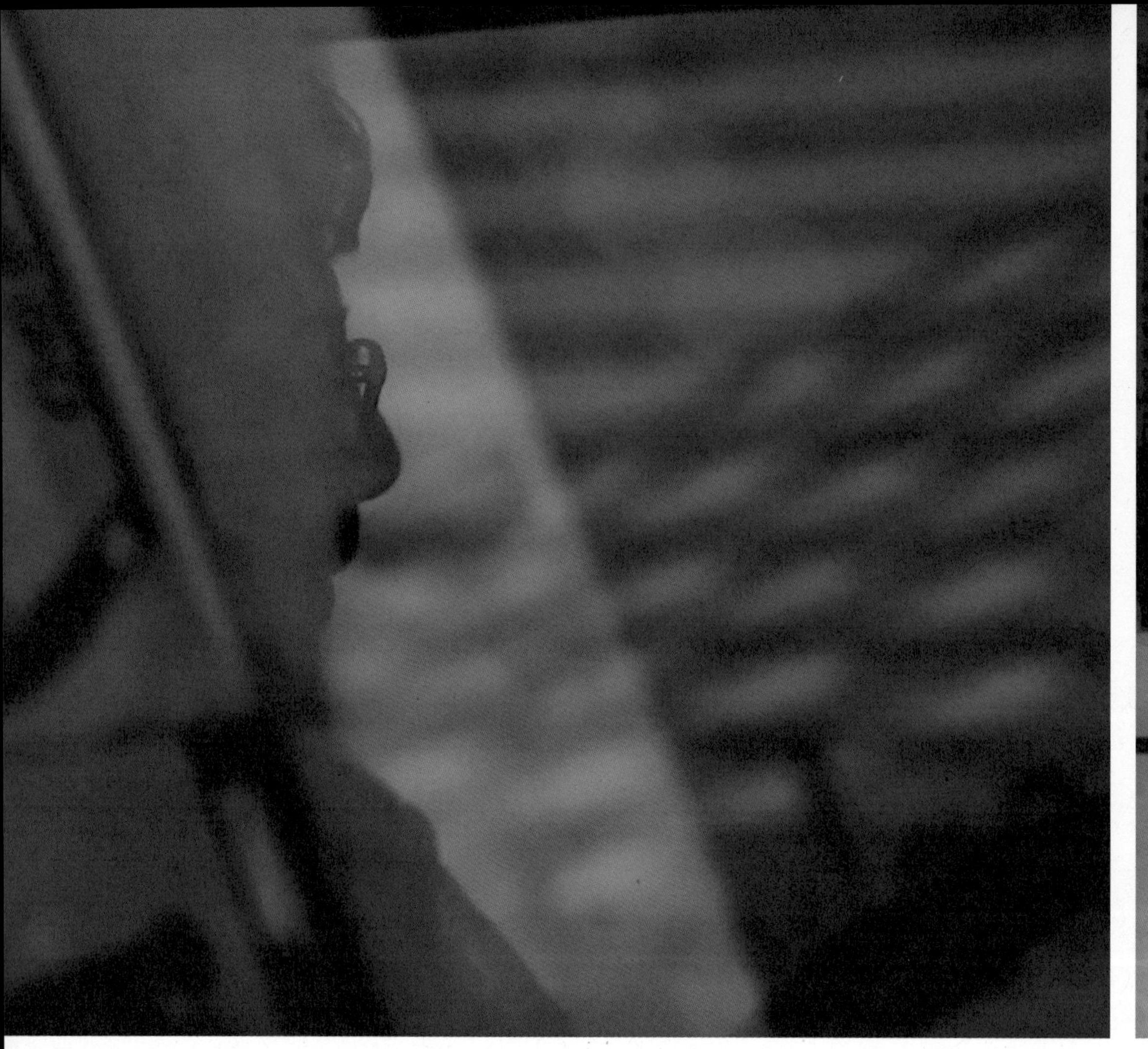

86

00' 00"

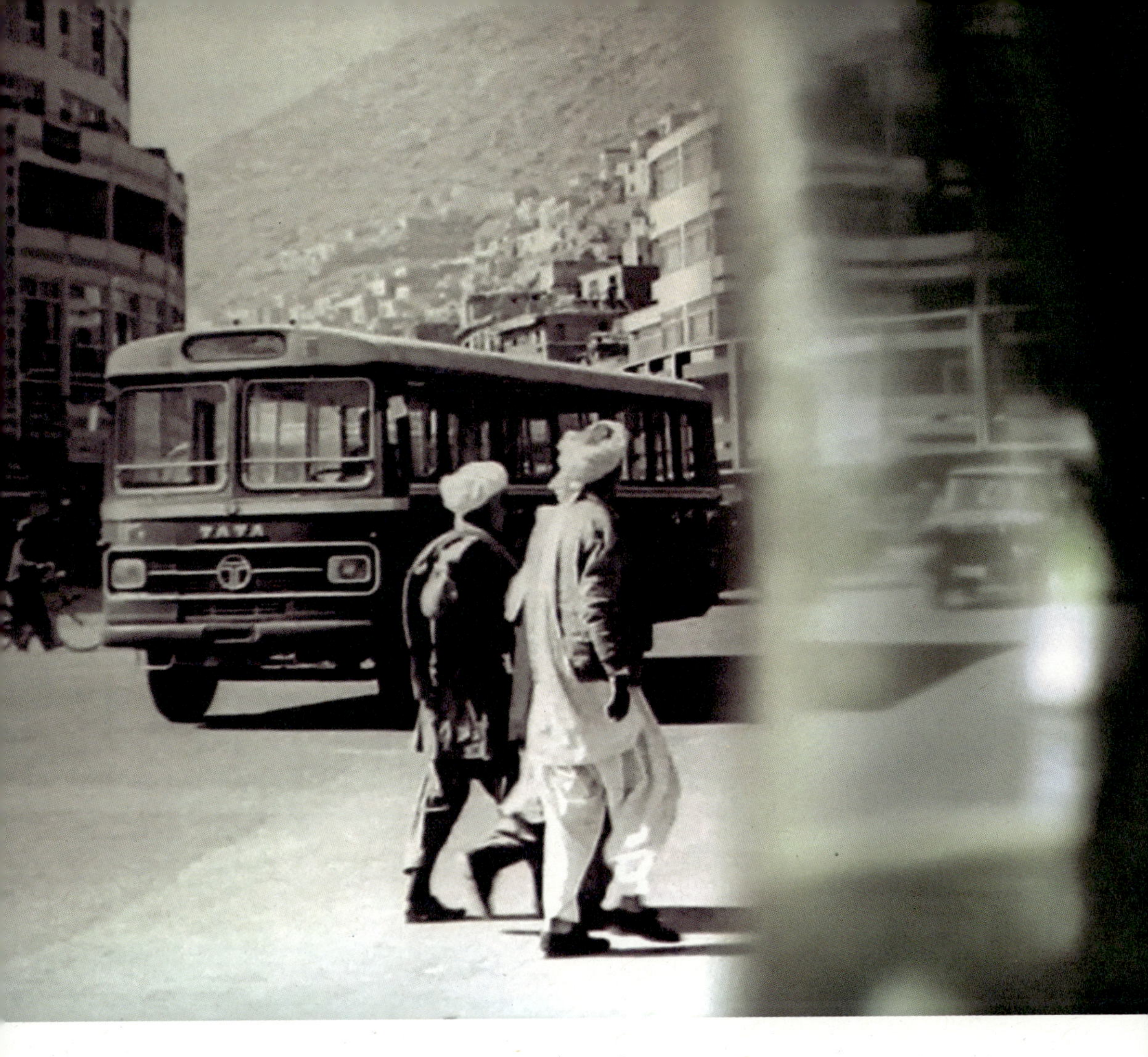

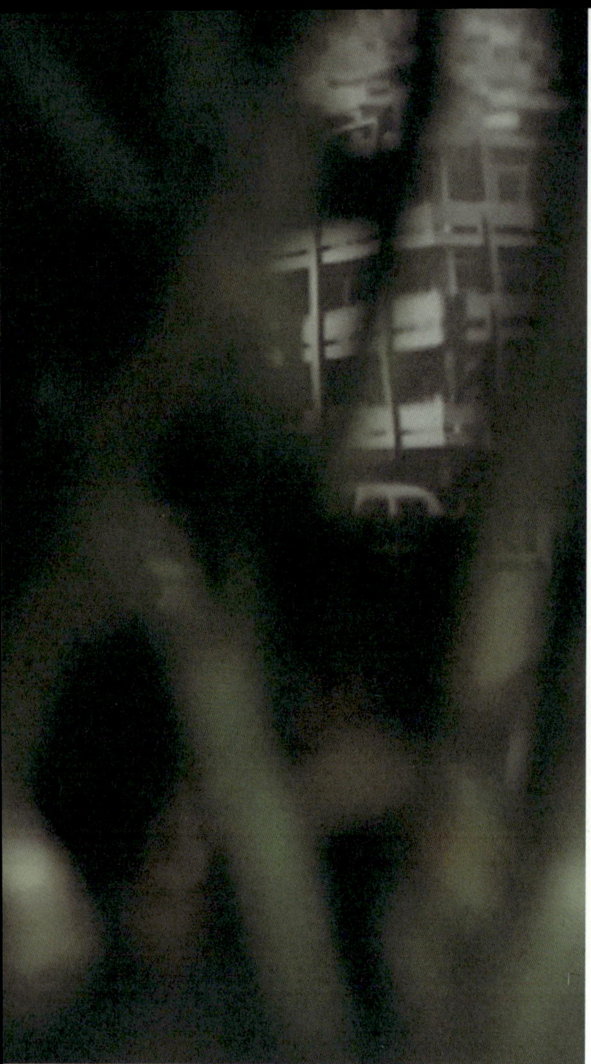

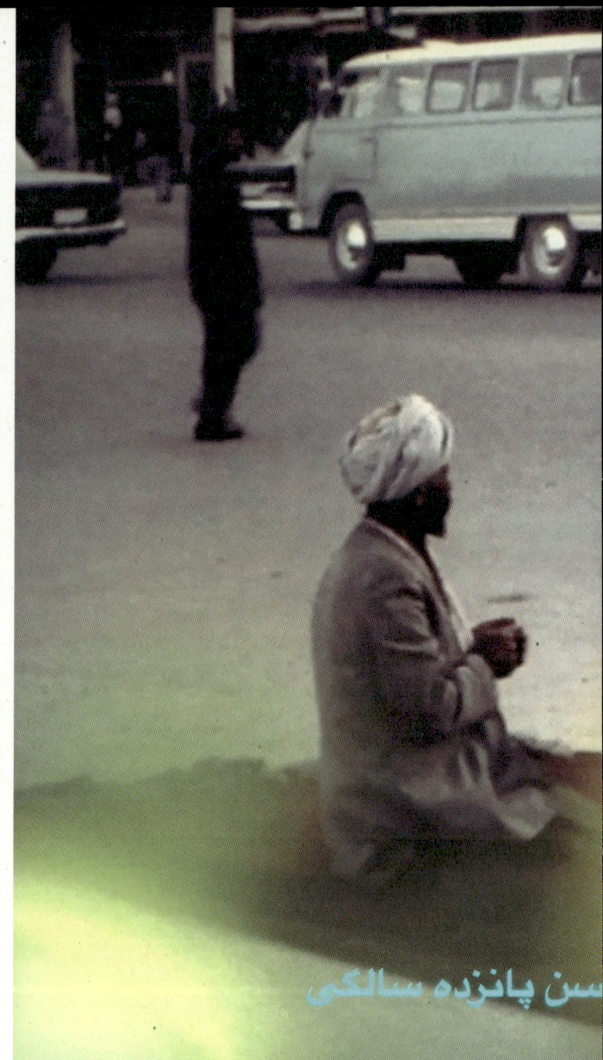

00' 00"

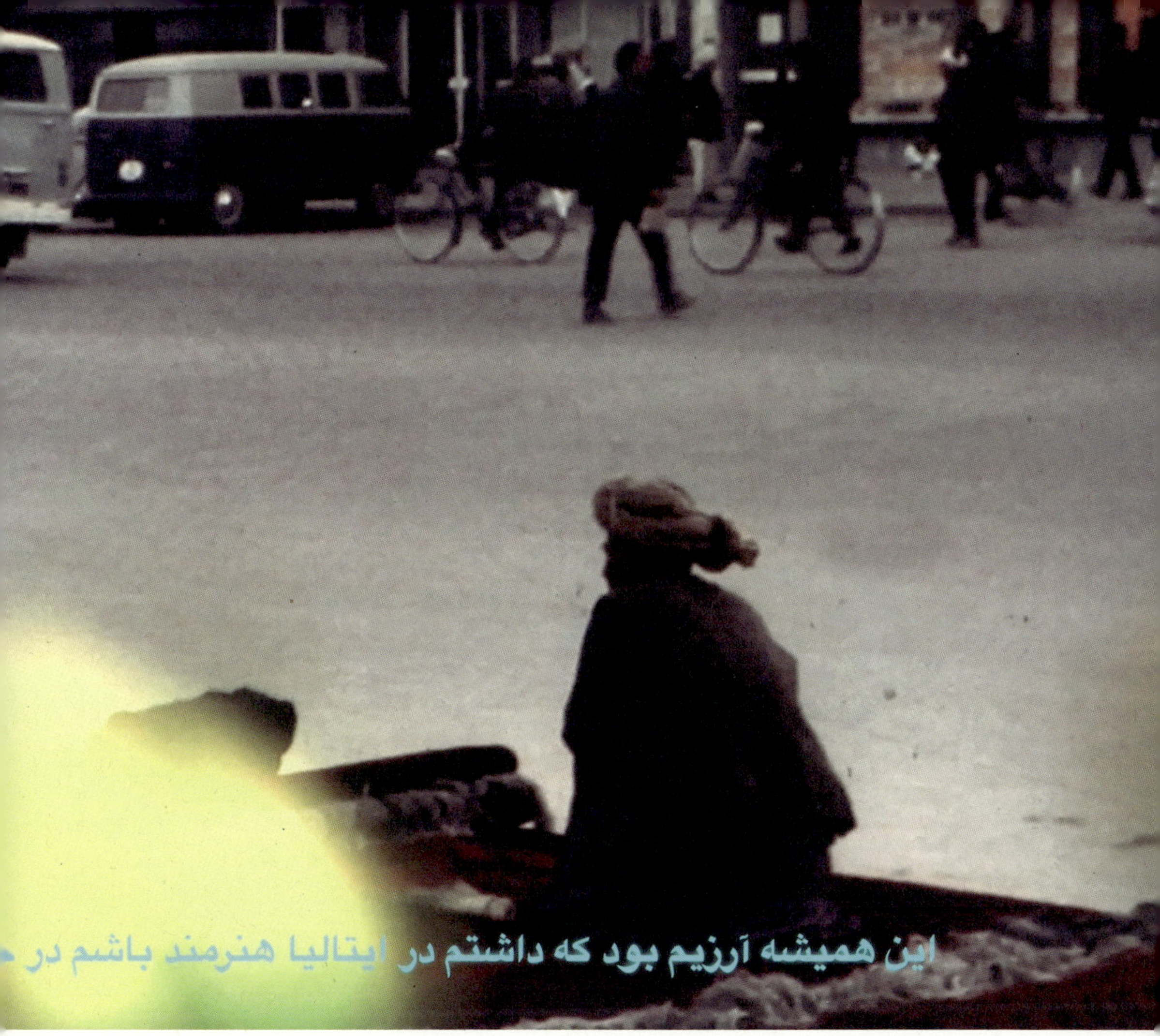

Art happened in some faraway place,
always somewhere else.

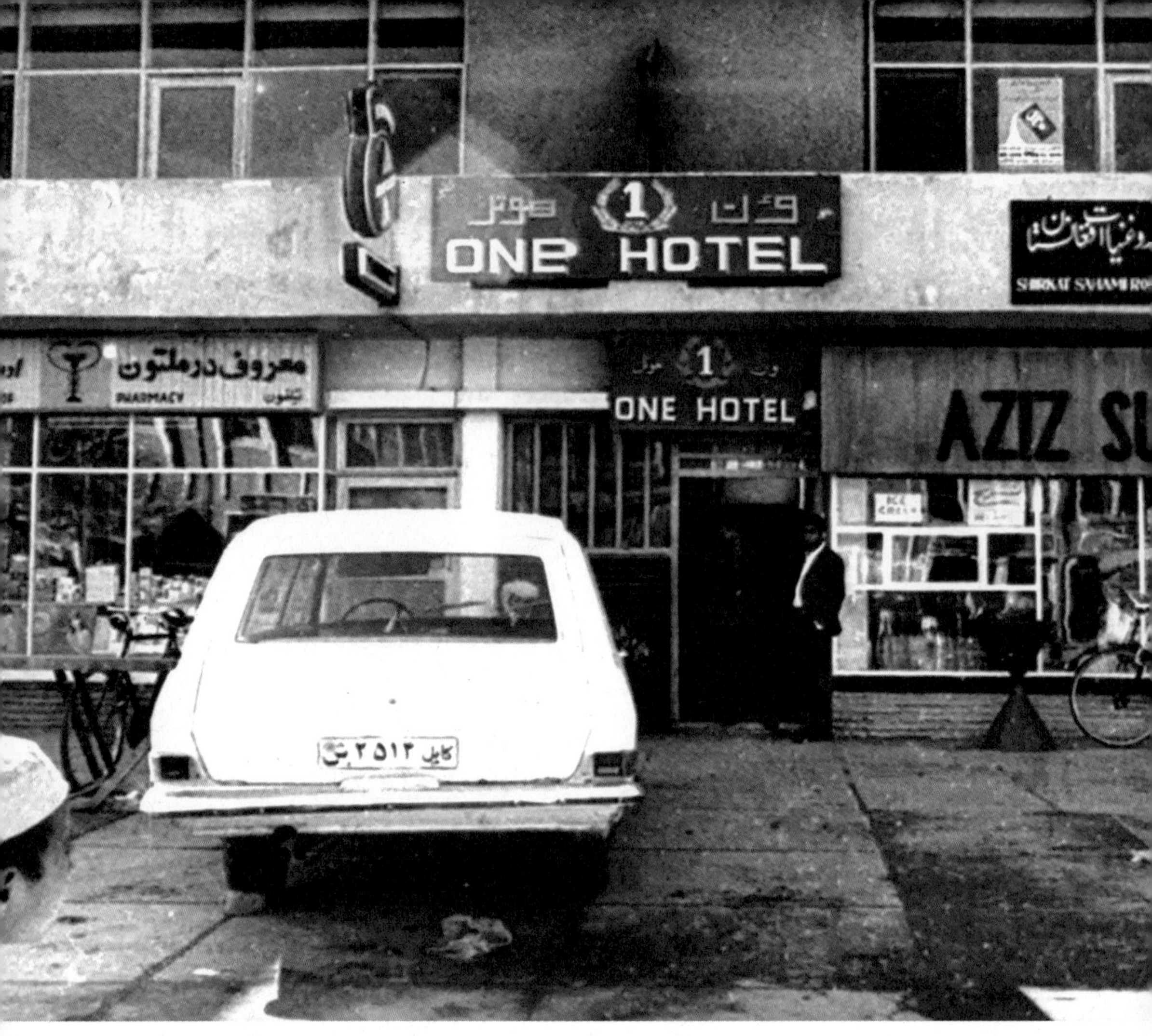

00' 00"

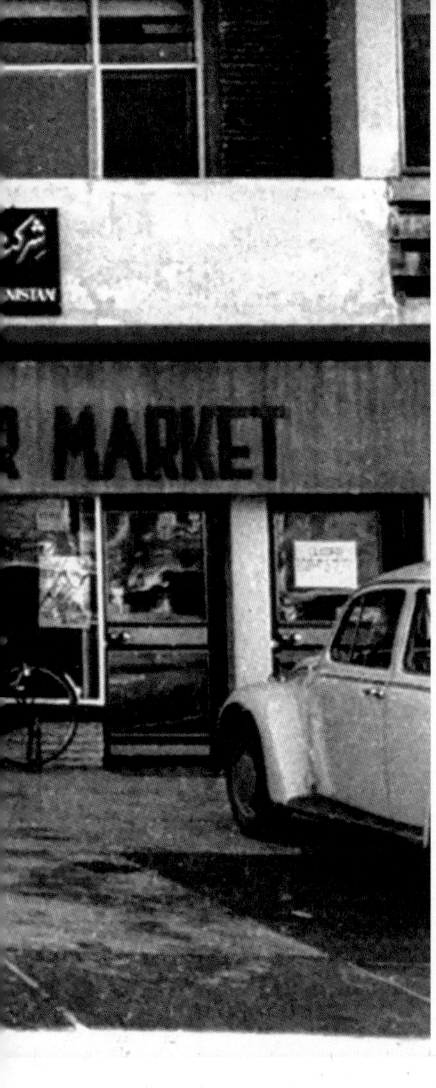

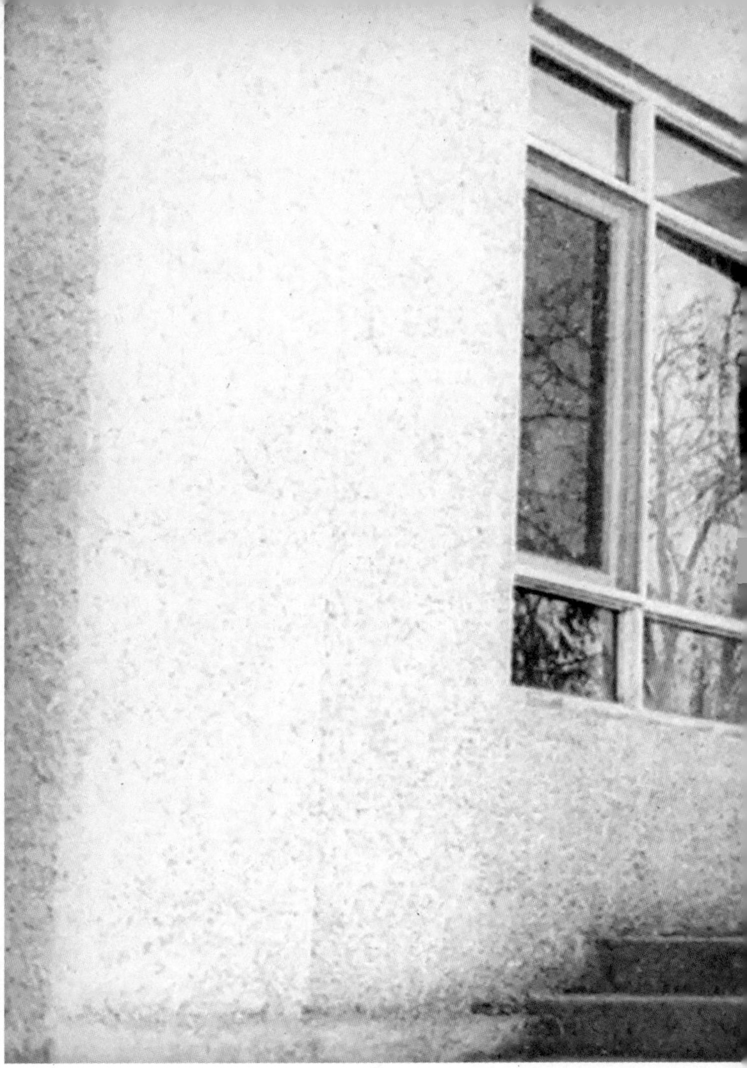

64' 00"

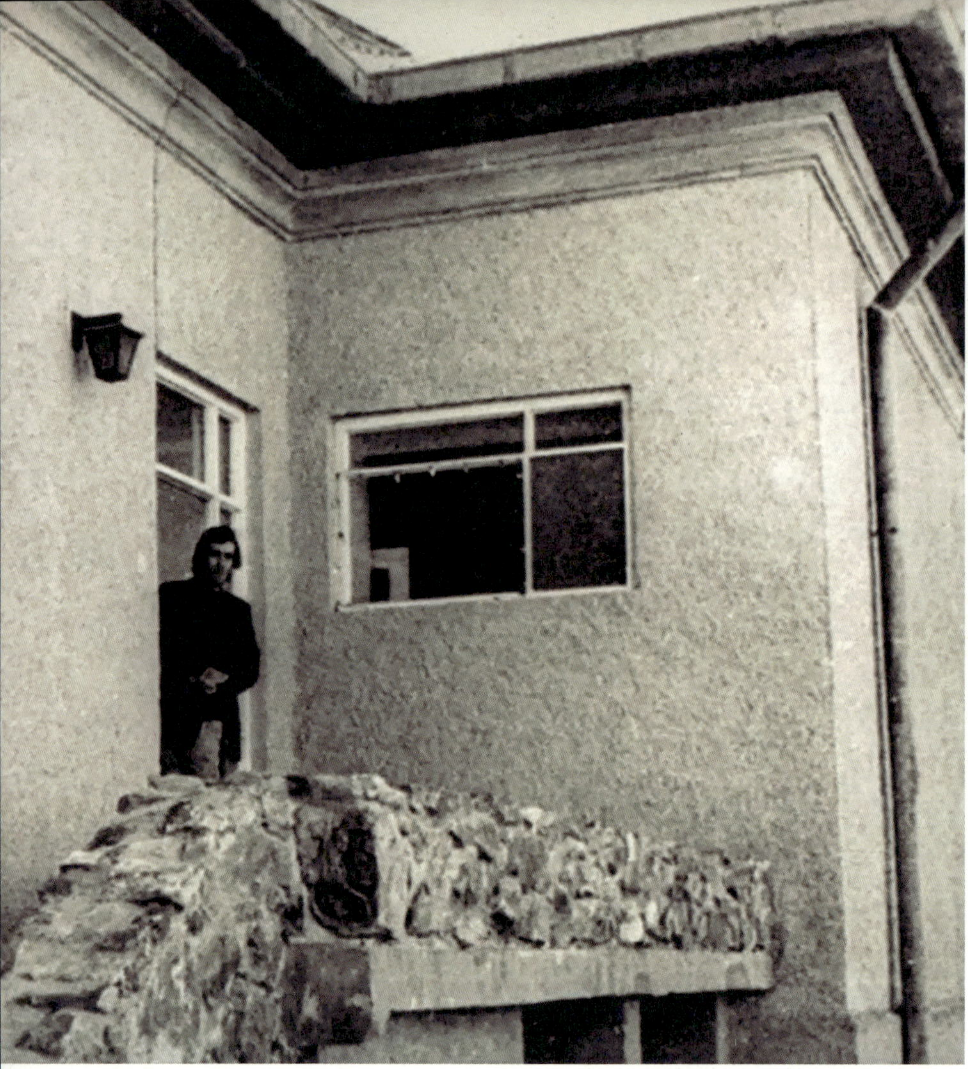

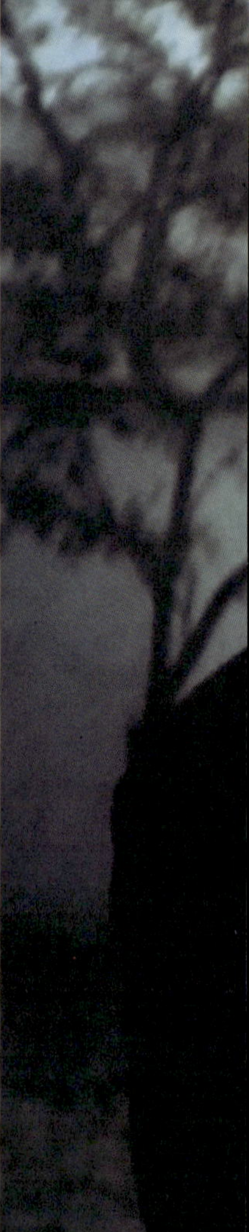

00' 00"

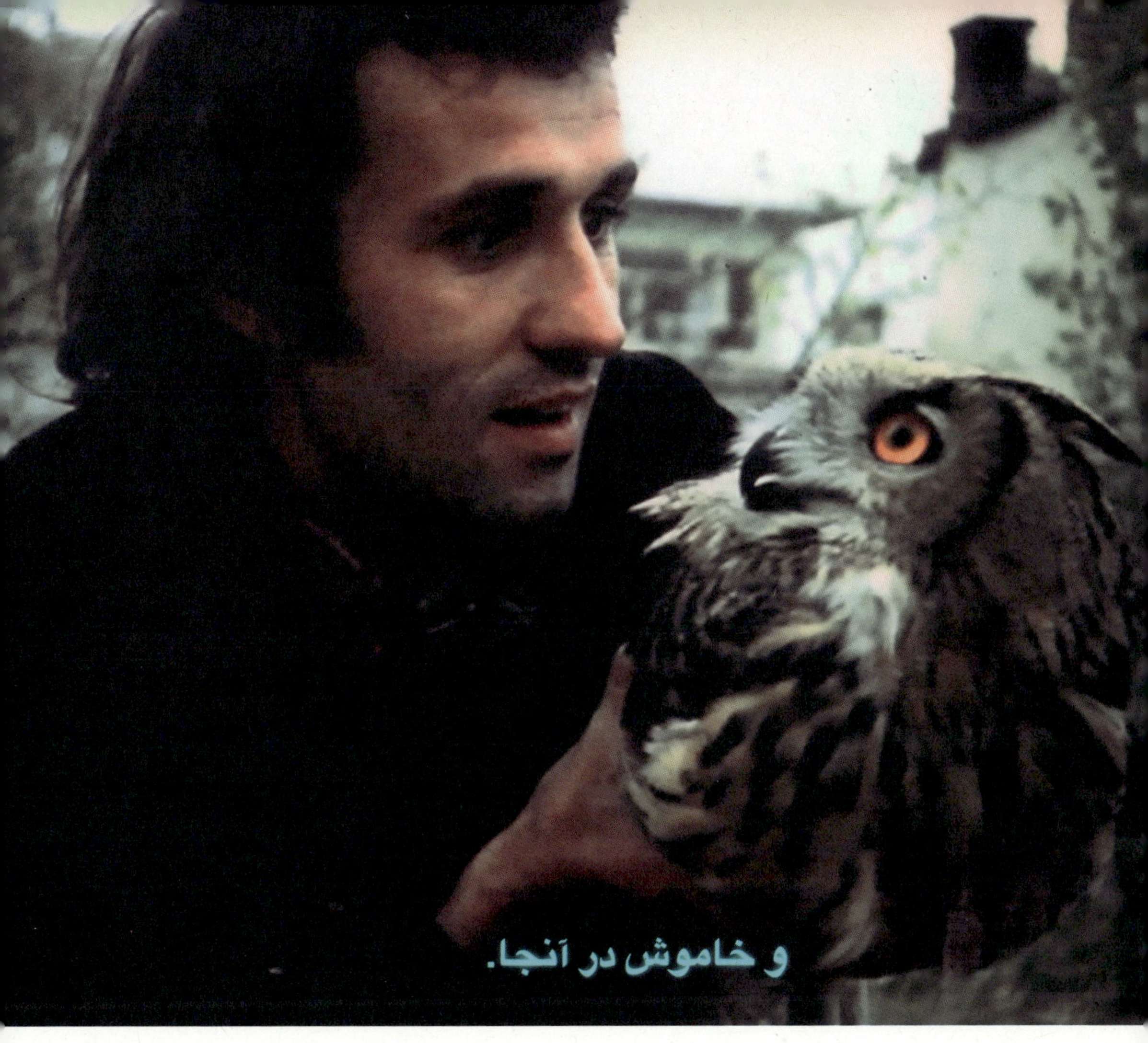

64' 00"

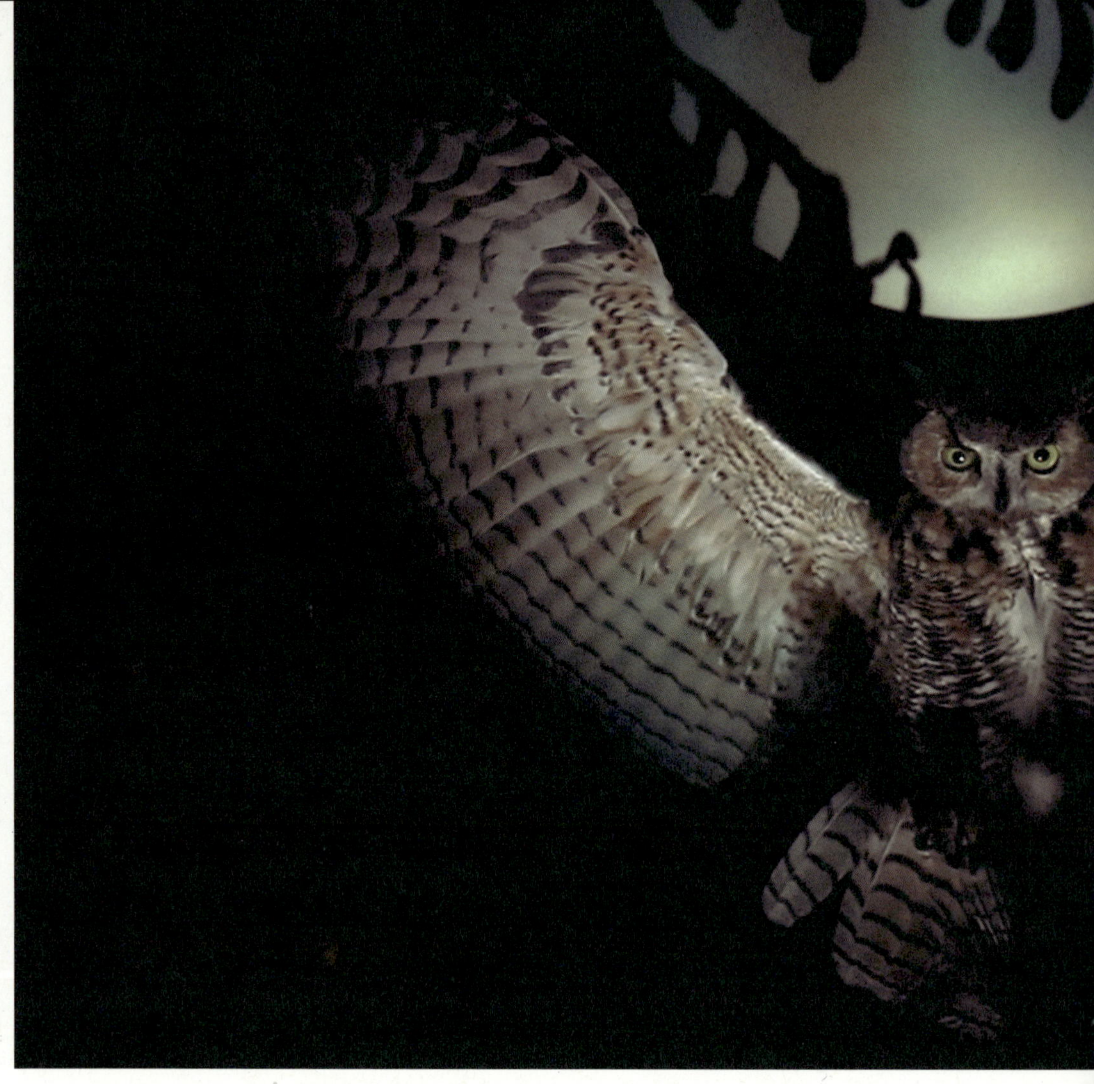

Artists that were also hosts have attracted
my interest for some time. I've dwelled on those
places, first through the accounts and memories
of other people, then retuning to those sites
while visiting them for the first time.

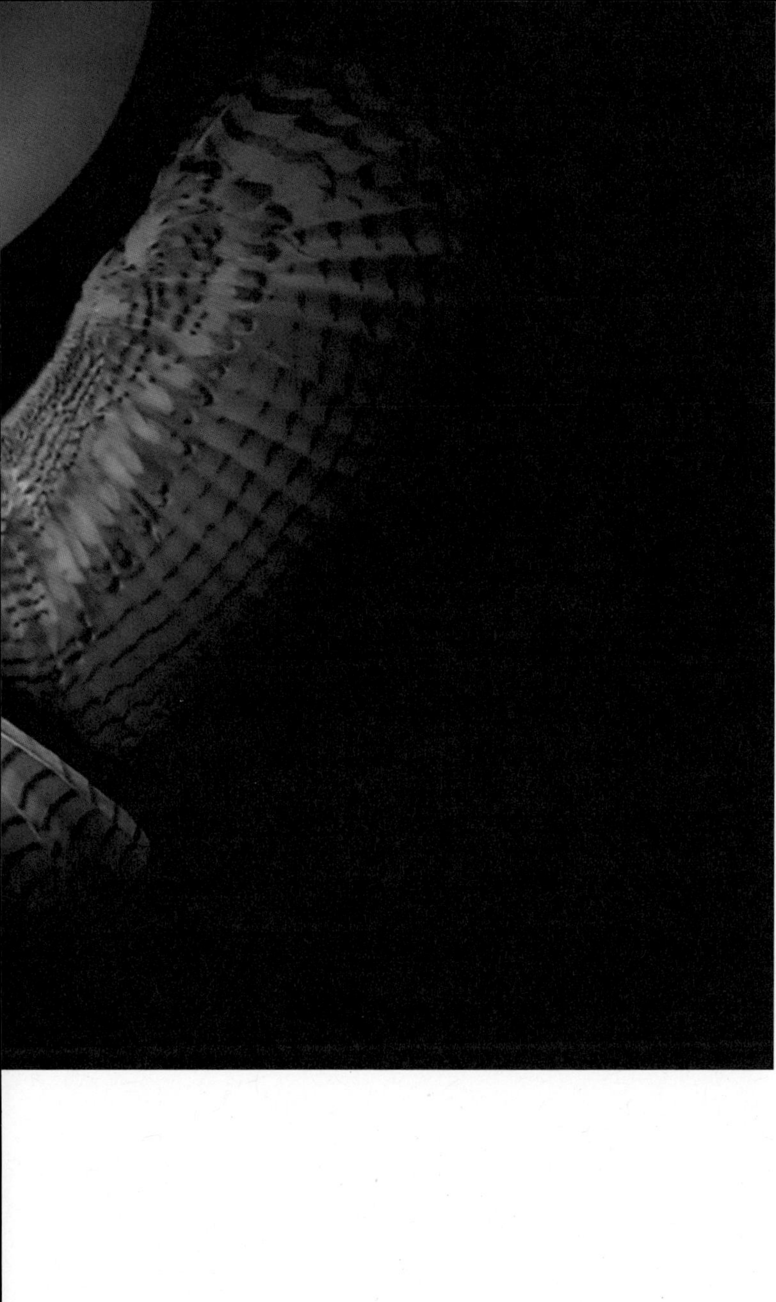

64' 00"

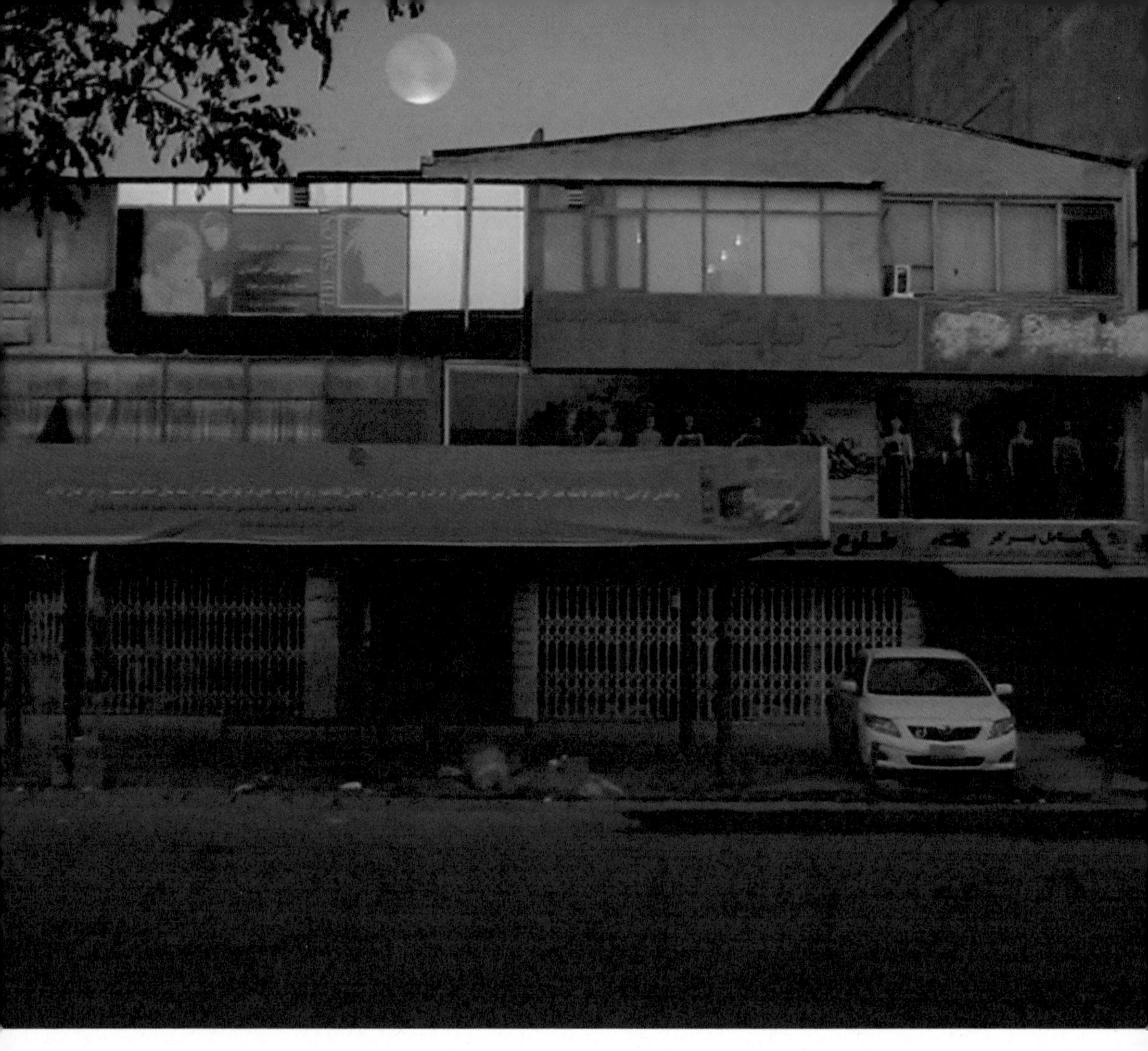

00' 00"

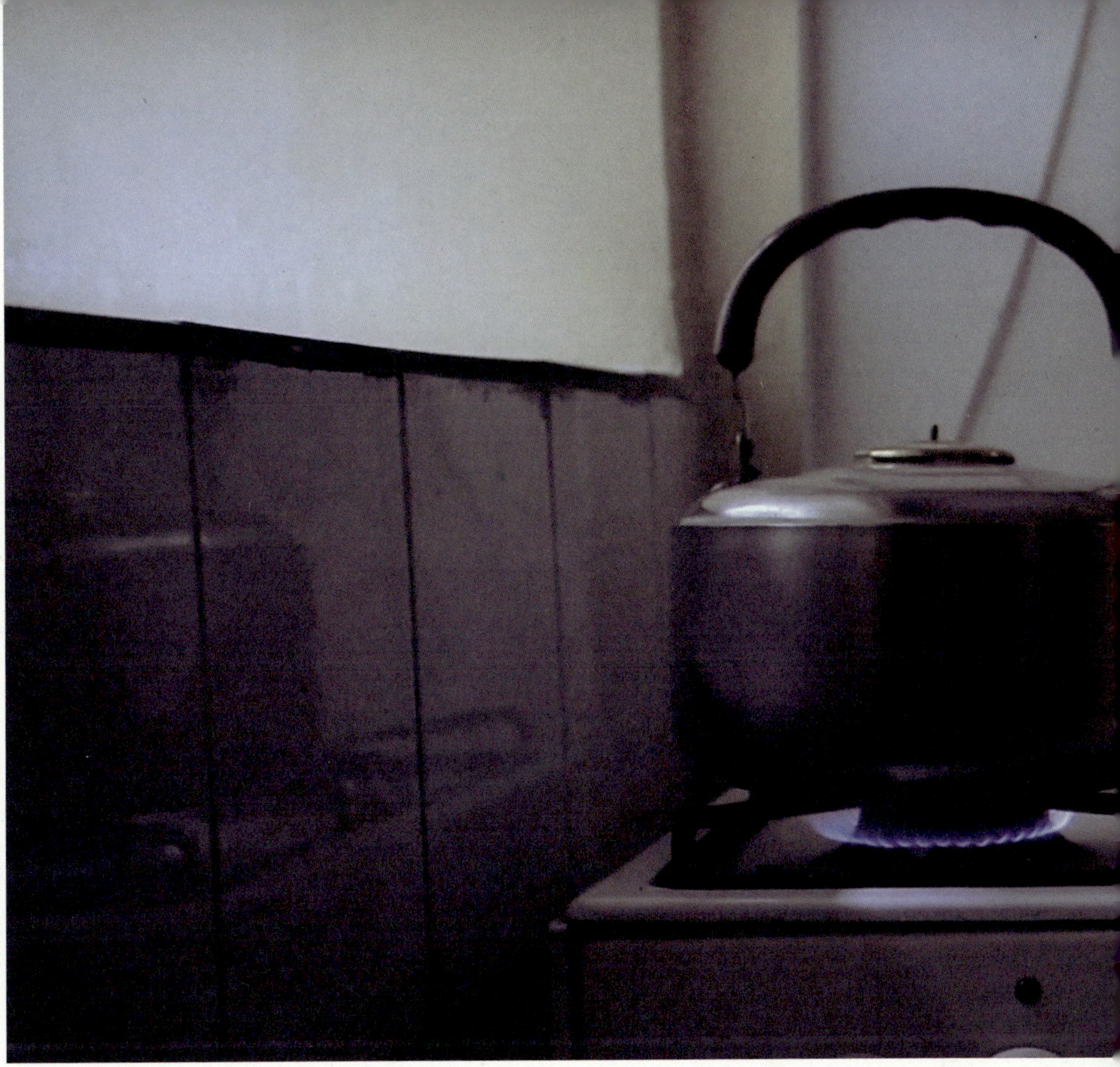

64' 00"

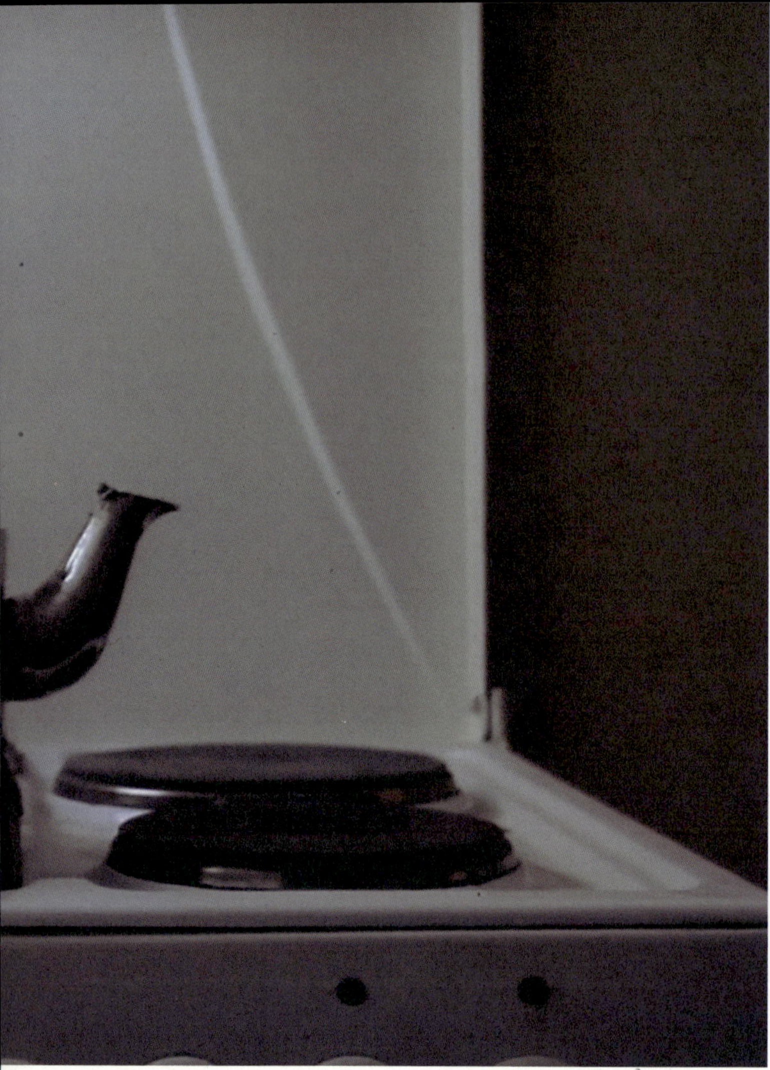

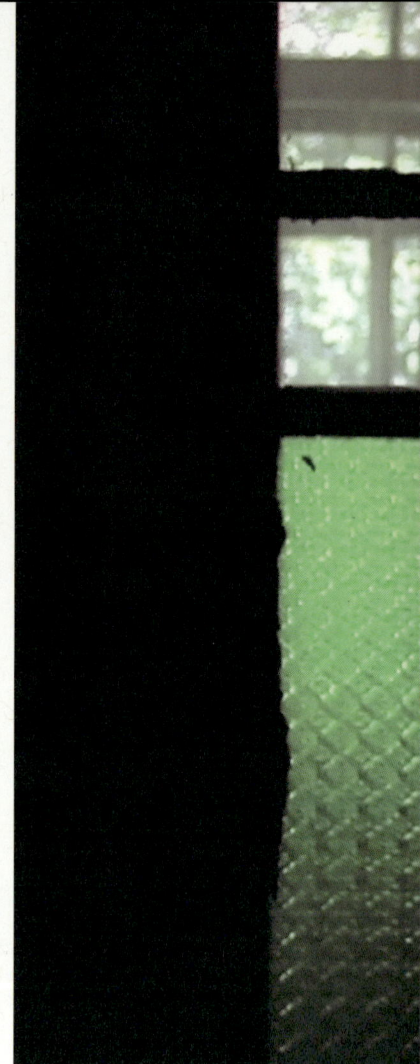

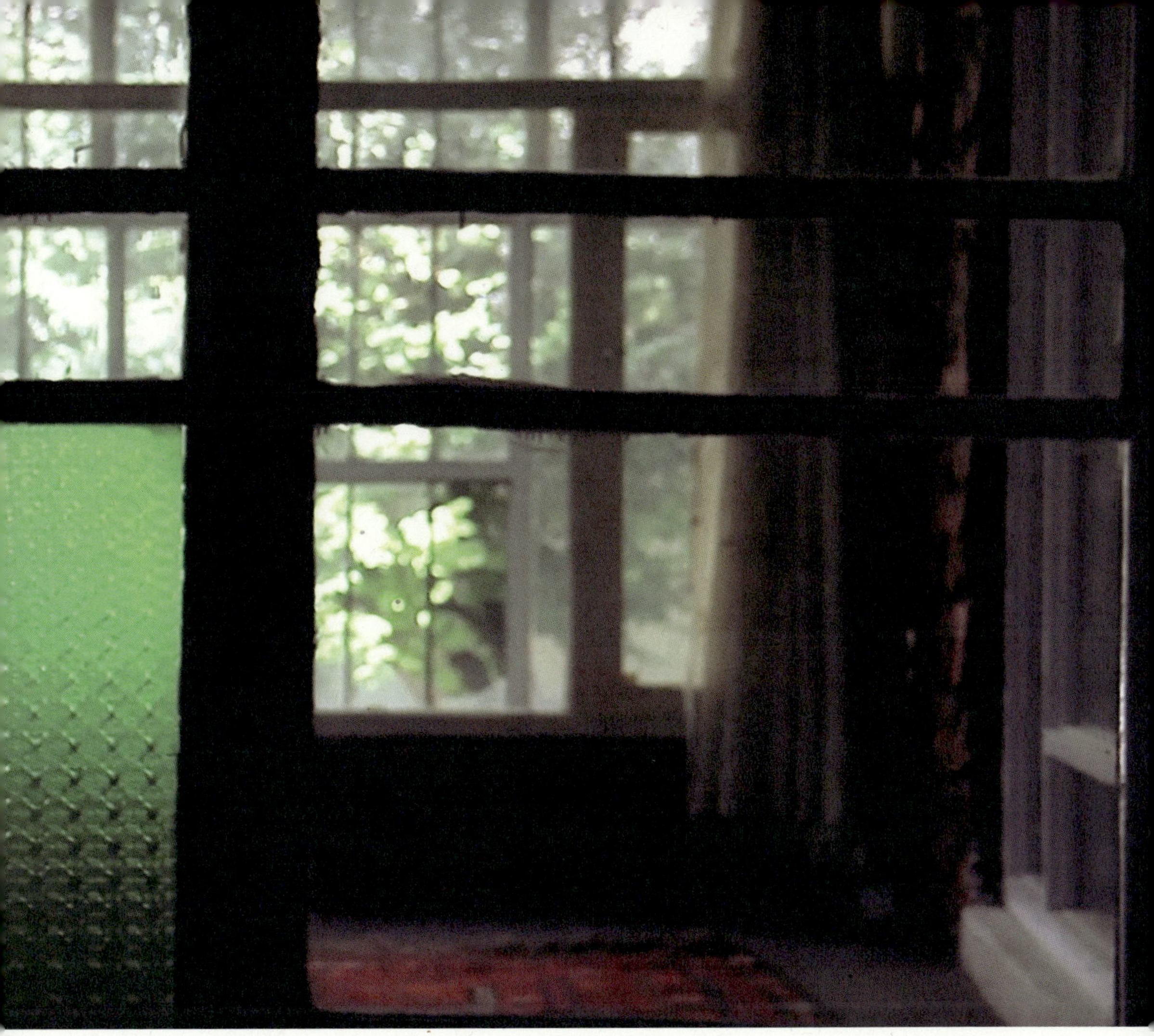

I might argue that I had been invited
to register at the One Hotel. The problem
was I'd come thirty-three years too late.

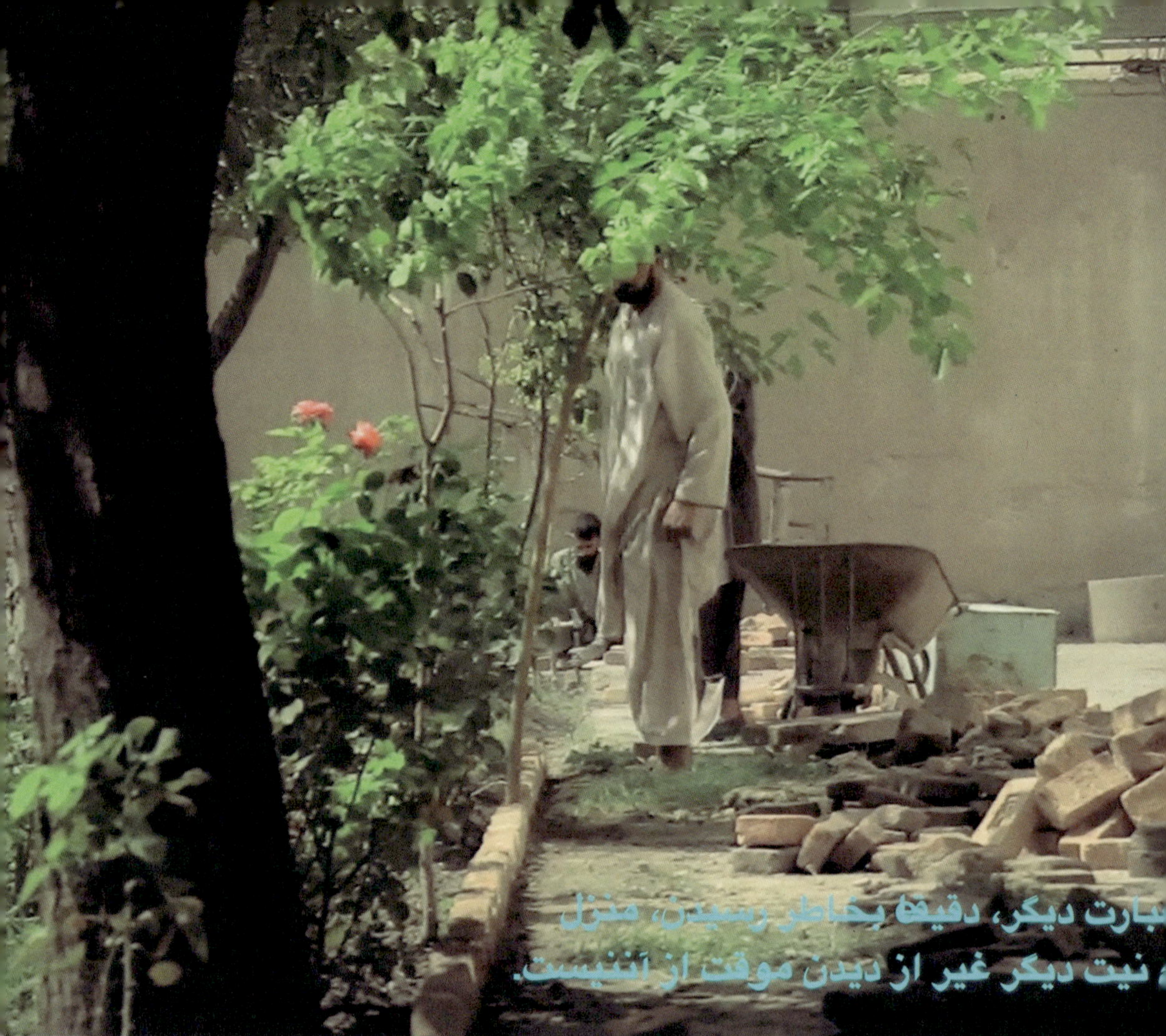

In other words, precisely because of having
arrived, the destination becomes a departure
and there is no other intention that comes up
than looking after it momentarily.

00' 00"

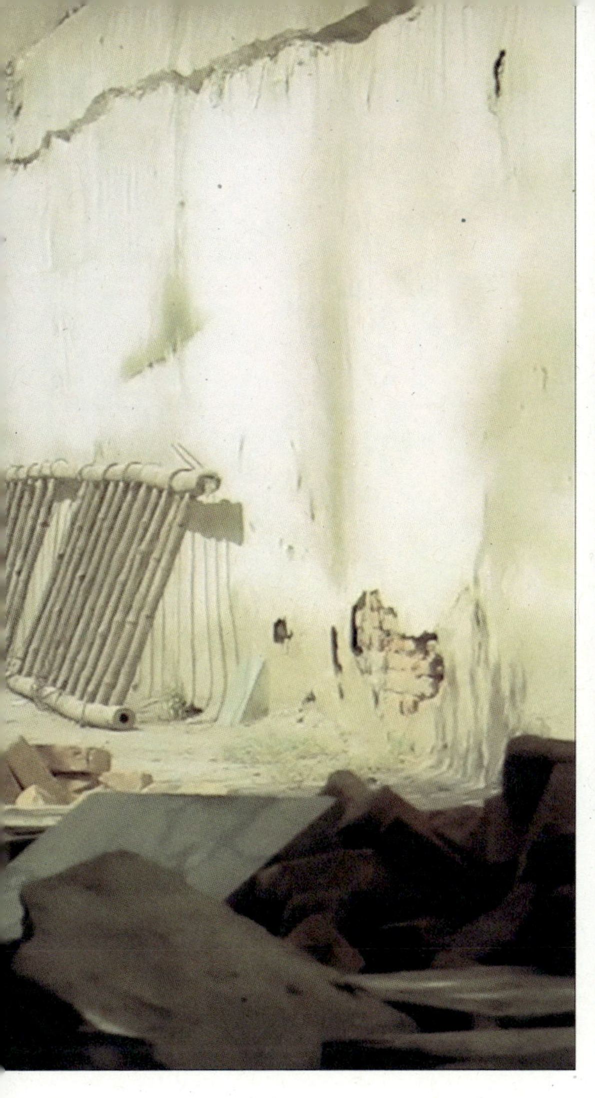

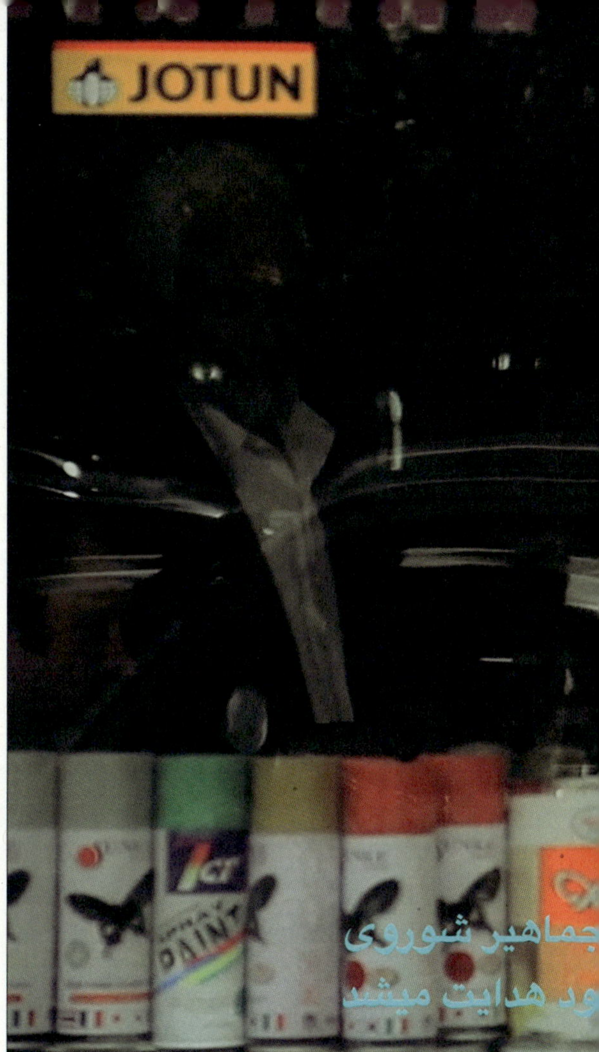

The only desire is to live like in any other place, and then to let it go.

64' 00"

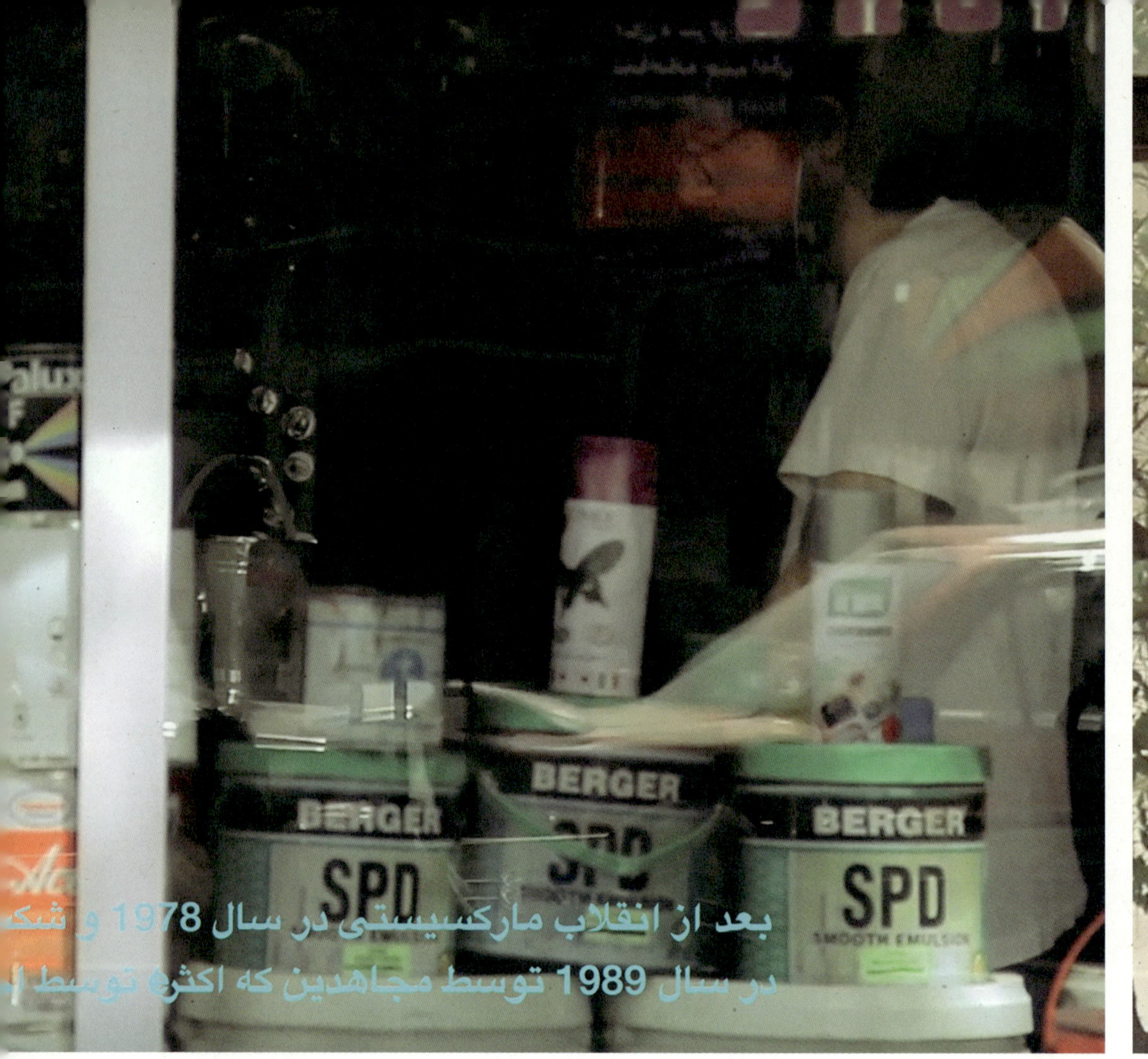
بعد از انقلاب مارکسیستی در سال 1978 و شکس
در سال 1989 توسط مجاهدین که اکثره توسط ا

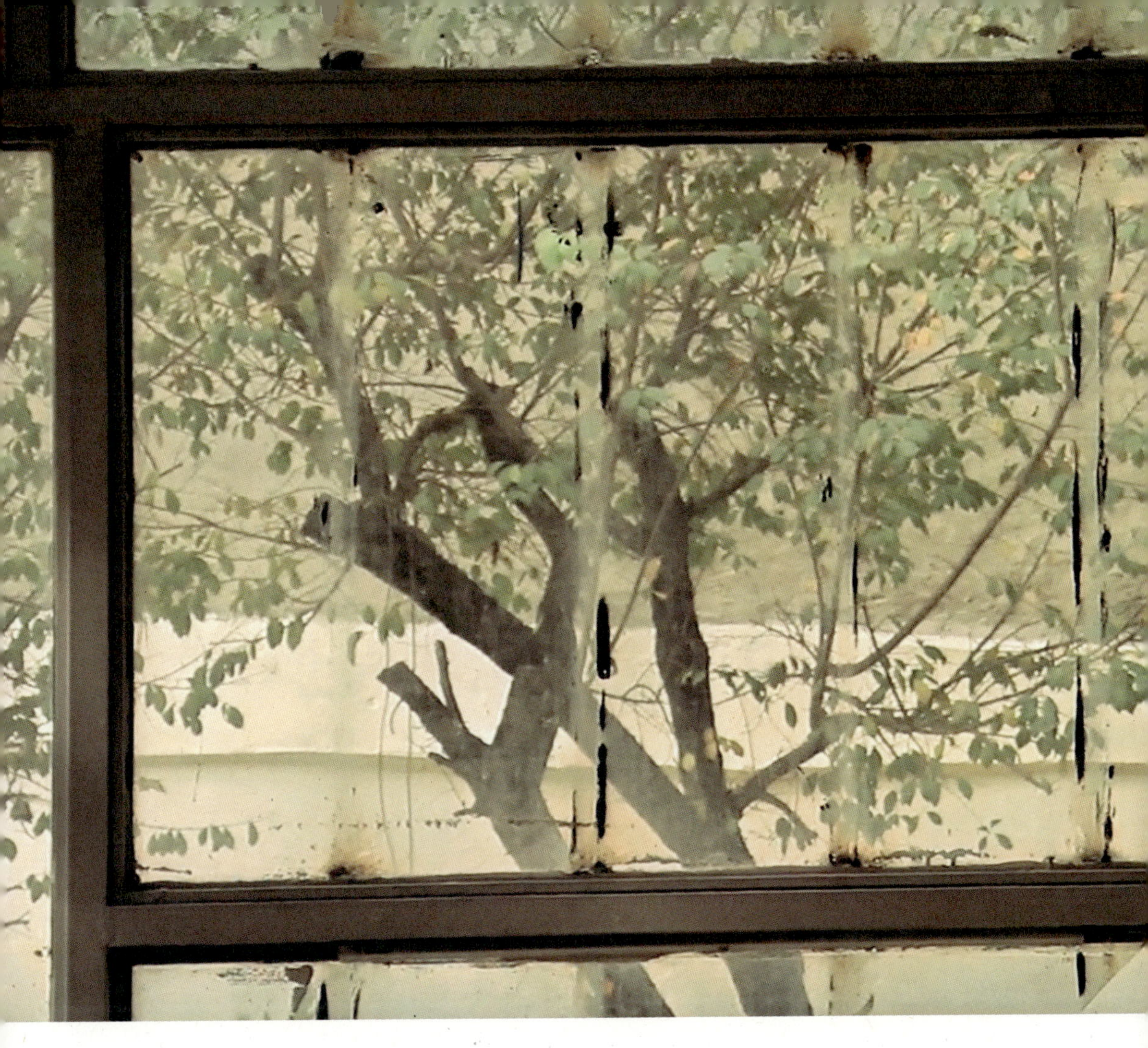

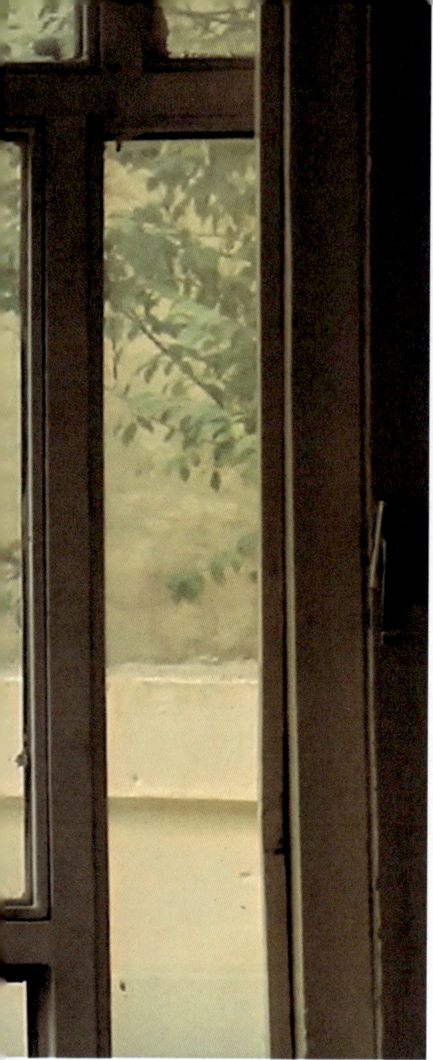

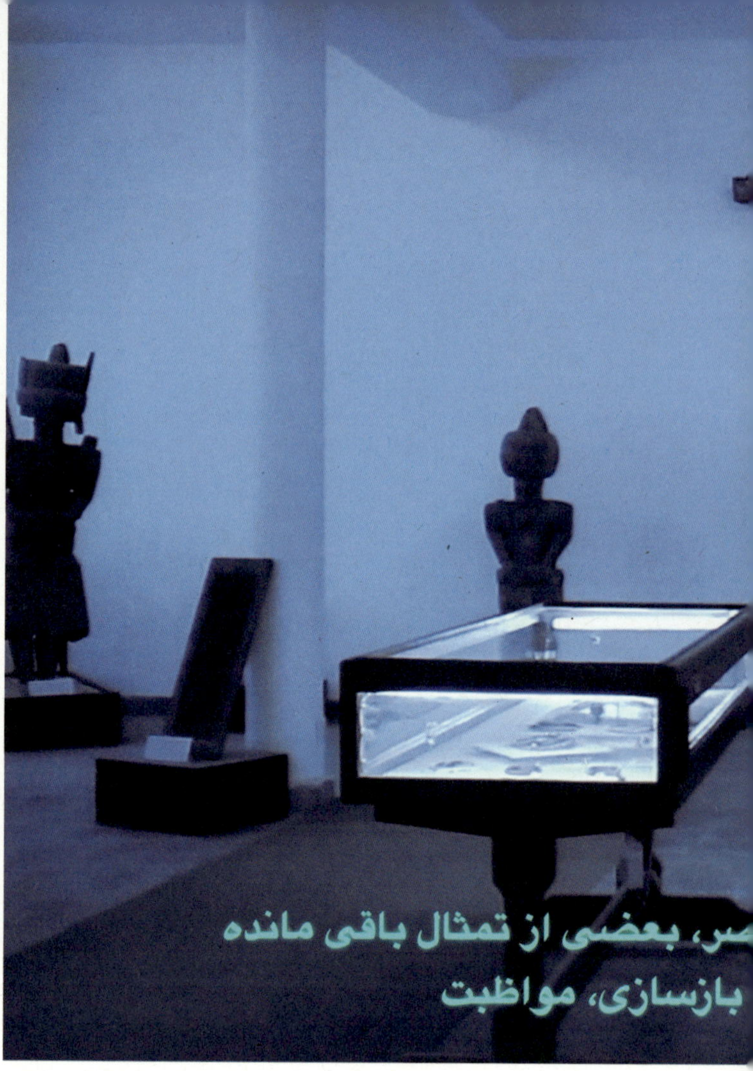

After all, what are museums if not places
where history and stories are collected, where
distances are shortened, and where the politics
behind time and place are continually debated
and put on display?

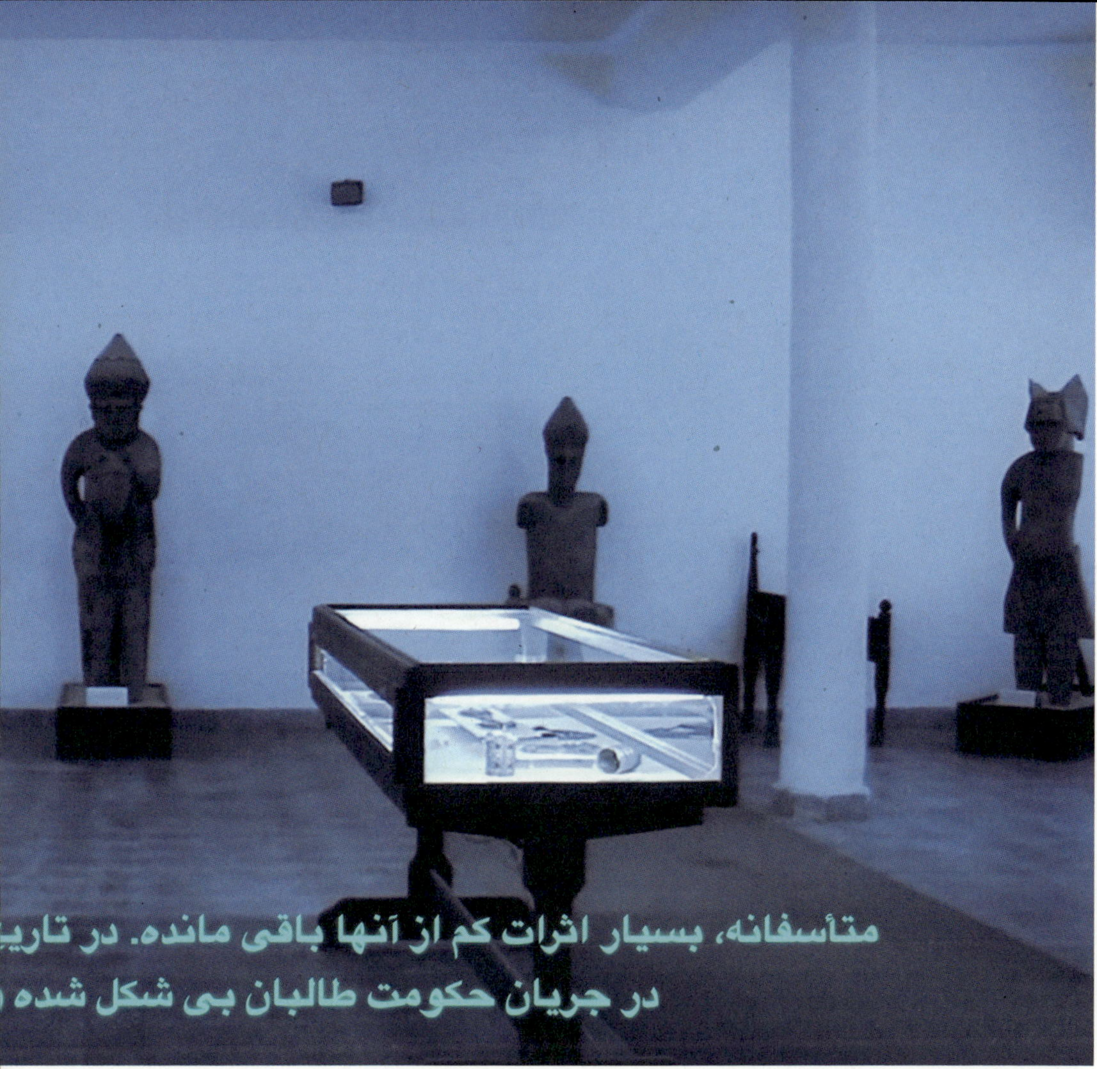

متأسفانه، بسیار اثرات کم از آنها باقی مانده. در تاری
در جریان حکومت طالبان بی شکل شده

64' 00"

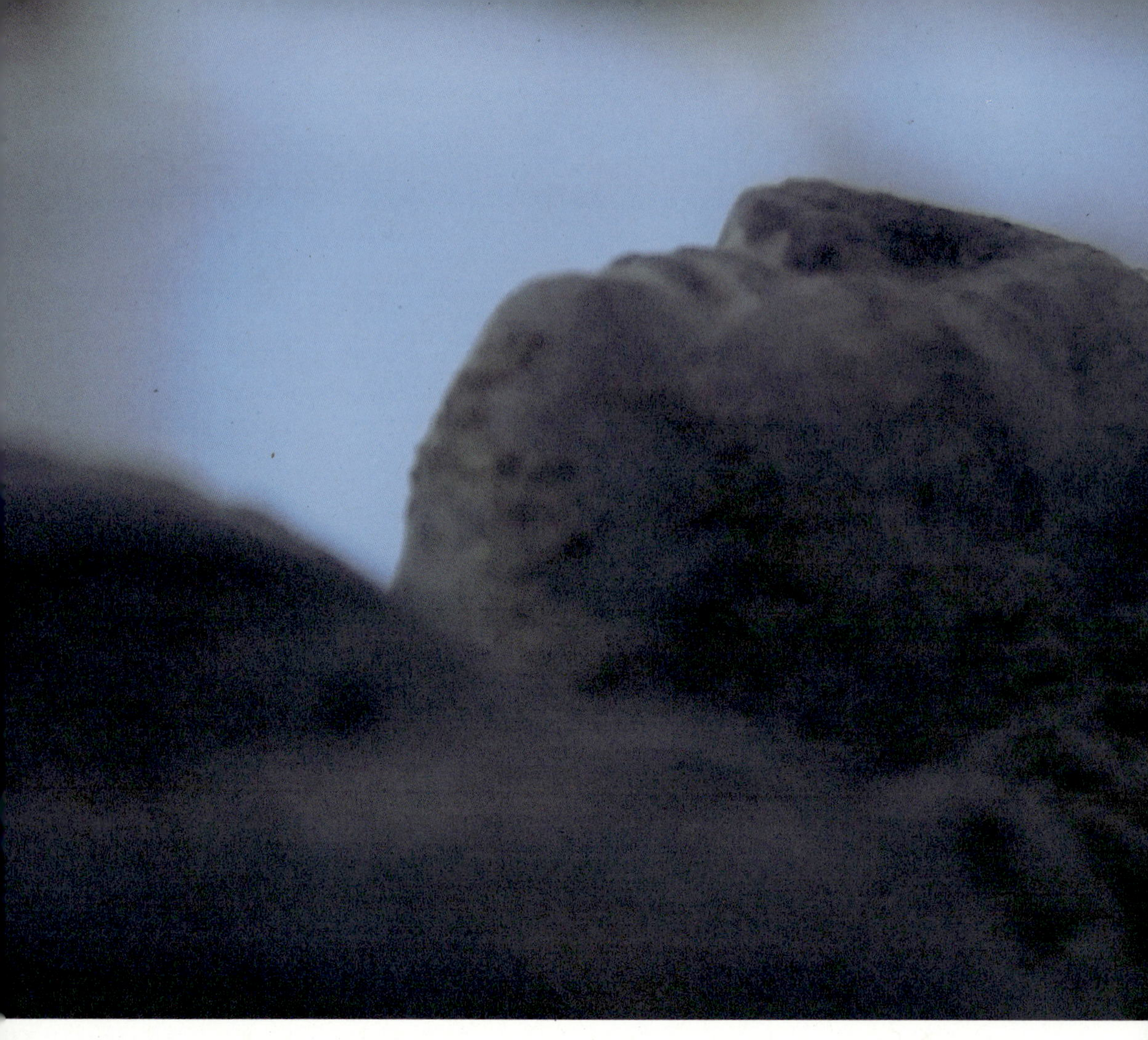

00' 00"

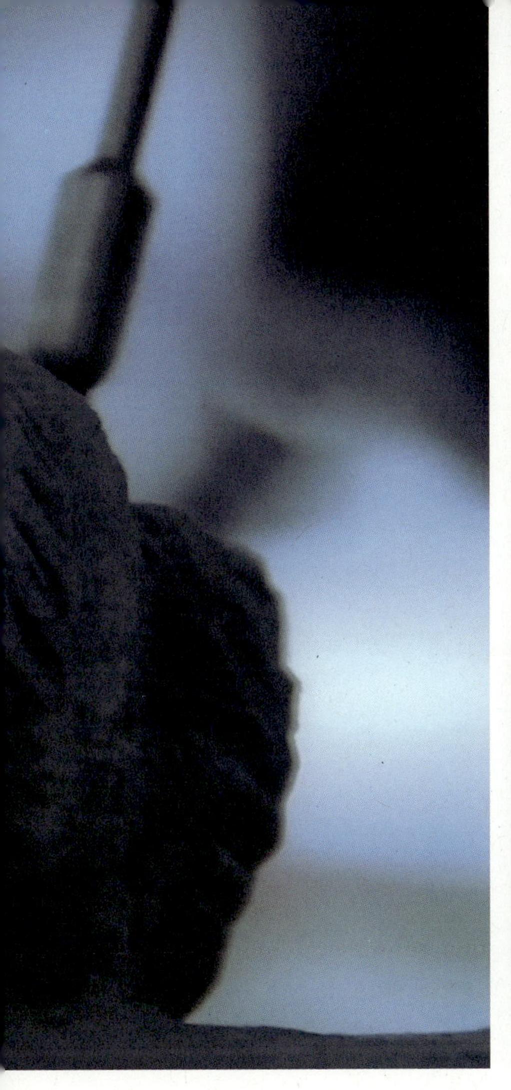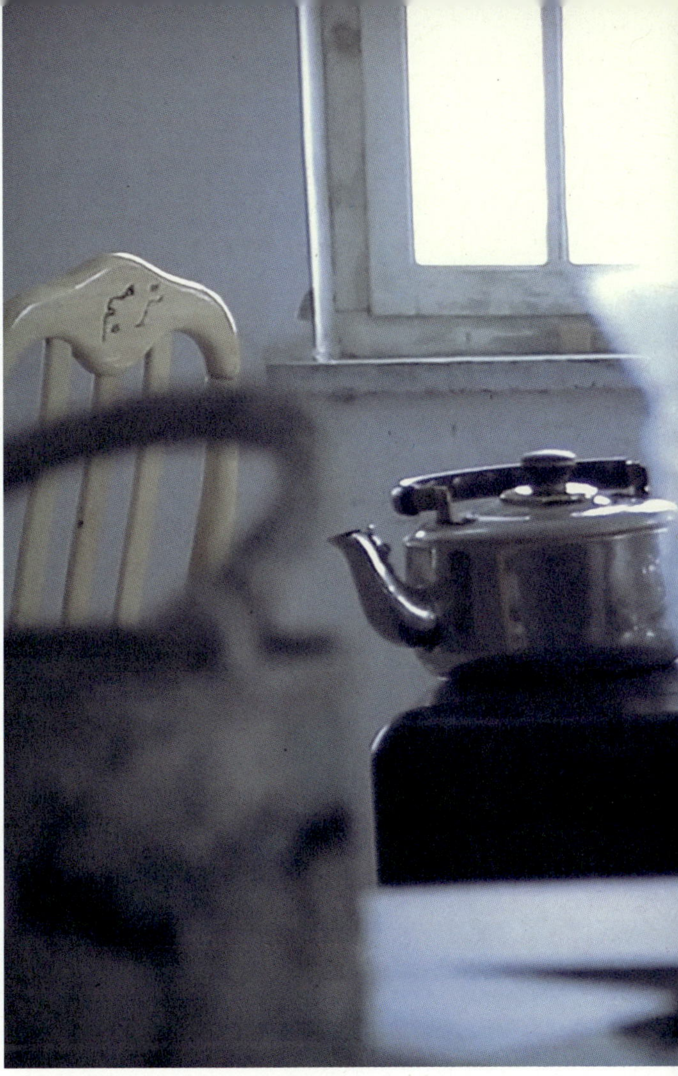

Winter is harsh in Afghanistan. It can even
put a pause on war. So people seem to be more
optimistic in winter.

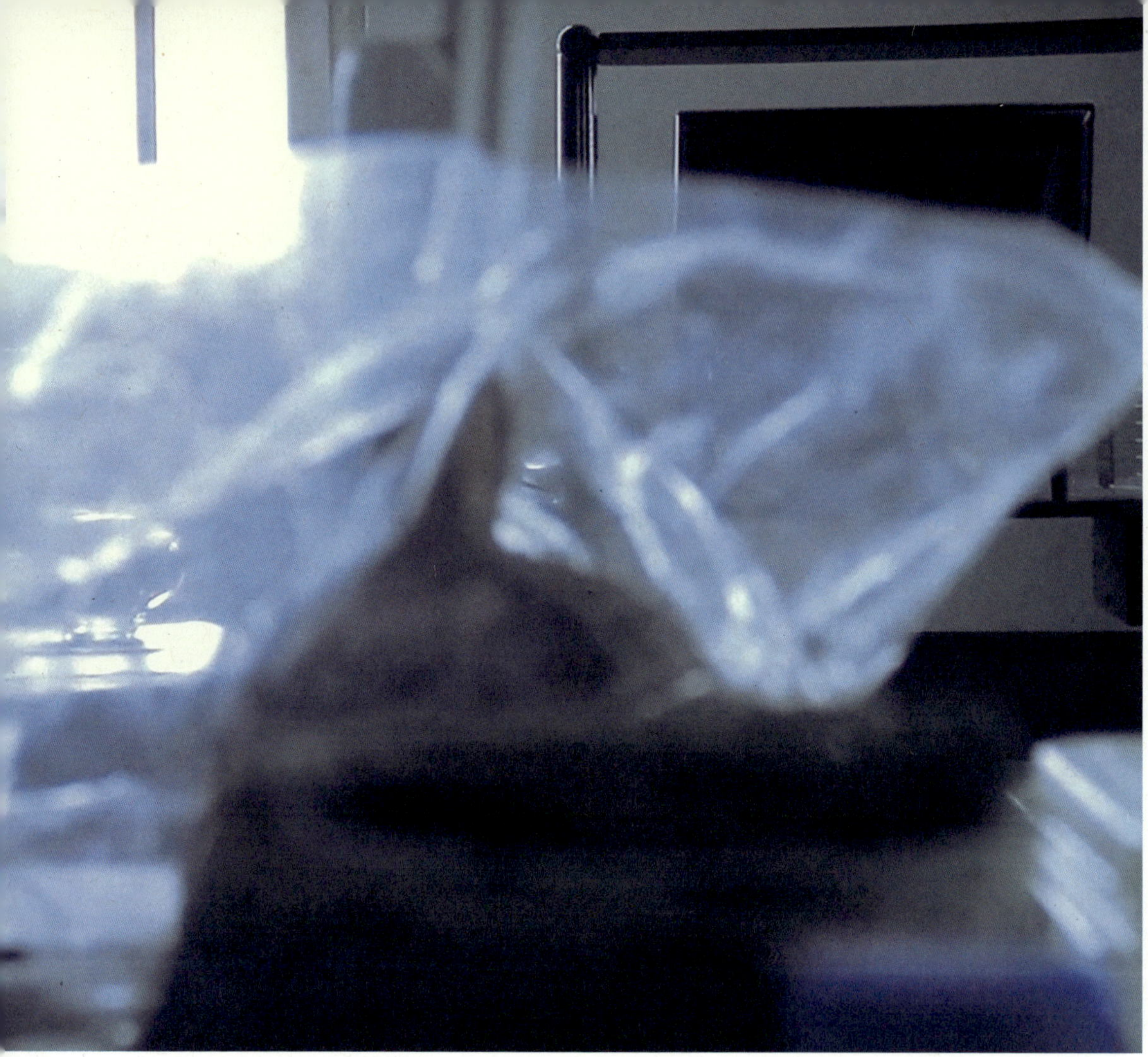

00' 00"

ان در اینجا حتی جنگ را مؤقتا متوقف میسازد.
ر این وقت سال، مردم زیادتر خوشبین به نظر میرسند

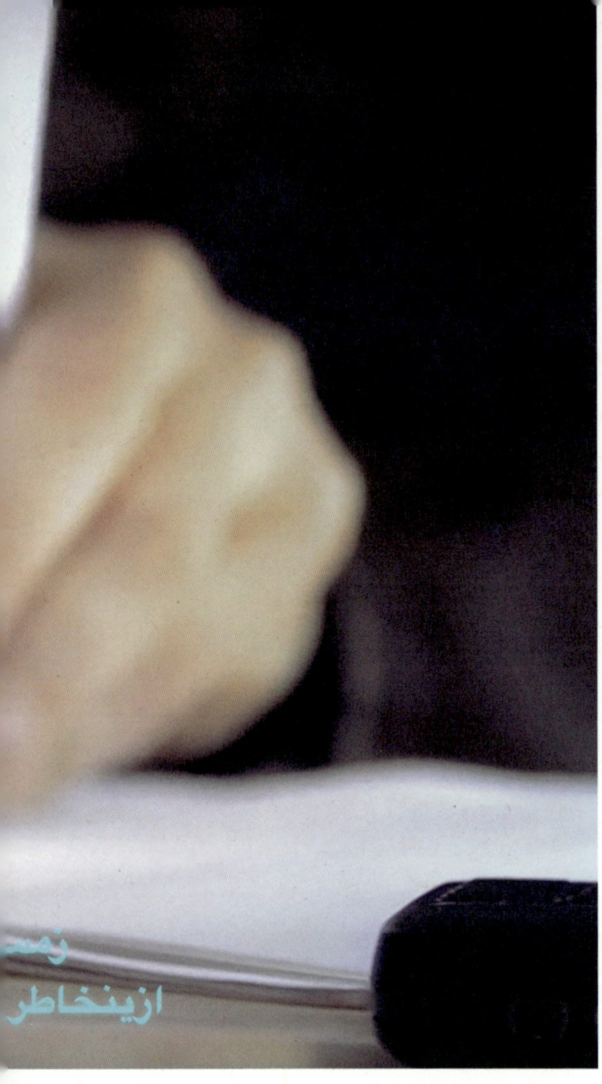

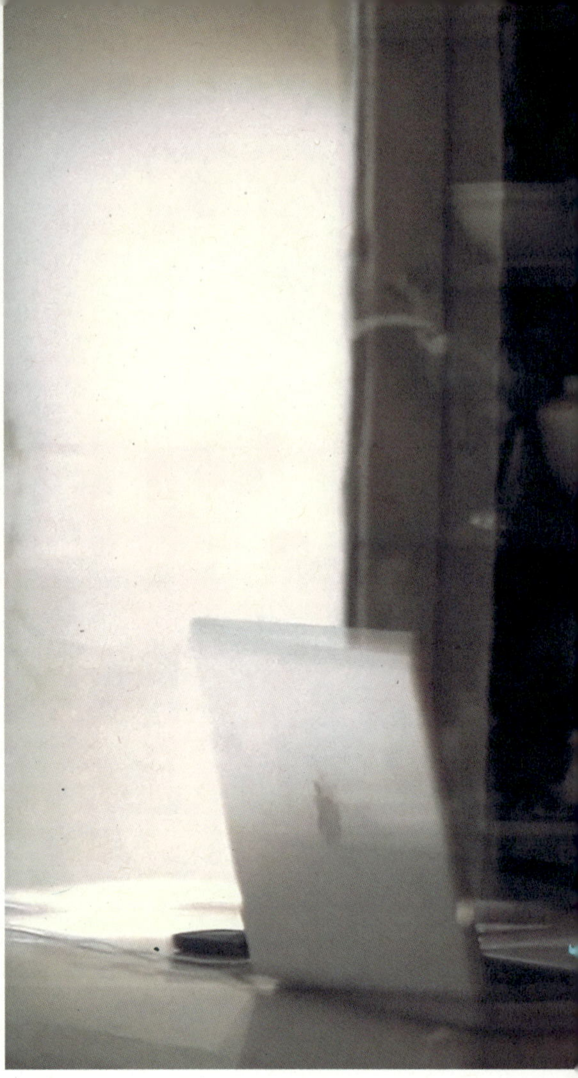

Such an unreachable gesture, or the attempt at it, keeps the exercise interesting after repeated attempts and encourages an exploration of the intricacies of storytelling as well as the veracity of history.

00' 00"

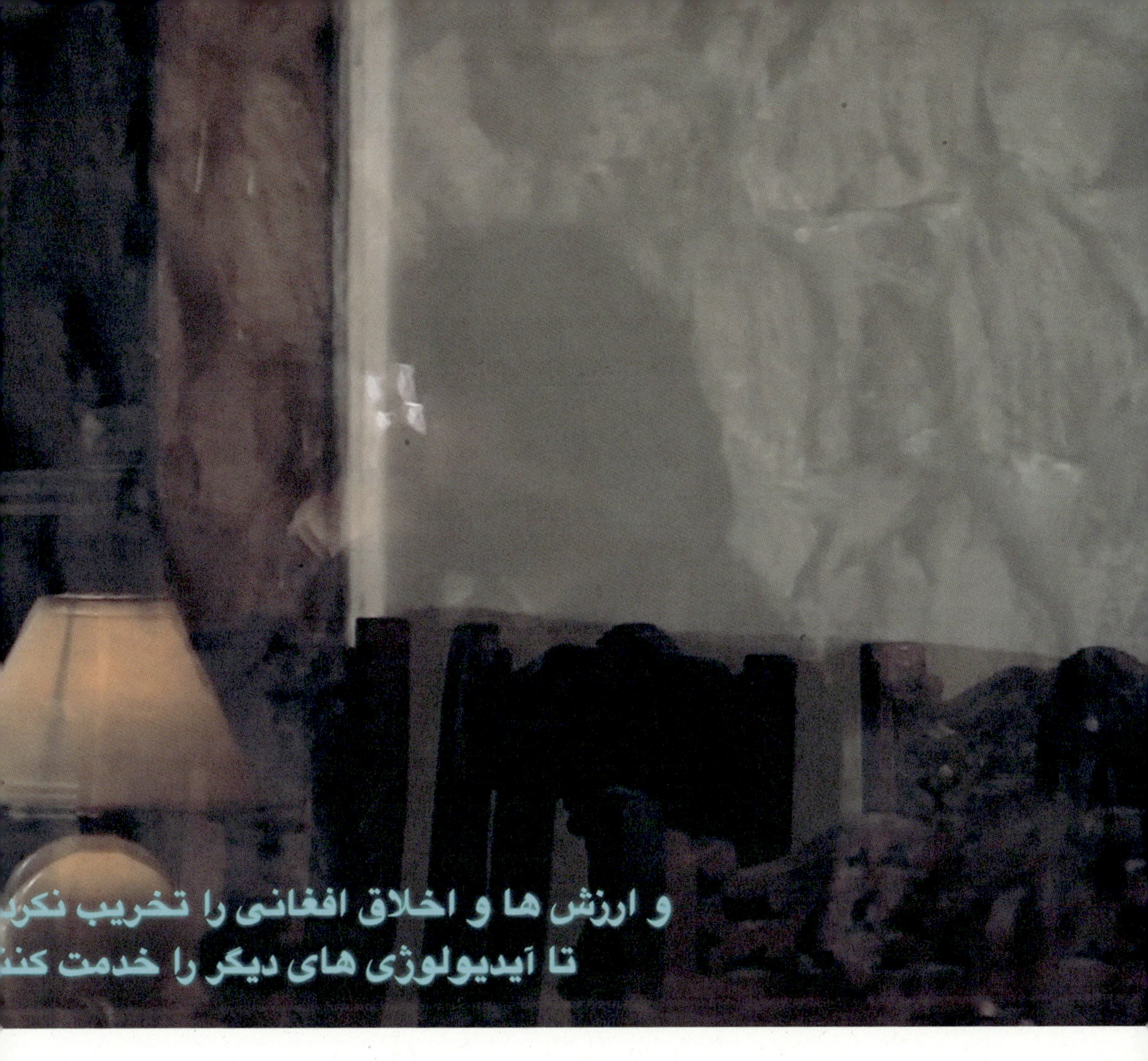
و ارزش ها و اخلاق افغانی را تخریب نکرد
تا آیدیولوژی های دیگر را خدمت کند

64' 00"

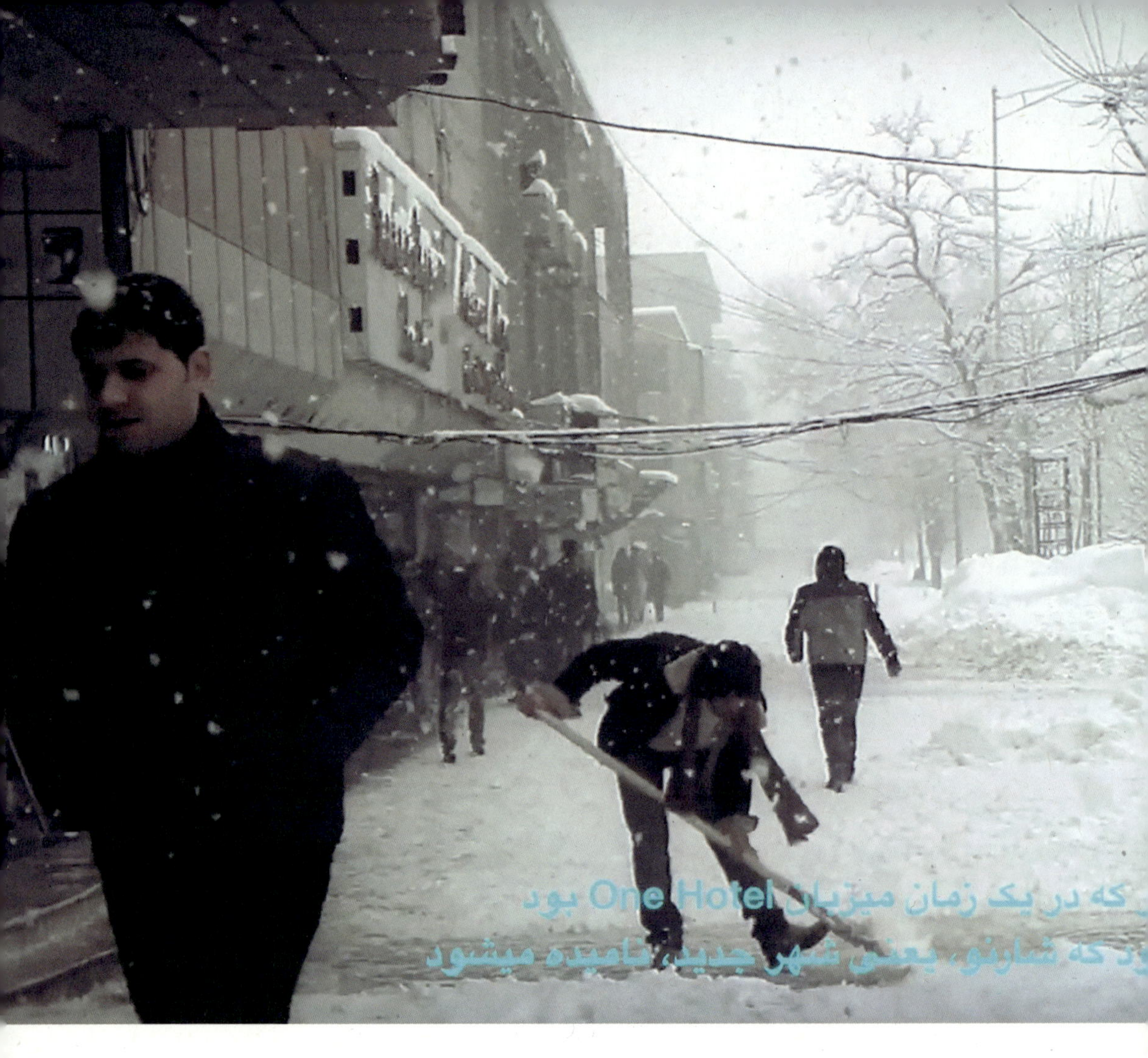

که در یک زمان میزبان One Hotel بود
که شارنو، یعنی شهر جدید، نامیده میشود

00' 00"

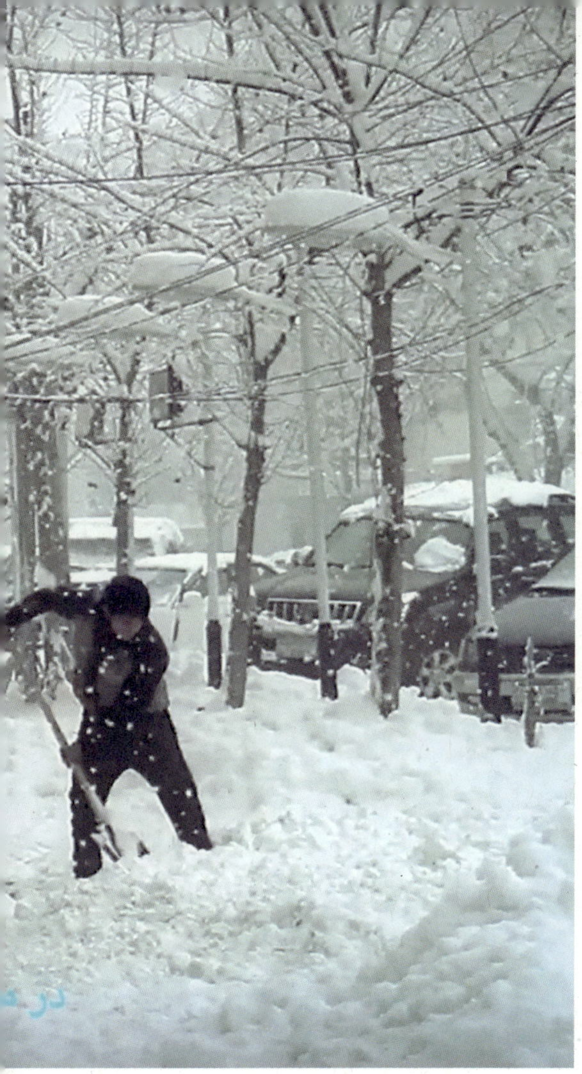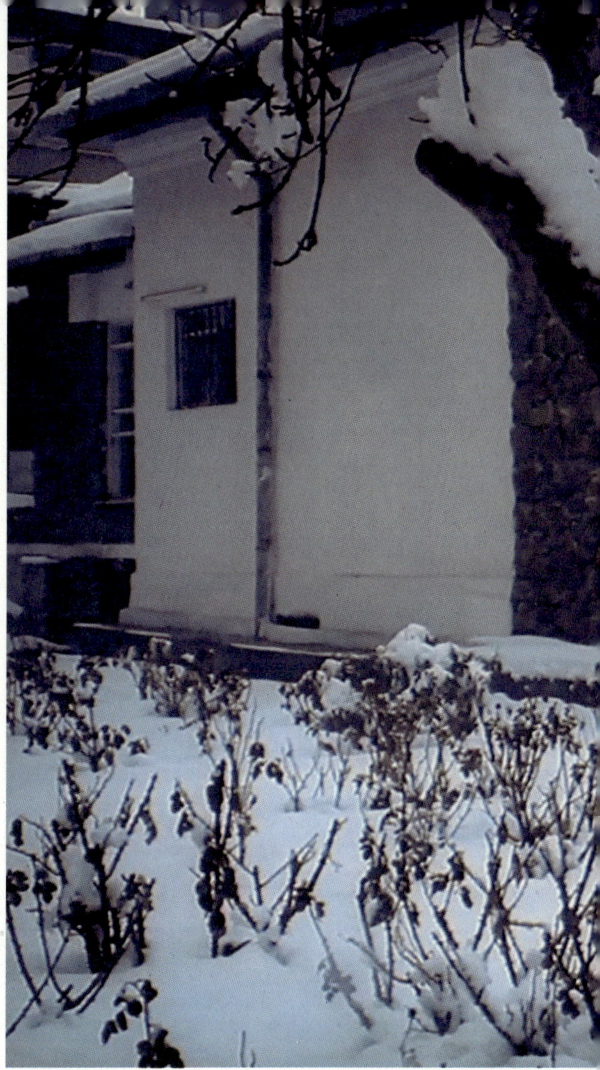

Did you see a man with a jacket and tie wearing
dark glasses in the piece of film we just saw?

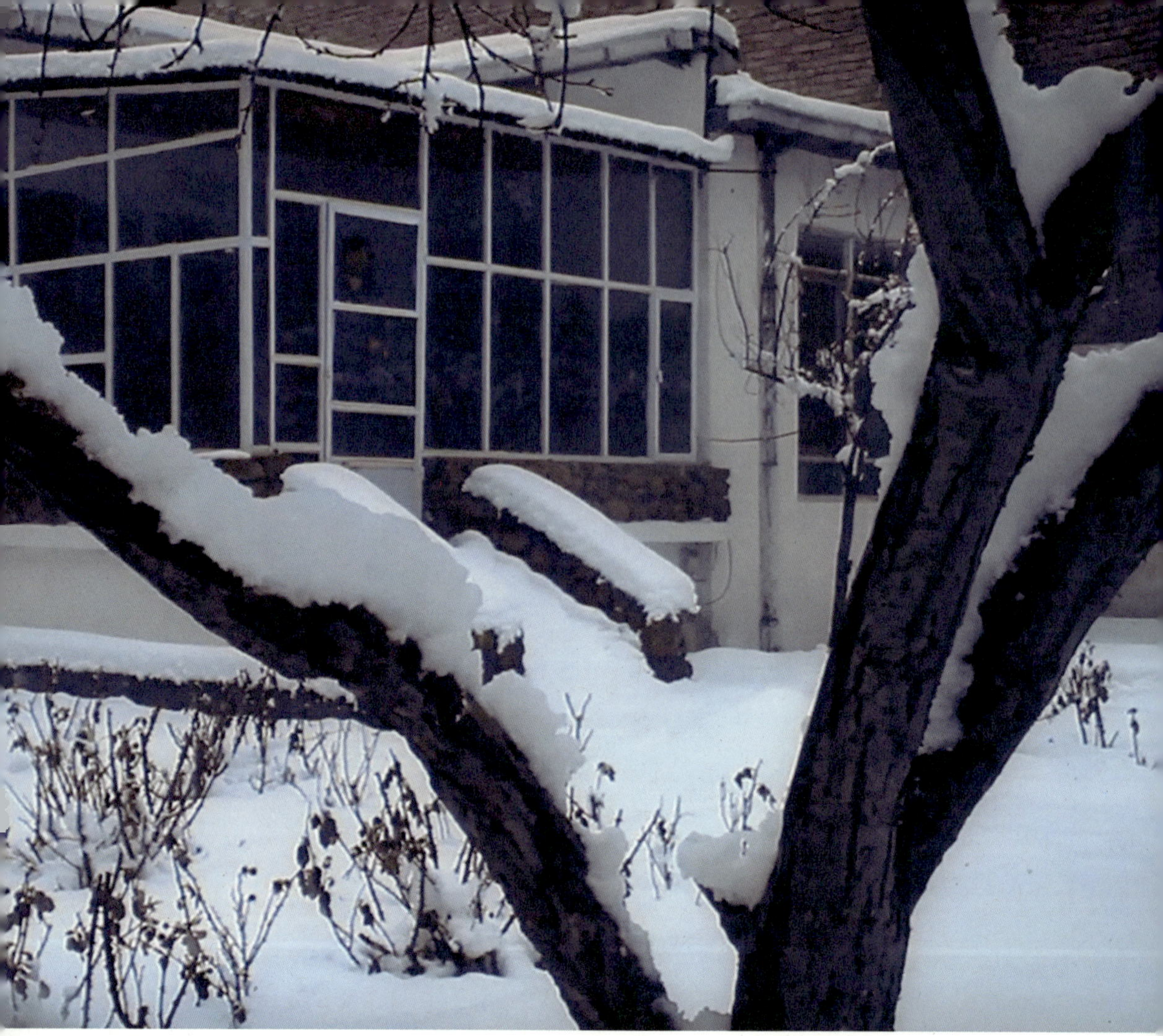

00' 00"

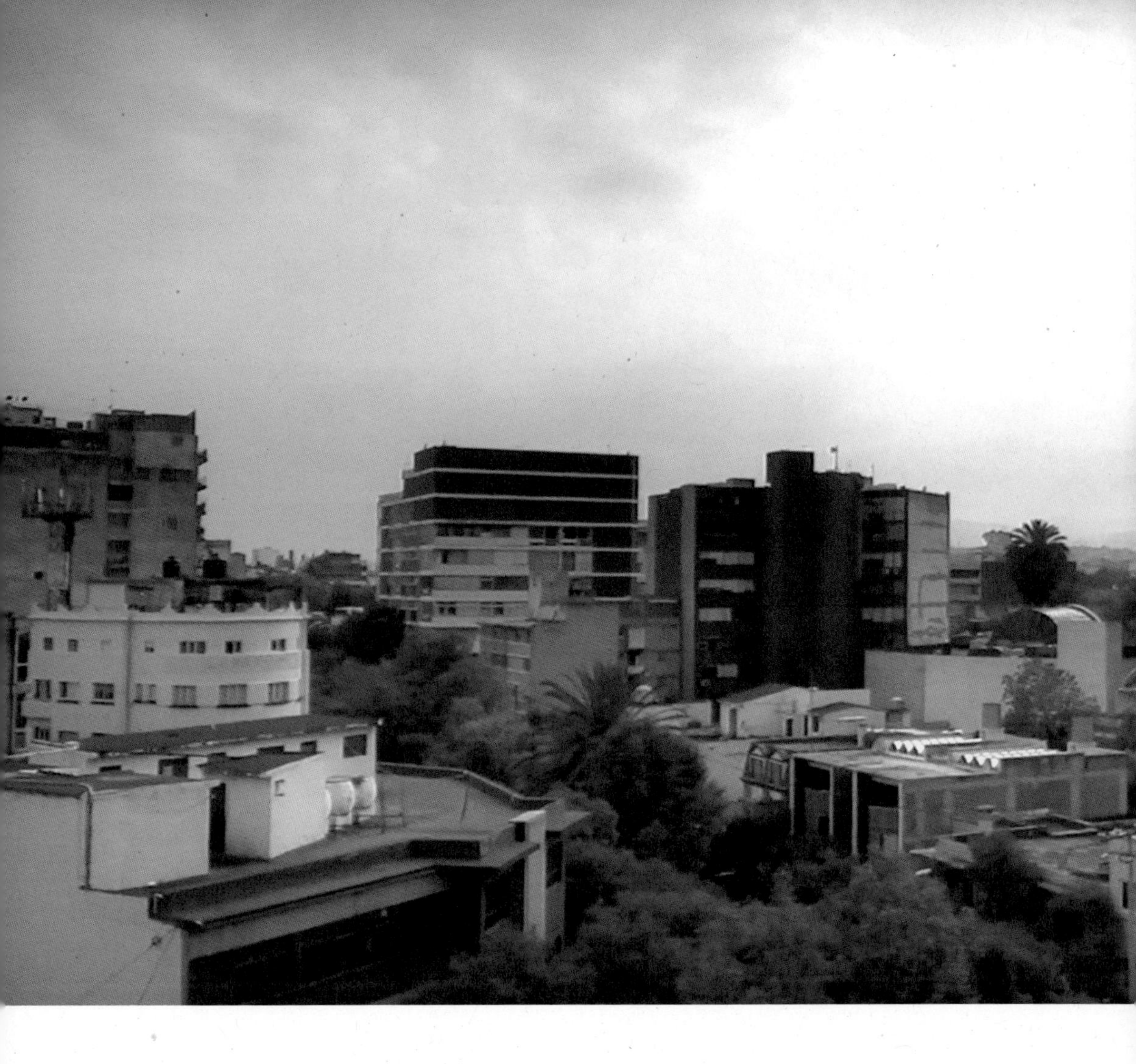

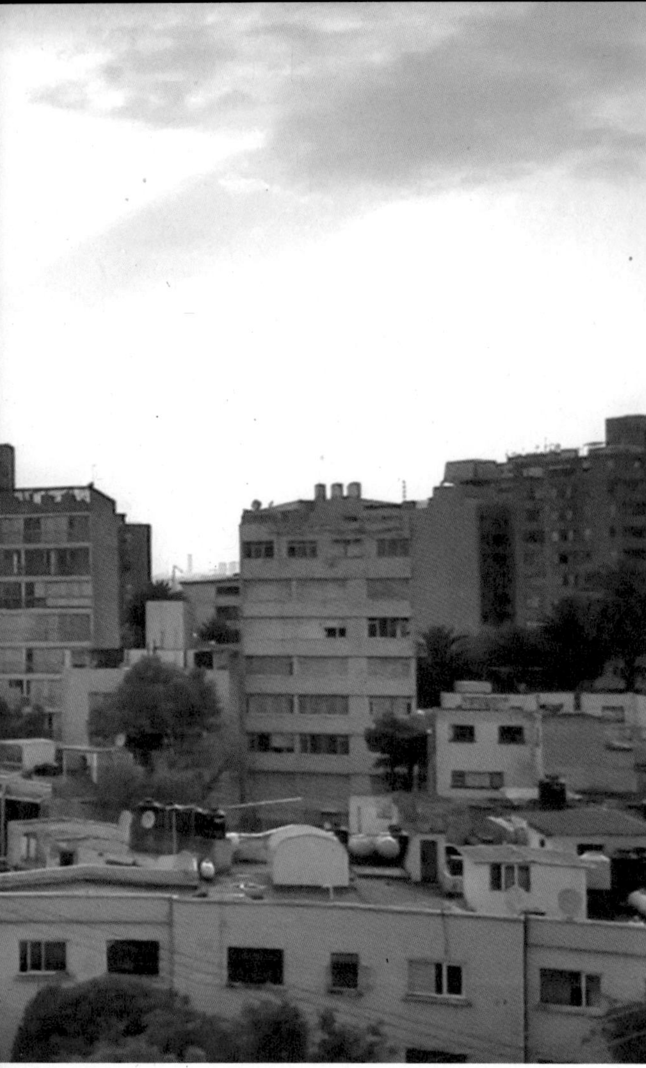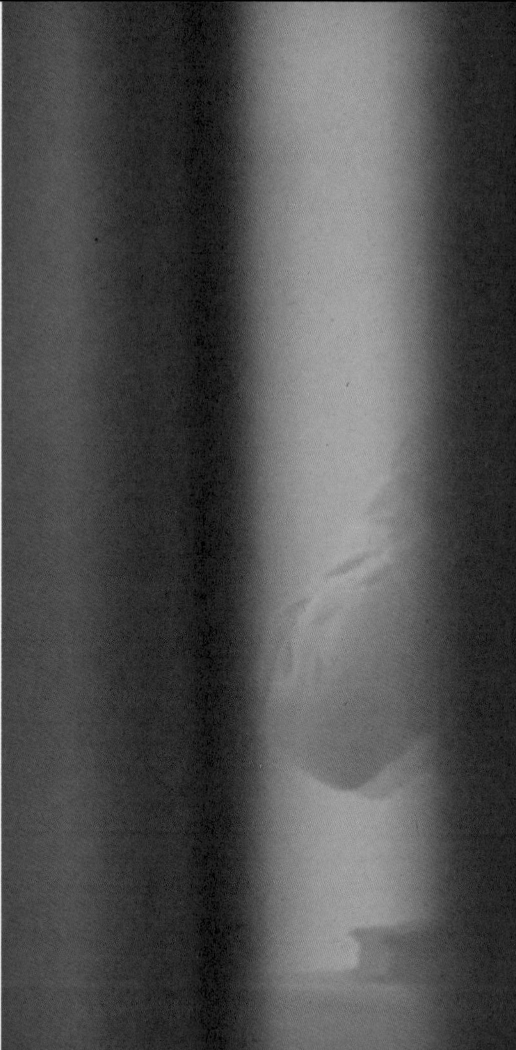

What makes the journey and the search
become an artistic gesture? It's probably not
the findings in themselves for here, much
of it is temporary anyway.

00' 00"

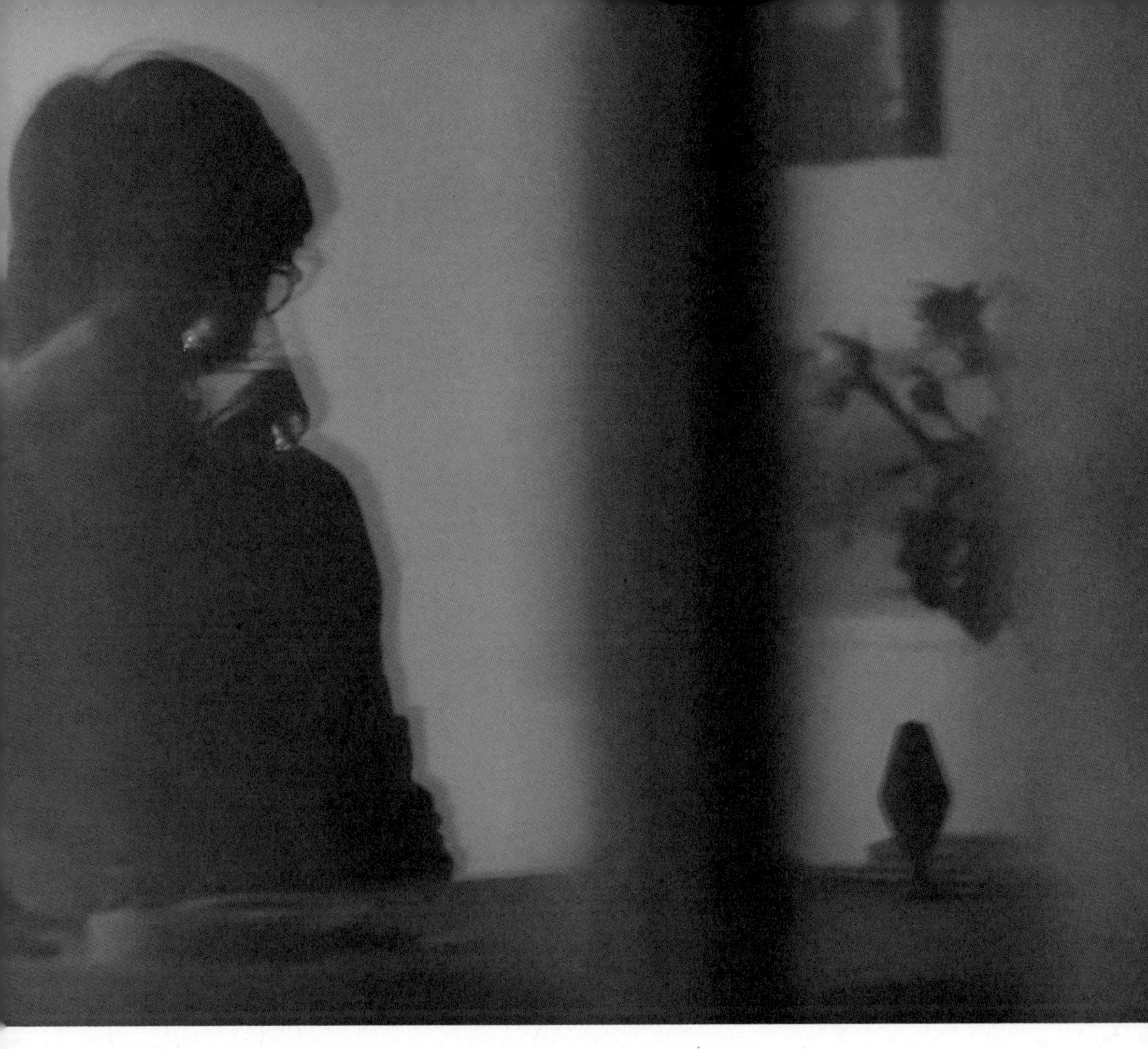

It's most likely their coming into being
as they steadily travel to a different place
and a different time.

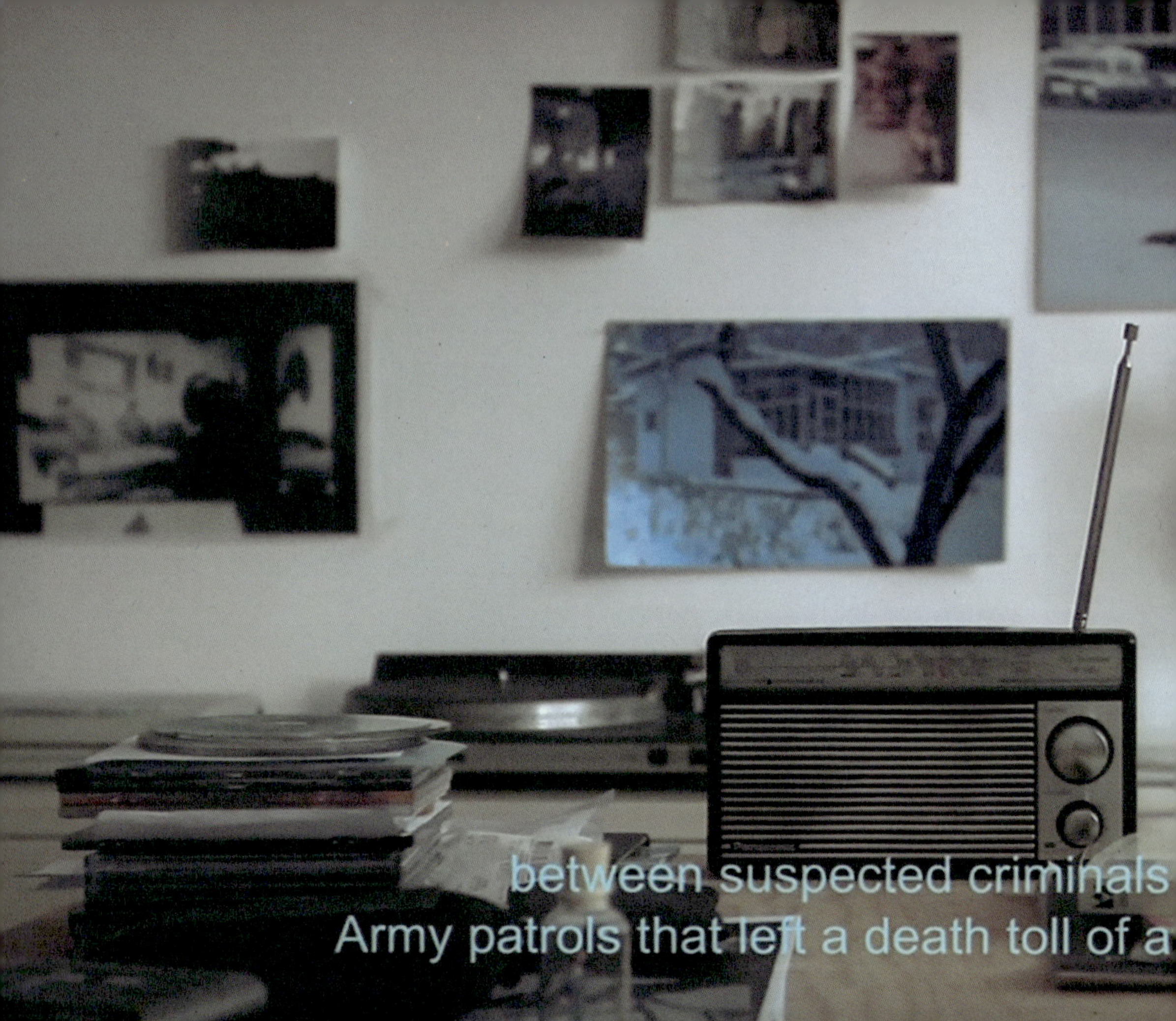
between suspected criminals
Army patrols that left a death toll of a

00' 00"

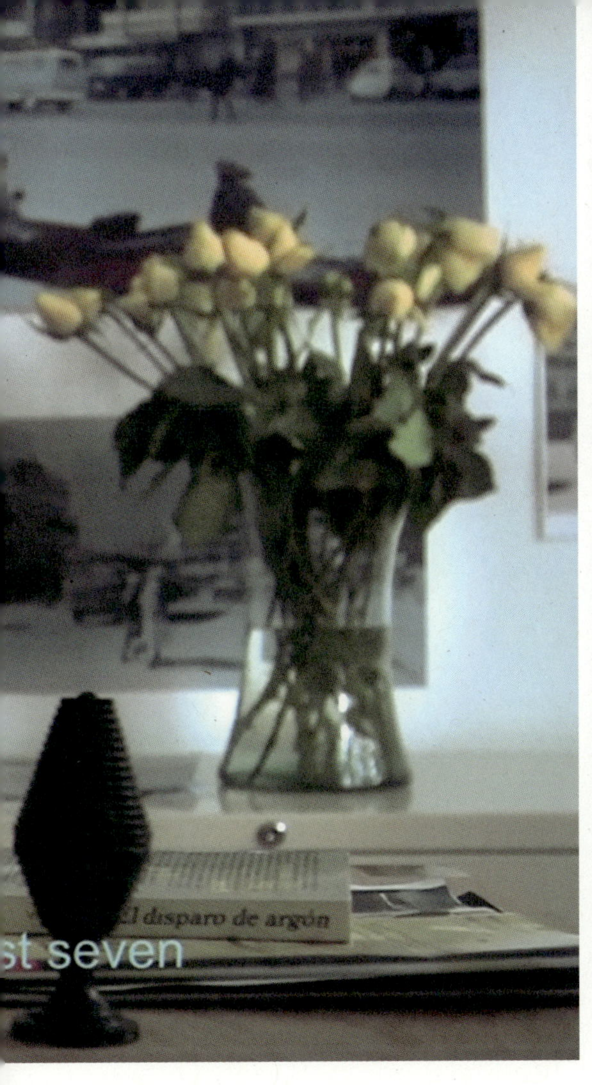

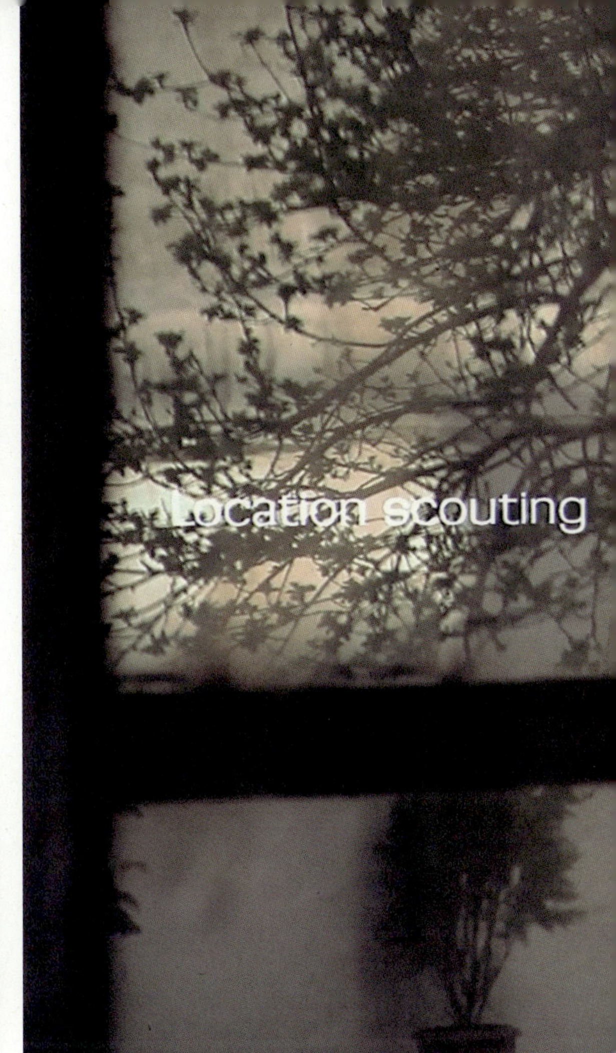

64' 00"

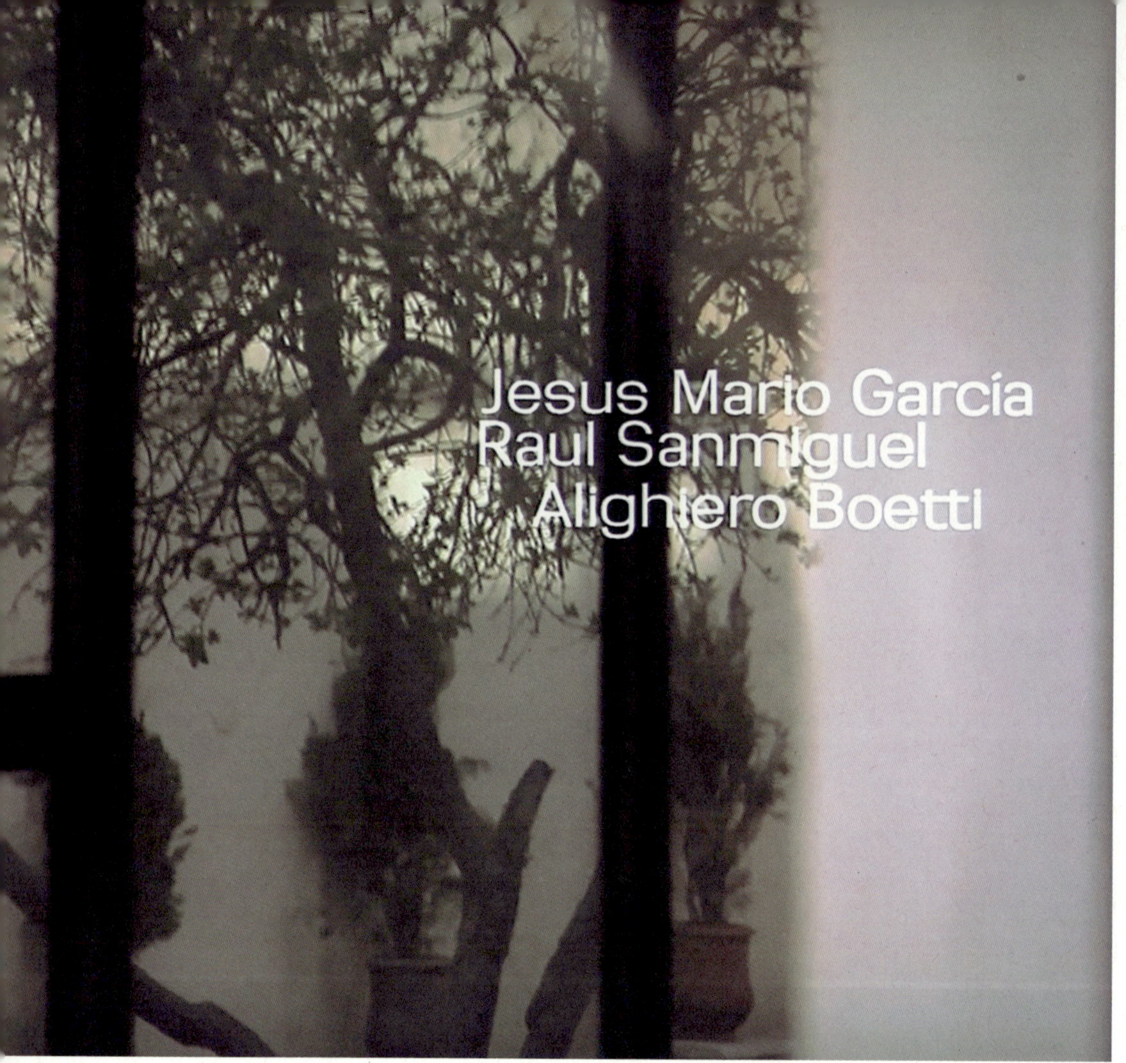
Jesus Mario Garcia
Raul Sanmiguel
Alighiero Boetti

Eva Wilson

Stepping into the Same River Twice: Mario García Torres's
The Way They Looked at Each Other

Rivers of No Return

Following the currents of the Río Consulado in the artist's native Mexico (a river piped and covered by a motorway and therefore hidden from view); cutting to the Danube as it passes through Budapest, Bratislava, and Vienna, home to TBA21 and the exhibition *An Arrival Tale*; and finally joining the Tigris, flowing through Turkey, Syria, and Iraq, Mario García Torres's film work *The Way They Looked at Each Other* (2016) strings together a narrative flux on the theme of the river. Carrying the viewer along a continuous flow, the work steadily bridges geographic, cultural, and contextual leaps. By fabricating this emphatic trajectory through a spoken narrative and a series of photographic images that do not always corroborate each other, García Torres creates a situated topology, at length arriving in Baghdad, the focal point or confluence of this unlikely sequence of streams. Here, in the last third of the thirty-four-minute film, the narrator introduces the incident toward which the work was gravitating all along. It is a lethal case of mistaken identity during the invasion of Baghdad in 2003, resulting in the deaths of two journalists, as well as the event's judicial and forensic aftermath eight years later, which ostensibly and remarkably (according to García Torres's reading) entered the realm of conceptual or aesthetic gesture.

For García Torres, the river, bypassing political borders, becomes a useful topographic marker to illustrate geopolitical, historical, and social constellations. The anonymous narrator of his film, speaking in the first person, embarks on a description of the transformative powers of the *image* of the river—as picture as well as metaphor. García Torres uses the river as a means to develop this metaphor of the movement of memory and perception through fact and fabrication. The waterway serves not only as the embodied figure of the passing of time but also as an ingredient of a perceptive gaze, becoming a tool to draw in a narrativized reading of image, time, and flux, and as such can be read as a perspicuous analogy for the medium of film. Within the metaphor's logic, this is a river of no return: even though both film and river seemingly offer the possibility of reversal—by rewinding or sailing upstream—this inverse movement fails to undo time and distance but rather delivers its subject at a point of arrival that is at once identical to and different from that of its departure, in that it is the subject itself that has been irrevocably bowed.

Within *The Way They Looked at Each Other*—a film that contains no moving images but consists entirely of still photographs that fade in and out at a meditative pace—the narrator speaks also of the transgressive force of photography, of the lens as a figurative bridge carrying the disembodied eye of the viewer to the opposite bank of a stream: into the image, through time, and coming to occupy the point of view of another viewer. "Optics sometimes help us reach places. They let us be in other places," the narrator explains.

Arriving in Baghdad, the narrator steers the slow images (or vice versa) to a point in space-time that is at odds with the one-directional, steady stream of time through space that suggests itself as the nature of the river. Film, flow, flux come to a halting point when narrator and viewer arrive at the bridges and buildings of the city. García Torres fades in various images: photography that he has sourced from photo agencies and stock image banks, variously ascribed to photojournalists or with no known author. These images have emerged from another kind of stream—the constantly moving, deterritorialized pool of disseminated pictures sourced from distributors of stock photography, detached from their original contexts and captions and accessible and exchangeable as fluid image currency. The artist strings together pictures of hotel complexes, a luxurious swimming pool, and other views of building sites along the Tigris showing the locations where these developments either would stand or once stood: a chronological enigma that is a first pointer to war as disruptor of a linear notion of time that could be correlated with "progress" or growth. A time lapse of Baghdad's cityscape is not legible in a continuous register. Neither does García Torres's string of images employ a linear development of diegetic time. The viewer floats back and forth between the riverbanks as well as between the disarranged or disrupted moments in time, following the photographers' perspectives.

García Torres remarks that the many conflicts shaking Baghdad since the invention of photography have led to recurring bursts in the frequency of documentation of the city by Western (war) photographers. Apart from being used by García Torres as a kind of circuitous scan, as a way of narrowing in on the scene and the city, this history of conflict and its by-product in the form of photographs, inversely, accommodates his endeavor to inhabit and represent the city of Baghdad entirely through the photographic history of the passing presence of other eyes. Photography in this sense not only creates documents of war but is also a statistical indicator of it as well as establishing a medial point of access through which to enter the city. And while war has led to an increase in images, it also disrupts their legibility, as it shifts, crushes, upends, and upsets the fabric of the city into a repeated pattern of destruction and reconfiguration, arrivals, departures, flight, and occupation.

García Torres plays with the evidential nature of contextual information as presented through voice and language, on the one hand, and its invisibility or unreliability within the register of lens-based documentation, on the other: even when the narrator mentions armed conflict as the reasons for the availability of the images appearing in the film, almost none of the images included in the work betray any evidence of military action. It is only at second glance that the spoken account and the visual indexes of the film begin to drift apart, the suggestiveness of both creating a third phenomenon, scenes appearing in viewers' minds, combining what is seen and heard with what is remembered and imagined.

Balconies and Bridges

As García Torres closes in on Baghdad as the setting of a slowly unfolding story, he introduces two protagonists: the Al Jumhuriya Bridge, which crosses the Tigris, and the Palestine Hotel, completed in 1982, on the east bank of the river. As the film alternates between viewpoints on both sides of the river, the bridge functions as an interruption of the film's flow, a place that enables a reversal of perspective. The hotel, in contrast, is a monument, an unmoving colossus located close to the center of the city—on the border of the Green Zone, the area cordoned off by Coalition forces after the 2003 invasion—offering ideal viewing conditions for photojournalists. Established as the preferred accommodation for international reporters during the 2003 invasion of Iraq for this reason, it in turn determined what would become iconic imagery of the war: namely, the buildings in the line of sight (and lenses) of the Palestine's balconies, with their honeycomb structure, such as, famously, the pyramidal Council of Ministers Hall, repeatedly struck and often photographed in the first days of the invasion.

Despite the absence of images of violence, the narrator of García Torres's film continues into an account of the events of April 8, 2003, when two journalists who were staying at the Palestine Hotel (Taras Protsyuk, a Ukrainian cameraman for Reuters, and José Couso, a Spanish cameraman for Telecinco) were killed and several others wounded while standing on the balconies of their rooms. They were hit by a shell fired from an American tank positioned on the Al Jumhuriya Bridge during the attacks on Baghdad, three weeks into the Allied invasion of Iraq and one day before Coalition forces formally occupied the city. The soldiers in the tank testified that they had fired at what they believed to be enemy combatants, even though it was known to army personnel at the time that the hotel was full of international press and should not be attacked. The incident effectively produced a media blackout from the point of view of the Palestine on the day that Baghdad fell to the Allied forces, sparking some speculation that the journalists might have been targeted with intent.

This case—causing international outrage and disputed in court several times—amplified the complexity not only of the representation of war, on the one hand, and the rules of war, on the other, but also more generally of perception and evidence, belief and subjectivity, and shot and countershot as techniques of vision as much as of ballistics. Shelling the Palestine Hotel— refuge and observation point for the journalists and front row for the global audience to the televised invasion—effectively fired through the forth wall of the spectacle and made the dangers of this proximity to combat evident and immediate (as in unmediated). Allegedly believing that Protsyuk, the journalist on the balcony watching the tank through binoculars, was a so-called forward observer directing Iraqi mortar fire against the Americans, the tank commander on the bridge received permission to attack. For the cameraman, the act of looking meant becoming a conspicuous pair of eyes, turning him into a target.

The title of García Torres's film, *The Way They Looked at Each Other*, hints at the immediacy of the encounter in this moment—journalists and soldiers eying each other, engaged in technologies of surveillance, documen- tation, and combat while also wrapped in momentary intimacy. This paradoxical, even grotesque intimacy and its correlation with (real, filmic, and photographic) time and its passing resonates with a Levinasian idea of the face-to-face relation: the defenselessness of the exposed face, especially in the context of a filmic iconography, presents itself as a signifier of the subject's encounter with time and death as an event of alterity in the face of the Other. The encounter with the Other in the momentarily locked gazes of journalist and soldier is rendered into a recognition of time as well as of death: "The situation of the face-to-face would be the very accomplishment of time; the encroachment of the present on the future is not the feat of the subject alone, but the intersubjective relationship. The condition of time lies in the relationship between humans."[1] In this reading, the mystery of the Other is analogous to the ungraspability, the alterity, and the eternal futurity of death. The crossed gaze between soldier and journalist as imagined in *The Way They Looked at Each Other* is both infinitely fleeting and infinitely prolonged: "death is never now."[2]

Late but Never Tardy

García Torres's interest is indeed not primarily in the events of April 8, 2003, or the trajectory of history that led to the deaths of the two journalists but rather in the future of these deaths and the way they arrived in the present in the form of (belated) images, thus suspended in time once and for all: this is the story of two pictures taken eight years after the attack by a Spanish Supreme Court judge in an effort to establish retrospective visual evidence in order to make a case against the soldiers who fired the shell. In January 2011 Santiago Pedraz, who had been involved in the case since 2003, arrived in Baghdad on a self-appointed mission: an attempt to re-create in images, if not reenact, the line of sight at the scene of the attack as it would have presented itself to the soldiers stationed on the bridge and the journalists at the hotel. In Baghdad, Pedraz first visited the Palestine and stepped onto the balcony of José Couso's room on the fourteenth floor, before proceeding to the Al Jumhuriya Bridge. One of the members of his entourage stayed back and positioned himself on the hotel balcony to be photographed from the bridge by the judge. The two images taken by Pedraz, the first from the hotel balcony and the second from the bridge—shot and countershot—were later analyzed by "specialists in optics and physics" and used in court, without, however, producing sufficient substantiation to reach a conclusive verdict. They were also published by *Público*, a Spanish

---

1   Emmanuel Levinas, "Time and the Other," in *The Levinas Reader*, ed. Seán Hand (Oxford: Basil Blackwell, 1989), 45.

2   Ibid., 41.

newspaper, where García Torres encountered them.

Adopting the role of the belated witness by attempting to inhabit both the position of the victims and that of the perpetrators, Pedraz's photographs endeavor to capture what the soldier firing the shell might or might not have seen in the moment of the attack as well as to replicate the view captured in the last seconds of film recorded by Couso before the fatal blow. Pedraz's aim was to find an effective method of creating evidence of the military's misconduct that would ensure the conviction of the soldiers he deemed guilty. For this purpose he seems to have relied on a supposedly self-evident correlation between seeing and knowing, endorsing a paradigm embedded in the very etymology of the term *evidence* (derived from the Latin *ex* and *videre*, "to see"): a form of proof that is objectively perceptible or visible and therefore supposedly obvious and self-explanatory. Accordingly, Pedraz banked on the mechanics of the optical medium of photography to materially aid and disseminate what he attempted to make apparent. The images made by him and brought into circulation are the product of the conflation of two epistemologies, those of vision and cognizance.[3]

Pedraz's apparent faith in the effectiveness of replicating and fixing photographically what the tank commander would have seen and experienced in the moments before the attack presupposes an idea(l) of the photographic that broadly validates an assumption about the medium's powers: it seems to sanction a simplified understanding of photography as an objective and infallible redeemer in the realm of representation and veracity, analogous to a mechanical, impartial, and timeless form of human vision. His action, however, also appears to disregard the forensic register within which it ostensibly sought to arrive. Many technical and circumstantial aspects seem to remain unconsidered: what kind of camera, lens, and zoom did Pedraz use? Did he account for ambient conditions, site- and time-specific factors that might have impacted the troops' and the cameramen's vision? Fundamentally, can two still photographs be compared with the tumultuous outlook that would have presented itself both to the soldiers and to the journalists through their various viewing devices on the day of the attack? And even if the photographs proved that the soldiers had a good view of the balconies, how could the court evaluate whether this translated into recog-

---

3 On the epistemologies of seeing and knowing and the employment and meaning of film and photography within this dichotomy, cf. the introduction to the anthology Heide Barrenechea, Marcel Finke, and Moritz Schumm, eds., *Periphere Visionen: Wissen an den Rändern von Fotografie und Film* (Munich: Fink, 2016), as well as Peter Geimer, ed., *Ordnungen der Sichtbarkeit: Fotografie in Wissenschaft, Kunst und Technologie* (Frankfurt am Main: Suhrkamp, 2002).

nition of the anonymous person on the hotel balcony, that is, whether *seeing* in this instance was actually *knowing* and, further, what this controversial knowledge might have involved?

An alternative reading, and one that García Torres suggests, is that Pedraz's act—while arriving in the performatively institutional guise of "science," "evidence," and "law"—actually utilized photography much as it has been used in the long history of conceptual art and its gestures: as the only material trace of an otherwise dematerialized event, one that has a limited scope of witnesses in real time but can be accessed indefinitely ex posteriori through the medium of photography and one that not only documents conceptual gesture but also *is* conceptual gesture itself. By proposing that Pedraz's photographs can be read in this register, as symbolic act, García Torres himself adopts the role of the (albeit nebulous) interpreter or critic, analyzing the pictures and the way they came into being within a familiar vocabulary that can become potent within his own practice precisely through the inversion of its context into that of art or critical discourse. While failing to provide decisive evidence in court, Pedraz's action proved successful as symbolic gesture directed toward public effect. García Torres, in the guise of the film's narrator, consequently describes the judge's act as a symbolic one, resonating more with the conventions of art than the logic of forensics.

García Torres's interest is ultimately engaged with an unlikely association, a resemblance he identifies between Judge Pedraz's gesture and certain methodologies of artistic practices that engage in or move between reenactment, performativity, and documentation. Pedraz challenged the contested accounts of the attack by reinscribing his present into the past (something that García Torres himself reverses in his work, bringing a moment from the past into the present), through visual storytelling, dramatization, documentation, and the retroactive creation of (partial or incongruous) evidence. A judge's professional responsibility to consider both sides of a conflict is assumed quite literally by Pedraz, who adopted the perspectives of both victims and aggressors. But performatively he extended the scope of his role: his use of the camera is reminiscent also of the war journalists present at the scene as unbiased witnesses or mediums, living tripods. Arriving eight years too late, Pedraz created a framework that allows for a delayed inhabiting of a past moment via an ultimately surreal suspension or superposition of time.

Part of the strength of Pedraz's gesture is the impact of his physical presence at the scene of the event, both as the institutional body of the law and as an individual (a presence that was well documented to this effect during his visit). Another central element of the symbolic act is the depiction of another living body at the site of the killing, exposing this body's vulnerability and the brutal reality of a human target. In the case of Protsyuk and Couso, the position of the victims' bodies behind the cameras meant that the cameramen themselves constituted a blind spot, had remained "hors-champ" of their own field of medial vision during the attack, even though they came close to recording (shooting) their own deaths.[4]

But Pedraz's documentation of the scene is not tinted by the chaos, violence, and bloodshed of the events of April 8, 2003. García Torres remarks that he feels more strongly drawn to these "innocuous" images than to the existing footage of the event and mentions his "distaste for the explicitness of the standardized skilled war imagery."[5] In *The Way They Looked at Each Other*, river as film or film as river, the slow fading in and out of images, and the calmness of the narrator's voice create a kind of stasis in time. The voice acts as a conductor between the personal, the subjective, the poetic, on the one hand, and the objective, the real, and the undeniable, on the other.

4   This "hors-champ" of war documentation is at the center of another recent work of art that deals with similar questions of visibility, war, and representation, Rabih Mroué's *Shooting Images* (2012, video, 09' 14"). Mroué reenacts a clip found on YouTube—a video recorded on a mobile phone in 2011 showing a Syrian regime sniper taking aim at the civilian filming the incident, the camera's line of sight directly encountering that of the gun in the moment of the shot. The death of the unknown cameraman remains invisible, "hors-champ," and is represented only in the falling movement of the camera before it hits the ground. In the nine-minute video by Mroué, the simulated and reiterated incident (reenacted by the artist and a friend) is deconstructed into countless cuts, slow-motion inserts, repetitions, zooms, and animations. Sound and image are disassembled and explicitly employed as reality effects instead of evidential substantiation. Mroué asks: "But is there a way to bring in the victim, the real Syrian cameraman, into the field of view, inside the frame?" and suggests the surreal possibility of a reflection of the victim's face in the killer's eye or in the deep pixels of the digital image caught on video in a kind of endless *mise-en-abyme* motion of zooming further and further into it, going far beyond the technical capacity of the camera's resolution and instead entering into the realm of the speculative and the poetic.

5   Abounaddara, an anonymous Syrian filmmakers' collective, has recently described "the shameless broadcasting of the bodies of slain Syrians" as an attack on Syrians' human dignity (concurring with García Torres's distrust of the explicitness of images of violence) and lays blame on a corrupted media. The collective has resorted to creating short films of everyday scenes filmed in Syria since 2011 and posts them online on a weekly basis. These films have become envoys of the collective's call for "a change in the standards of representation: the right for each individual to a dignified image": "We are appealing to the citizens of this world: the time has come to seize the weapons of art, cinema, and journalism in order to protect society and to allow it to produce its own image beyond power's grasp. The scales must be shifted in such a way that there is a right to one's own image that is based on the principle of human dignity and the right to self-determination." Abounaddara, "We Are Dying—Take Care of the Right to the Image," available online at http://www.documenta14.de/en/notes-and-works/1523/we-are-dying-take-care-of-the-right-to-the-image. Abounaddara's films are uploaded weekly on documenta 14's website.

The Way They Looked at Each Other speaks and operates from a remote position of geographic as well as poetic distance. In a text written by the artist and published in *frieze*, preceding the film but bearing the same title,[6] García Torres quotes Theodor W. Adorno: "the viewer who always comes too late can never be tardy after all."[7] Here Adorno is elaborating on the variety act (compared by him to the eternal repetitions produced by the film industry), in which "something happens and nothing happens at the same time."[8] Similarly, in Pedraz's images, something happens and nothing happens. The formal re-creation of the sight lines of the killing renders its images at once more rewarding for an encounter interested in the discursive implications and complications inherent to them as well as making the surrogate event accessible for constant revisiting, creating a virtual freezing and suspension of time in the envisaged moment of the encounter of the bodies and their apparatuses. Herein lies the unconventionality of Pedraz's move: disregarding (or having reached the limits of) an analytical logic of material evidence based in forensics and testimony, he resorts to *poiesis*, the generative bringing forth of (self-substantiating or self-legitimizing) evidence that is multivalent and thus subject to discursive interpretation. In the reflected gazes from balcony to bridge and back, the event is (unintentionally?) sent into an endless loop, no longer really striving for any resolution in the form of a verdict but letting the unresolved and ultimately inaccessible moment play out restlessly and perpetually. García Torres identifies the "unintended disillusionment" of Pedraz's gesture as one that nonetheless reaches beyond its forensic failure, introducing indeterminacy as a productive condition.

Writing about indeterminacy as a state of limbo, the artist and theorist Hito Steyerl suggested Erwin Schrödinger's famous thought experiment as a tool as well as a symptom.[9] The cat trapped in Schrödinger's black box together with a flask of poison and a radioactive source could be killed at any moment. According to a specific interpretation in line with quantum mechanics, after a while the cat is *simultaneously* alive *and* dead. This entanglement, or quantum superposition, lasts as long as the situation in the box is indeterminate. It ends only when the box is opened and an observer

6   Mario García Torres, "The Way They Looked at Each Other," *frieze*, January, 1, 2012, available online at https://frieze.com/article/the-way-they-looked-each-other.

7   Theodor W. Adorno, "The Schema of Mass Culture," in *The Culture Industry: Selected Essays on Mass Culture*, ed. J. B. Bernstein (London: Routledge, 2005), 70.

8   Ibid.

9   Hito Steyerl, "Missing People: Entanglement, Superposition, and Exhumation as Sites of Indeterminacy," in *The Wretched of the Screen* (Berlin: Sternberg, 2012), 139.

witnesses the cat *either* dead or alive, reality collapsing into a definite outcome. Importantly, it is the observer who determines the state of indeterminacy in the act of seeing. In the context of legal matters, it is vital for the prosecutors that a legal investigation is kept open for it to stand a chance of successful prosecution. Pedraz's case was closed by Spanish and American courts several times. Paradoxically, in the case of García Torres's thought experiment, Schrödinger's closed black box is analogous to Pedraz's open investigation, indeterminate as long as it remains unresolved, aided by the two phantom photographs featuring a stand-in and a reinhabitation: the two images, forming a parenthesis for the dichotomous states of the case (alive/dead, visible/invisible, identified/misidentified, guilty/innocent) from a moment beyond its immediacy, uphold the state of superposition from an oblique angle.

Perception Is Subjective

García Torres's interest in this ambiguous act and the resulting images—"demonstrations of the impossibility of untangling a moment in the past"[10]—itself results in an open and ambivalent work. It ends with a montage of the two alternating photographs, fading from color into black and white, emphasizing their location in limbo time as well as the fact that it is not entirely clear what we are looking at (or what we see). His reading of Pedraz's appearance in Baghdad as a symbolic gesture renders it the subject of an artwork that is interested in the workings and intricacies of this gesture as seen from the field of art. García Torres states that the pictures taken by Pedraz "might be more persuasive than scientific evidence in that they actually empower our subjectivity and thereby our understanding of the visual politics of our times through a more humane and less logical paradigm."[11] The film, however, refrains from delving too far into or analyzing the larger consequences of this transposition of epistemologies: it does not address the question of the legitimacy or effects of resorting to a symbolic but ambiguous gesture within the legal framework and public perception of a court case handling a potential war crime; nor does it scrutinize the significance and scope of its reading within the context of artistic practice.

10   Mario García Torres, "The Way They Looked at Each Other," *frieze*, January, 1, 2012
11   Ibid.

What does it mean for images to be "persuasive" and what does
the "empowerment" of our "subjectivity" entail? In his frieze article, García
Torres links Pedraz's action with Sol LeWitt's 1968 "Sentences on Conceptual
Art"—"Irrational thoughts should be followed absolutely and logically"—
thereby making a connection to a school of thought interested in the generation of propositions with open ends, in the unsolidified potential of experience and subjectivity, narrative and discourse. In the twenty-first century,
however, LeWitt's "Sentences," among them "Perception is subjective," are
no longer only a promise of liberation but must also be read in the context
of a political and discursive double bind.[12] The paradigm of perception's
subjectivity has in many ways found its way into a cul-de-sac of infinite
discourse, of a myriad of multitudes and as many subjective experiences
of reality that remain unaccountable and impassable precisely because of
the unshakeable subjectivity of perception. Incidentally, *The Way They Looked
at Each Other* retraces an incident that took place in the aftermath of a war
begun under speculative and ultimately false pretenses which nonetheless
have since shaped reality as we know it, and a political era under George W.
Bush that famously proclaimed the end of the "reality-based community."
This phrase, coined by Karl Rove, senior adviser to the Bush administration,
in a conversation with the journalist Ron Suskind in 2004, was followed by
the statement: "We're an empire now, and when we act, we create our own
reality. And while you're studying that reality—judiciously, as you will—we'll
act again, creating other new realities, which you can study too, and that's
how things will sort out. We're history's actors [...] and you, all of you, will be
left to just study what we do."[13] And while the relationship between the Bush
administration and reality seems all but innocent from today's perspective
of false news and filter bubbles, the sentiment described by Rove—which
cannot be as easily unpacked into a "good" vs. "evil" dualism as it may seem—
has powerful ramifications for anyone engaged in the interpretation as well
as the creation of reality and experience in their multiplicities, dialectics,
and ambiguities.

Which side of this empire does Pedraz fall on? *The Way They Looked
at Each Other* adopts an indeterminacy characteristic of a postconceptual

131

12   Sol LeWitt, "Sentences on Conceptual Art," *Art & Language: The Journal of Conceptual Art 1*
     (May 1969): 11–13.
13   Ron Suskind, "Faith, Certainty and the Presidency of George W. Bush," *New York Times
     Magazine*, October 17, 2004, http://www.nytimes.com/2004/10/17/magazine/faith-
     certainty-and-the-presidency-of-george-w-bush.html.

approach, embodying a "hegemonic hangover"[14] that reacts to a legacy of avant-garde practices that generally sought radical reinvention of a given aesthetic and social status quo but have since been seen to come to rest on similar ideological foundations they had hoped to undo. The discursive tools provided by a history of (critically motivated) self-reflexive aesthetic experience and conceptual art seem to have become viciously circular. After conceptualism, what can a work of art communicate beyond itself and its experience? Can it engage with the viewer without becoming complicit in the corruption of all communication? What technologies, languages, and gestures need to be created in order to affect the course of the river?[15]

Hito Steyerl has made the case for the "poor image." Identifying the image's resolution as a symptom of hegemonic power, she invokes the powerless, the low-res, the compressed and mobile image instead, circulating on less than official channels, developing speed from brevity and reduced data load, severed from its author and open for appropriation and reinterpretation. (Self-)representation comes at the cost of resolution: "A poor image is an image that remains unresolved—puzzling and incon-clusive because of neglect or political denial, because of lack of technology or funding, or because of hasty and incomplete recordings captured under risky circumstances. It cannot give a comprehensive account of the situation it is supposed to represent. But if whatever it tries to show is obscured, the conditions of its own visibility are plainly visible: it is a subaltern and indeterminate object, excluded from legitimate discourse, from becoming fact, subject to disavowal, indifference, and repression."[16]

The footage used by García Torres is not easily locatable on the spectrum of rich to poor images. Commercialized stock photography is subject to quality and data control as long as it is confined to circulation within the framework of its proper terms and conditions of use. The judge's pictures, too, are rich images insofar as they emanate from a position of sanctioned state authority and are awarded extensive legal and forensic

---

14 David Levine, during a panel discussion on the occasion of the exhibition *That Time*, Kópavogur, Iceland, October 29, 2016.

15 There have been numerous recent approaches within artistic practices that ask similar questions and come to very different conclusions. Prominently, the theory and research originating from the Forensic Architecture agency adopts a widely positivist stance toward the integration of artistic practice and forensic science and offers up its work in the service of political and legal forums. The agency is invested in "articulating notions of public truth" and works with NGOs, political organizations, and international prosecution teams to "provide evidence," as stated on the agency's website, http://www.forensic-architecture.org/.

16 Steyerl, "Missing People," 156.

attention. They seem to have adopted a second identity though, one that is enforced by their use in García Torres's film and their circulation through media and Internet. Within this second register, as "a copy in motion"[17] (i.e., as poor images), the entire narrative—the deaths of Couso and Protsyuk and the impossibility of the prosecution of their killers—is compressed into these two photographs, keeping the case afloat and inextinguishable as mobile signifiers of an investigation in low resolution with no resolution.

Similar to the experiment of Schrödinger's cat, in García Torres's work, seeing is key for the outcome of reality, even though it is not necessarily correlated with knowing. Optics, the translation of specific wave frequencies into shape and color on the retina, are the effect of the reflection of light on opaque surfaces, just as photography is the inscription of light onto an interface. Finally, it seems that the Other—that other interface— is reflexive to all light, producing an image of itself while remaining mysterious, unknowable. Levinas writes, "The other's entire being is constituted by its exteriority, or rather its alterity, for exteriority is a property of space and leads the subject back to itself through light."[18] Here, vision and image are not equivalent to knowledge but on the contrary describe the limits of what can be known. García Torres's *The Way They Looked at Each Other* orbits this exteriority, refracting the photographers' perspectives back and forth until all light is dispersed.

---

17   Steyerl, "In Defense of the Poor Image," in *Wretched of the Screen*, 32.
18   Levinas, "Time and the Other," 43.

The Way They Looked at Each Other

n.d., HD video, color, sound, English with Arabic subtitles,
38' 00", commissioned by TBA21, Thyssen-Bornemisza
Art Contemporary Collection, Vienna

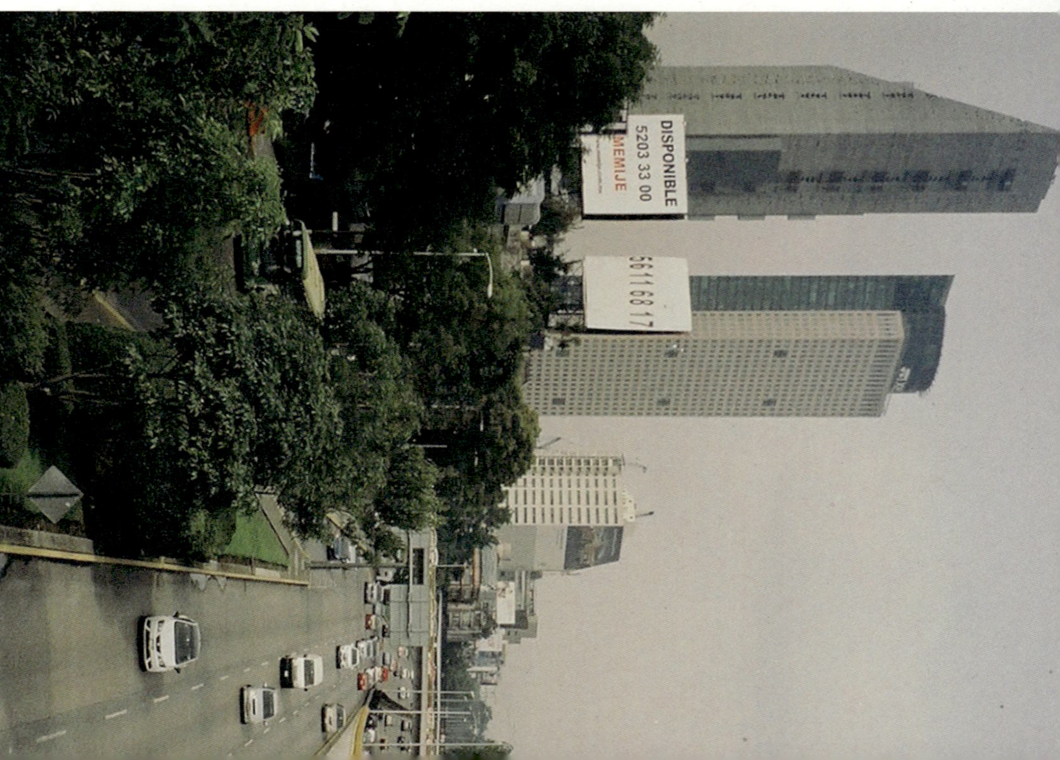

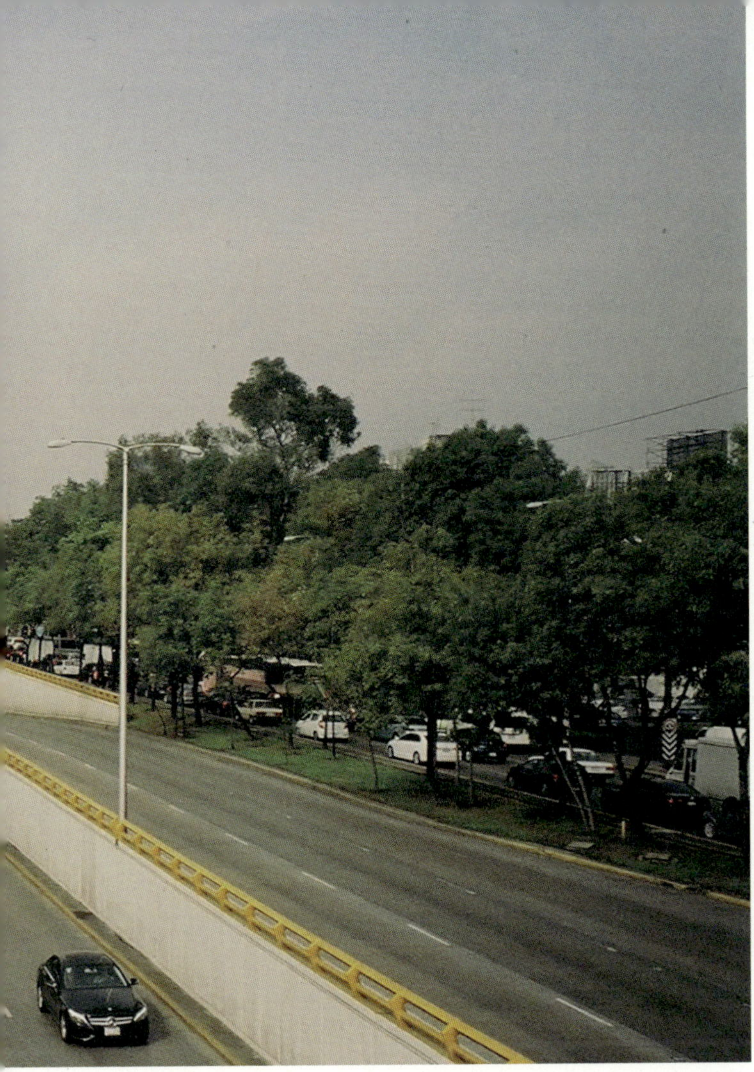

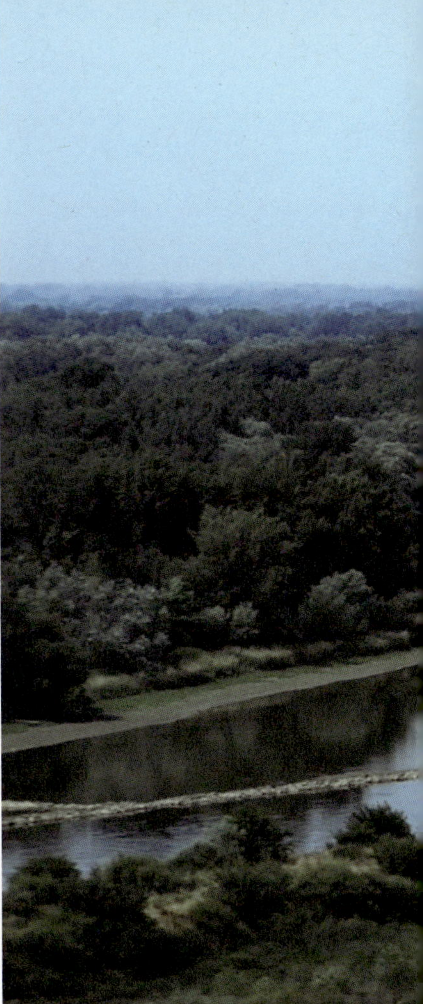

It's called Consulado River, and constitutes
the confluence of the San Joaquin and
Los Morales rivers. It was tubed in 1944,
in what they called the modernization
of Mexico City.

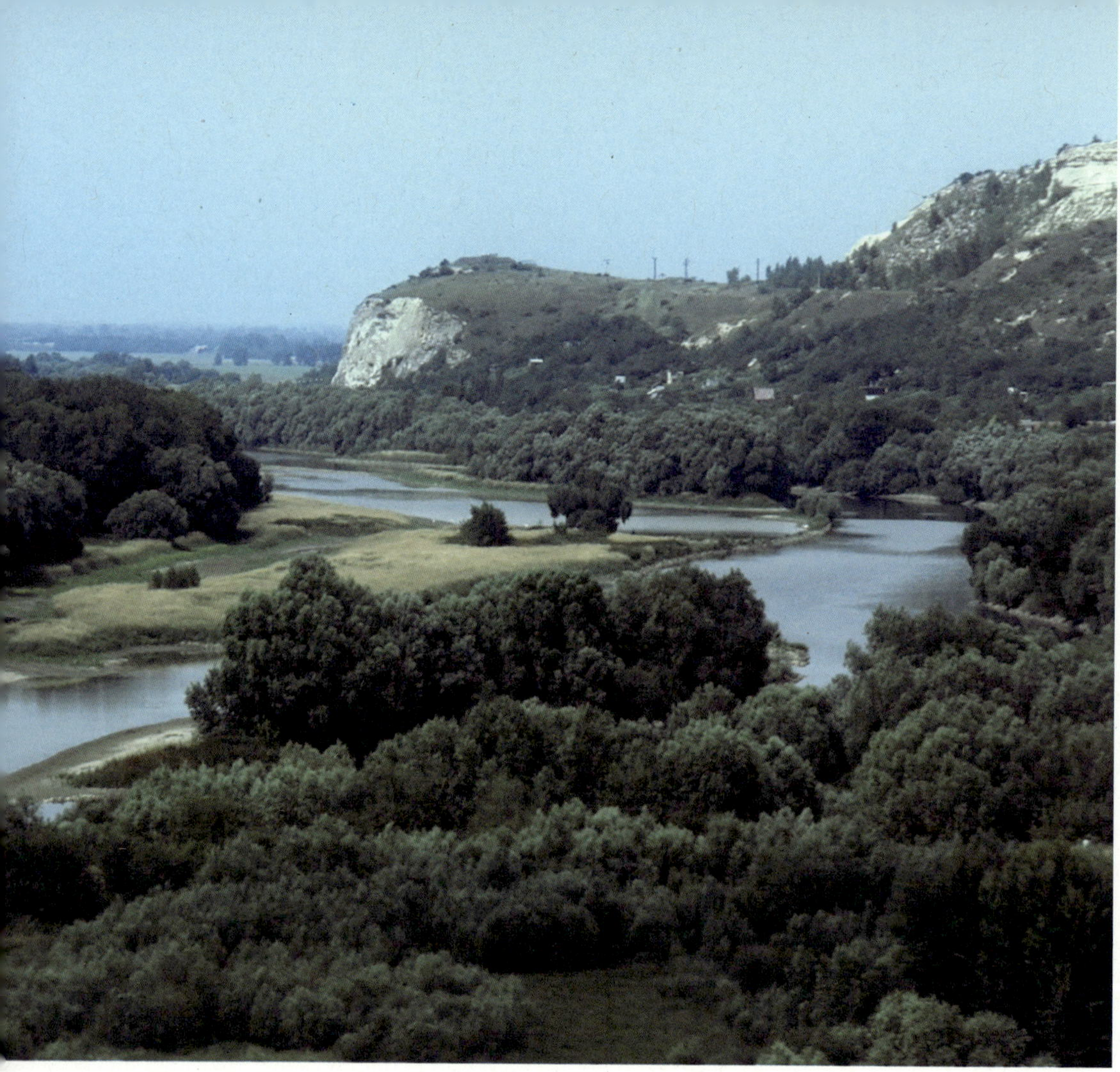

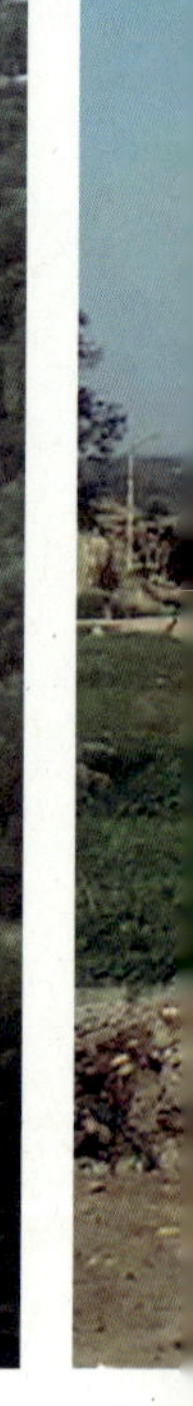

00' 00"

... وأكثر من النهر نفسه
أحب أن انظر بمقربة الى تلك المنطقة التي تظهر بوضوح أقل .

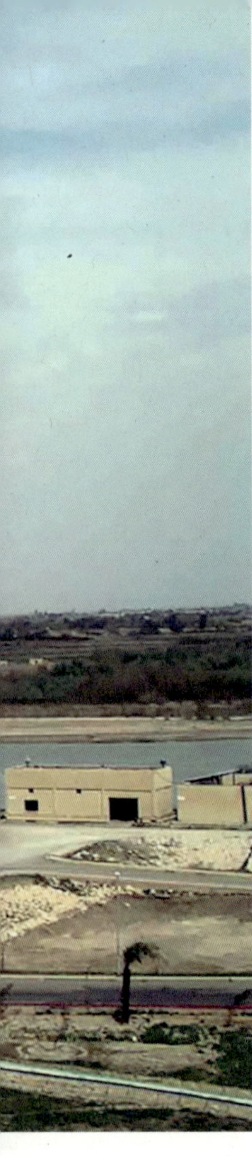

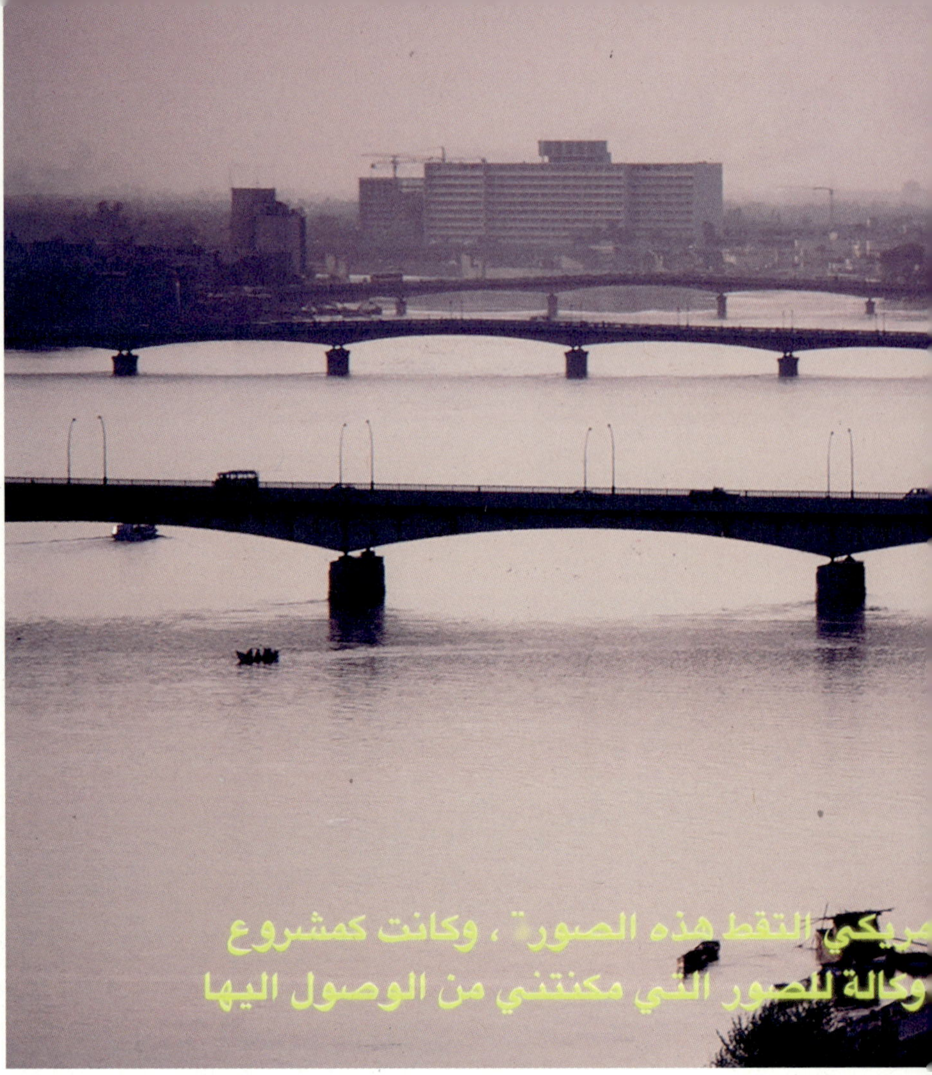

When one reviews the history of the images
from Baghdad, it's easy to recognize that each
time there has been a conflict in the area, since
the invention of the camera, there has also been
a burst of images from Western photographers.

00' 00"

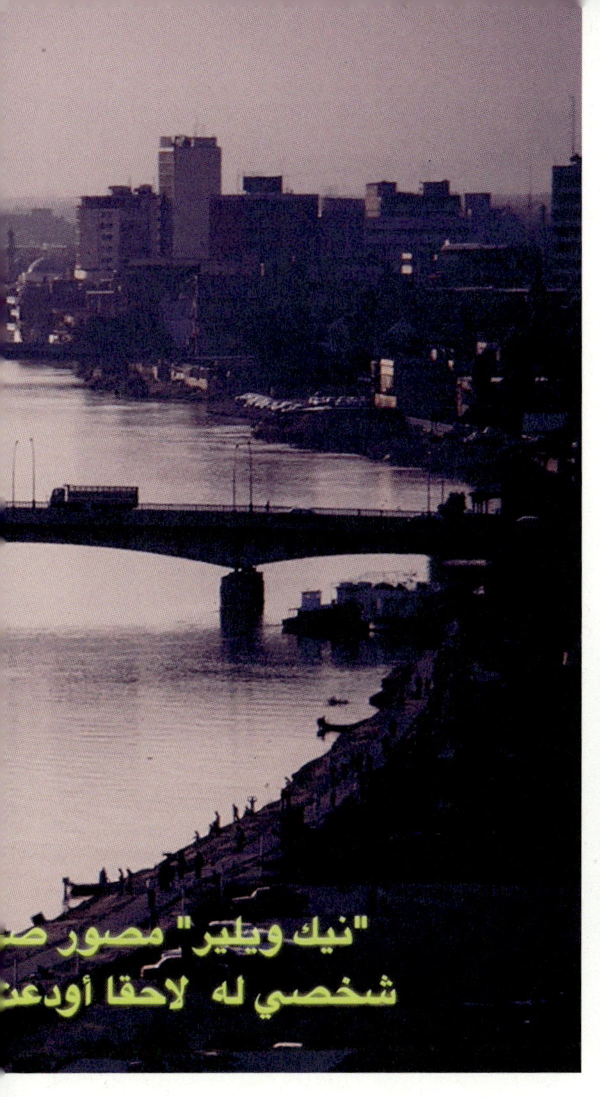

"نيك ويلير" مصور ص
شخصي له لاحقا أودعن

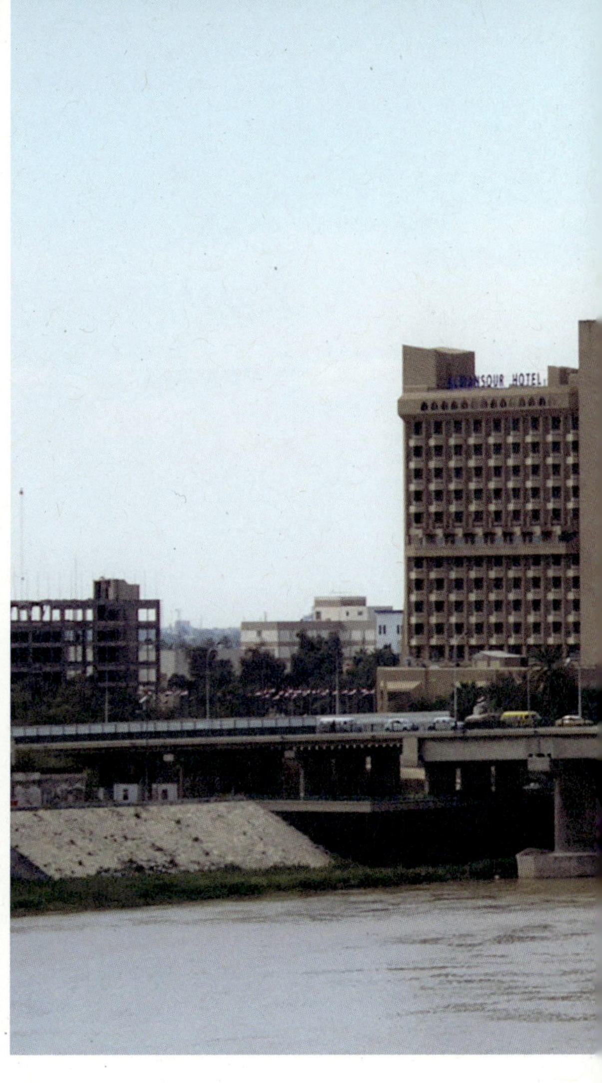

AL MANSOUR HOTEL

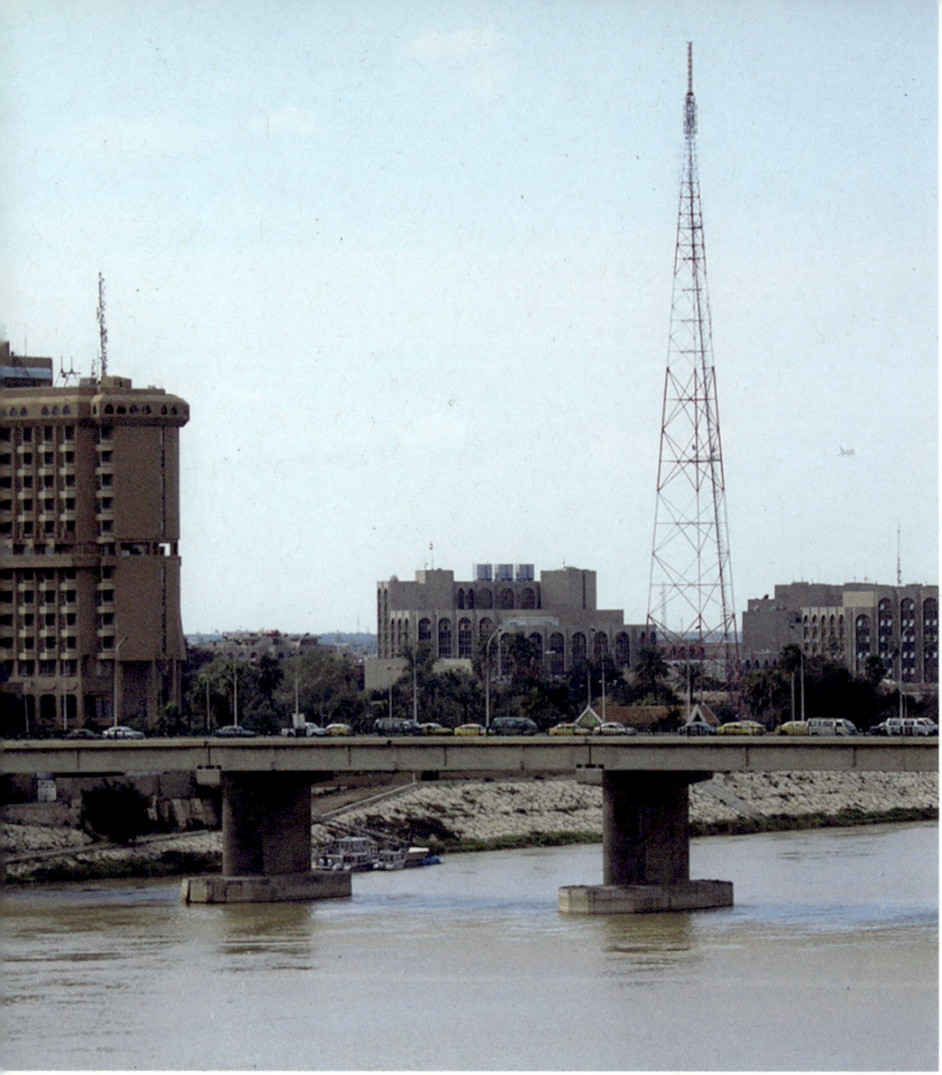

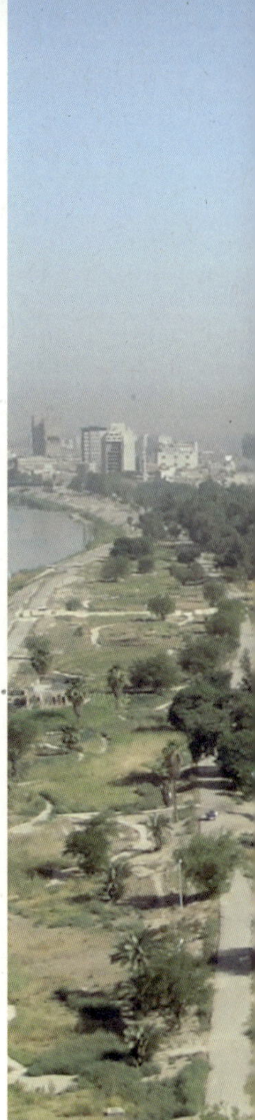

00' 00"

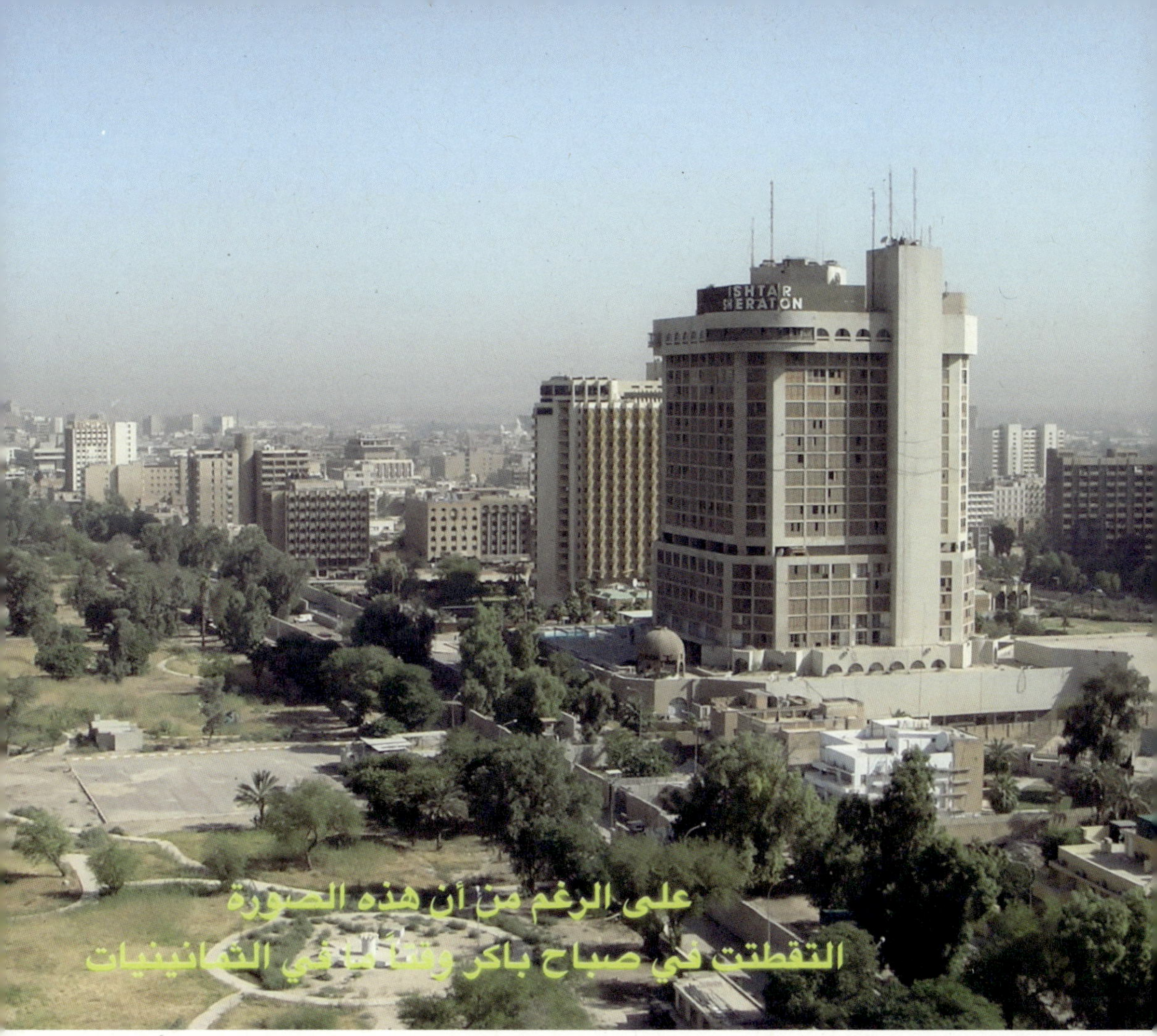

على الرغم من أن هذه الصورة
التقطت في صباح باكر وقتاً ما في الثمانينيات

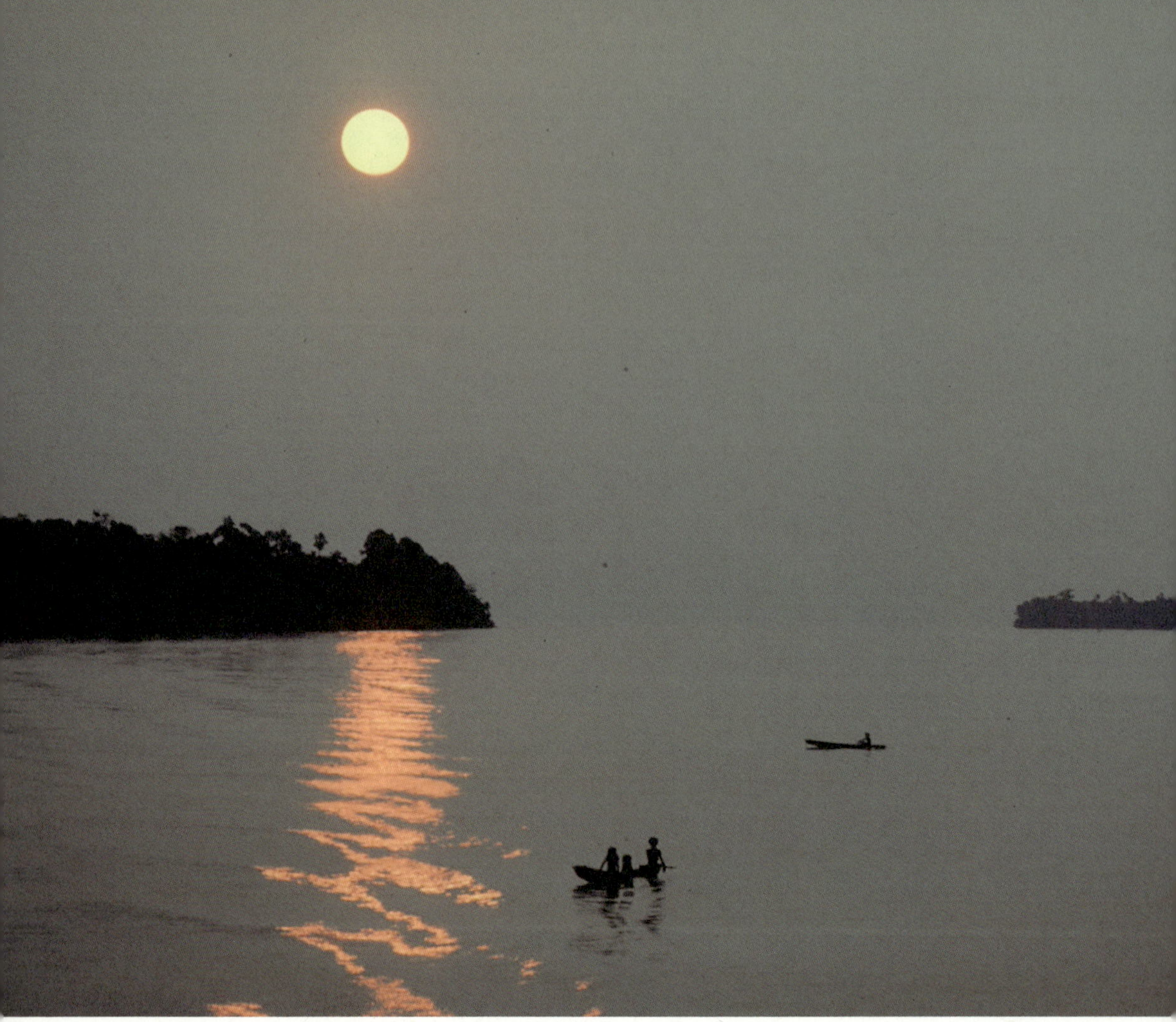

When I stare long enough at a picture of
a river, I forget what I was looking for, and
sometimes I feel like it turns into a moving
image. The water starts to actually drift and
make sounds, and boats start to disappear
in the bends.

00' 00"

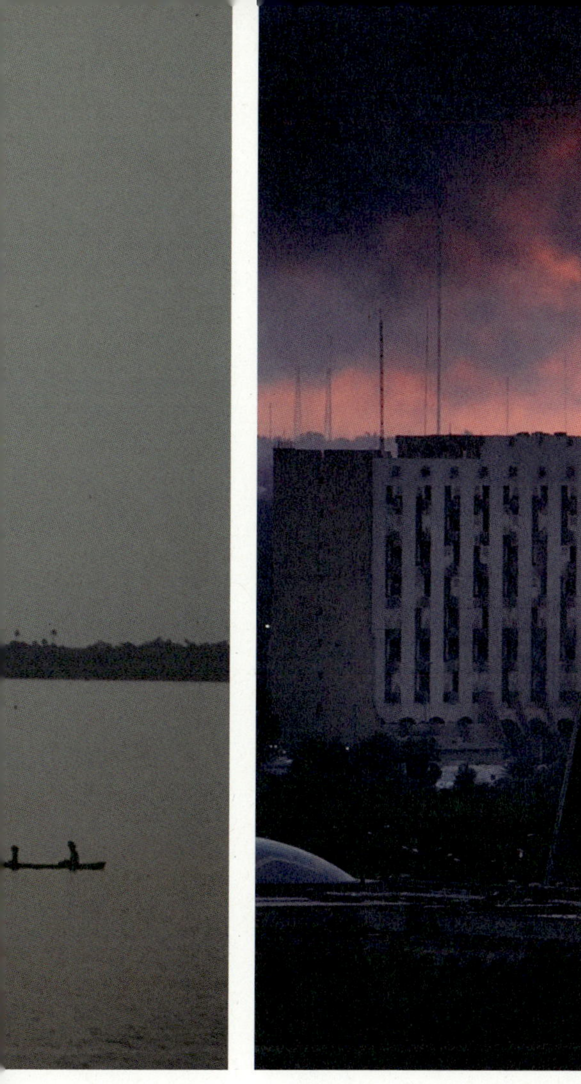

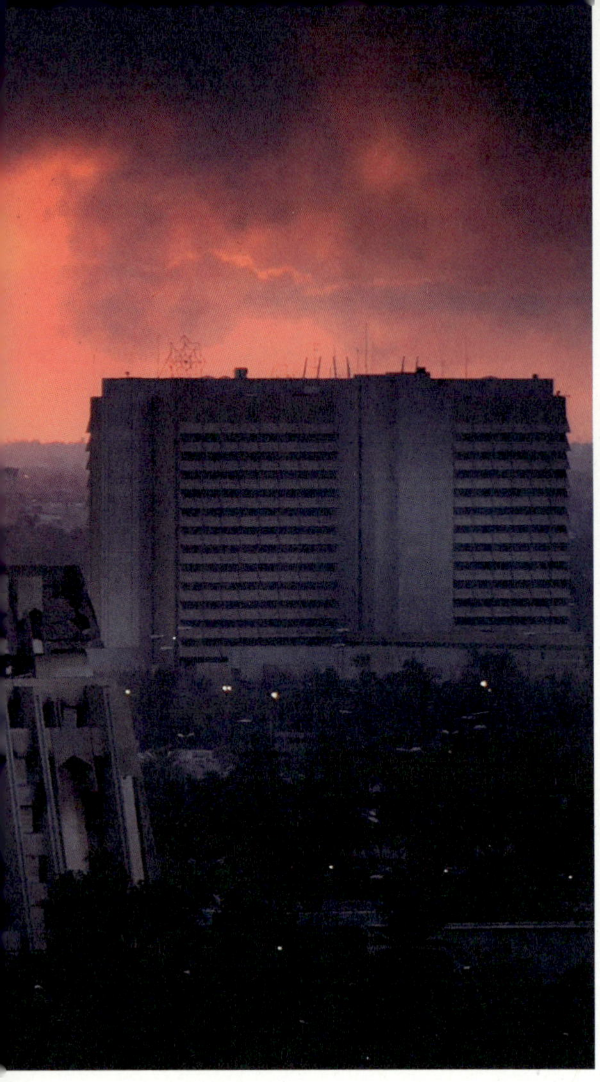 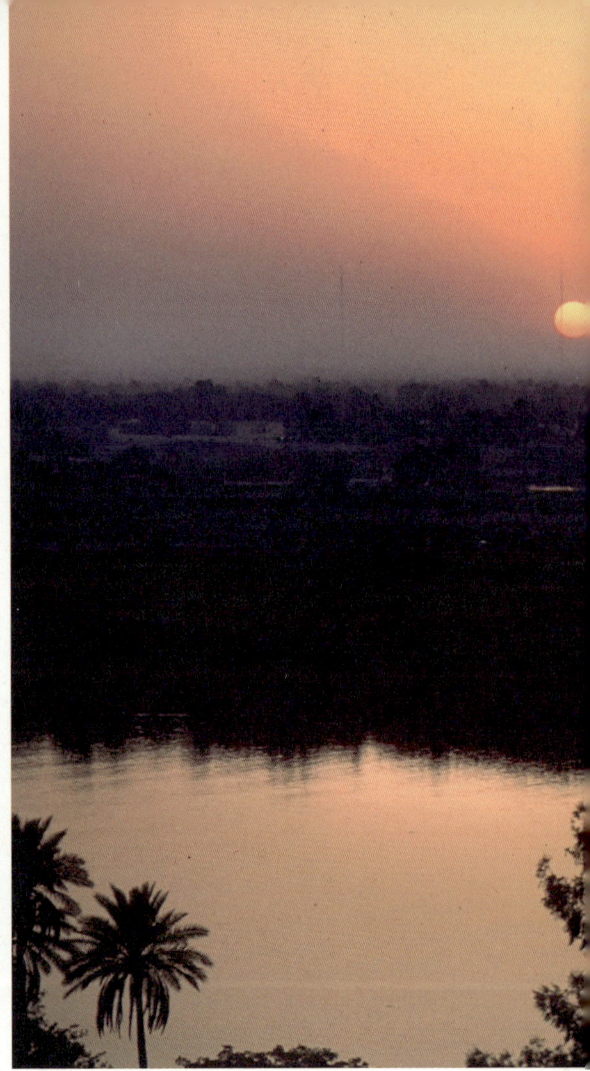

00' 00"

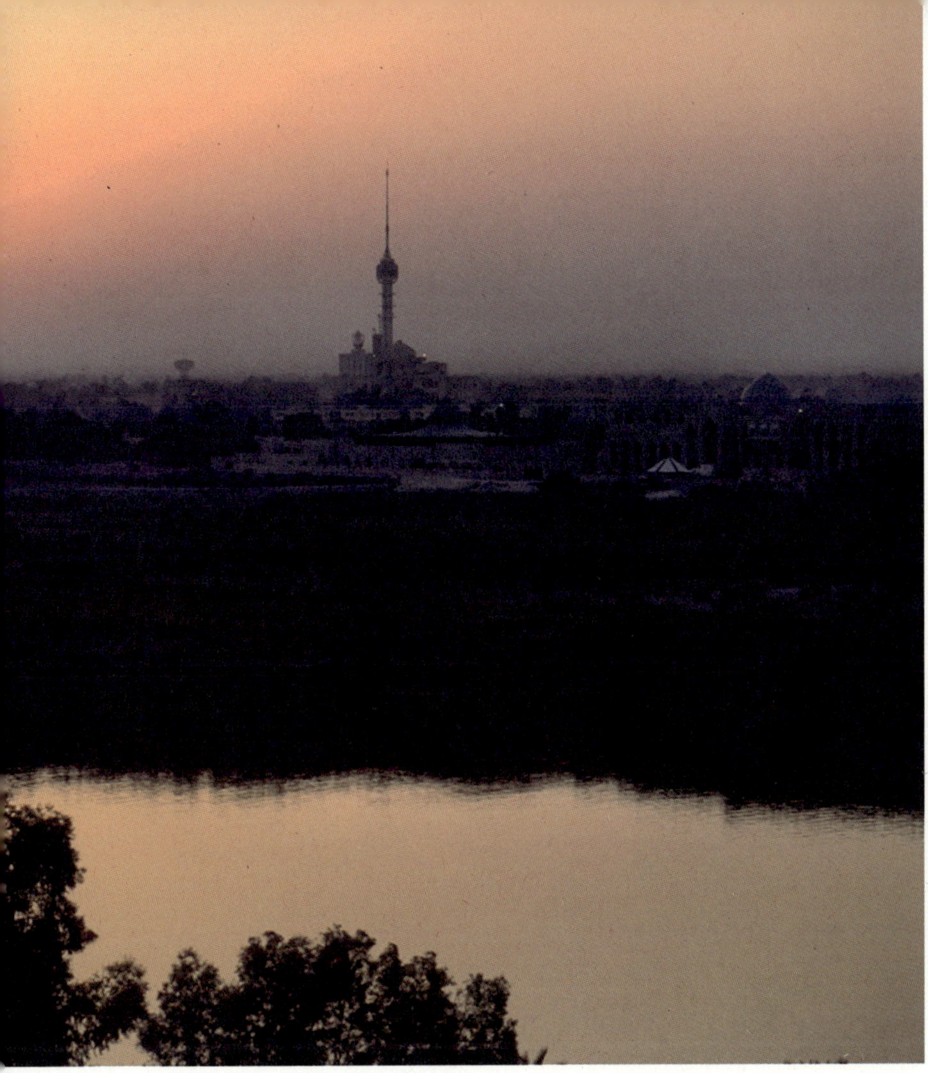

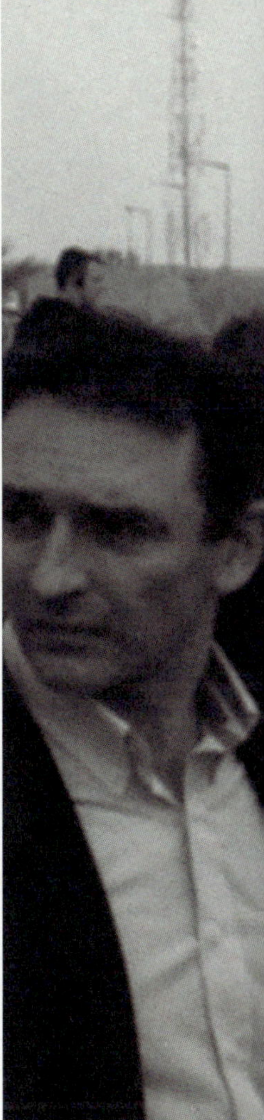

Pictures tells us more than what is depicted
in them. Why was this picture taken?
Why did the photographer feel the need to make
this precise image? What does the very act
of doing it tell us once the image circulates?

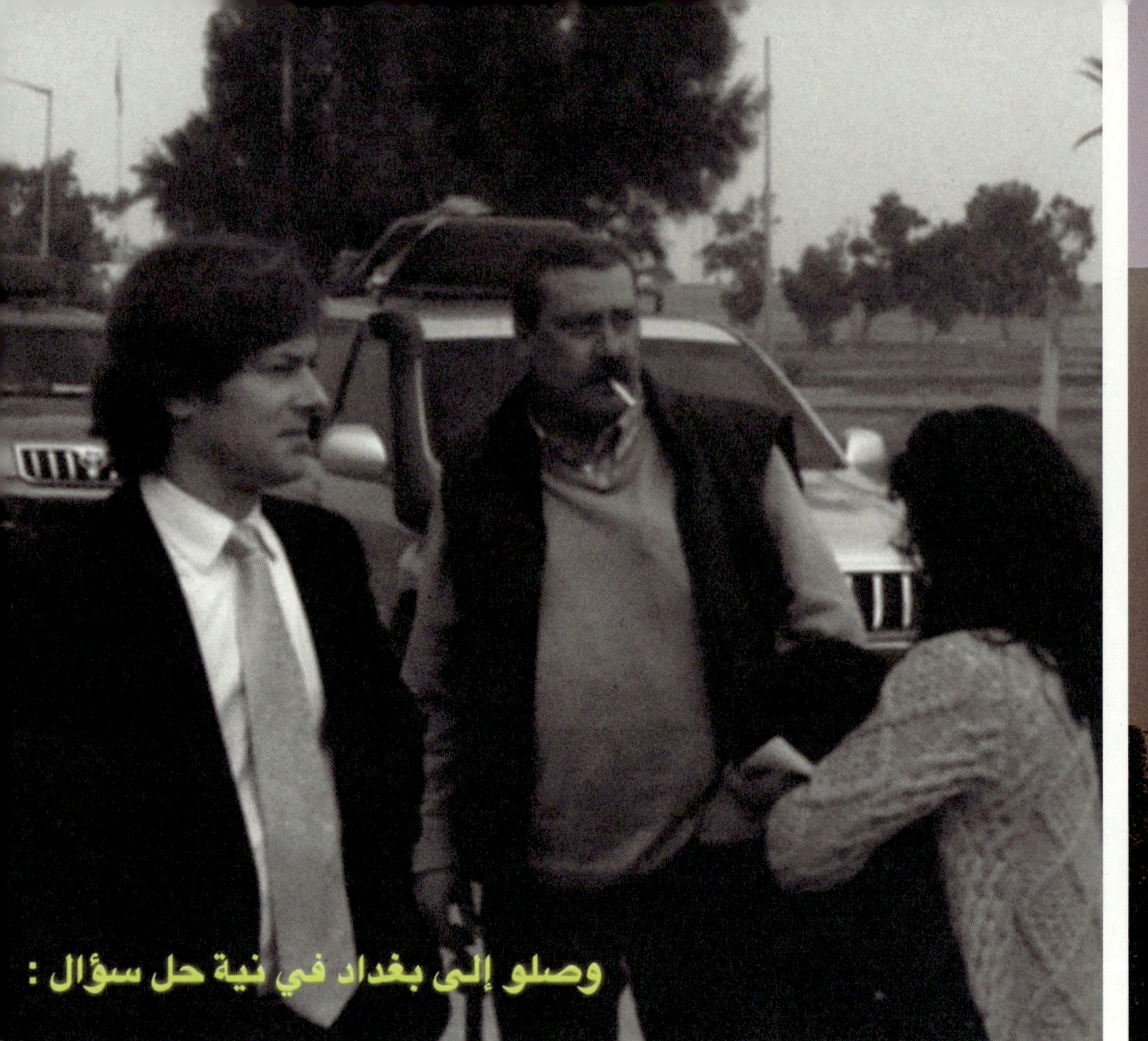

00' 00"

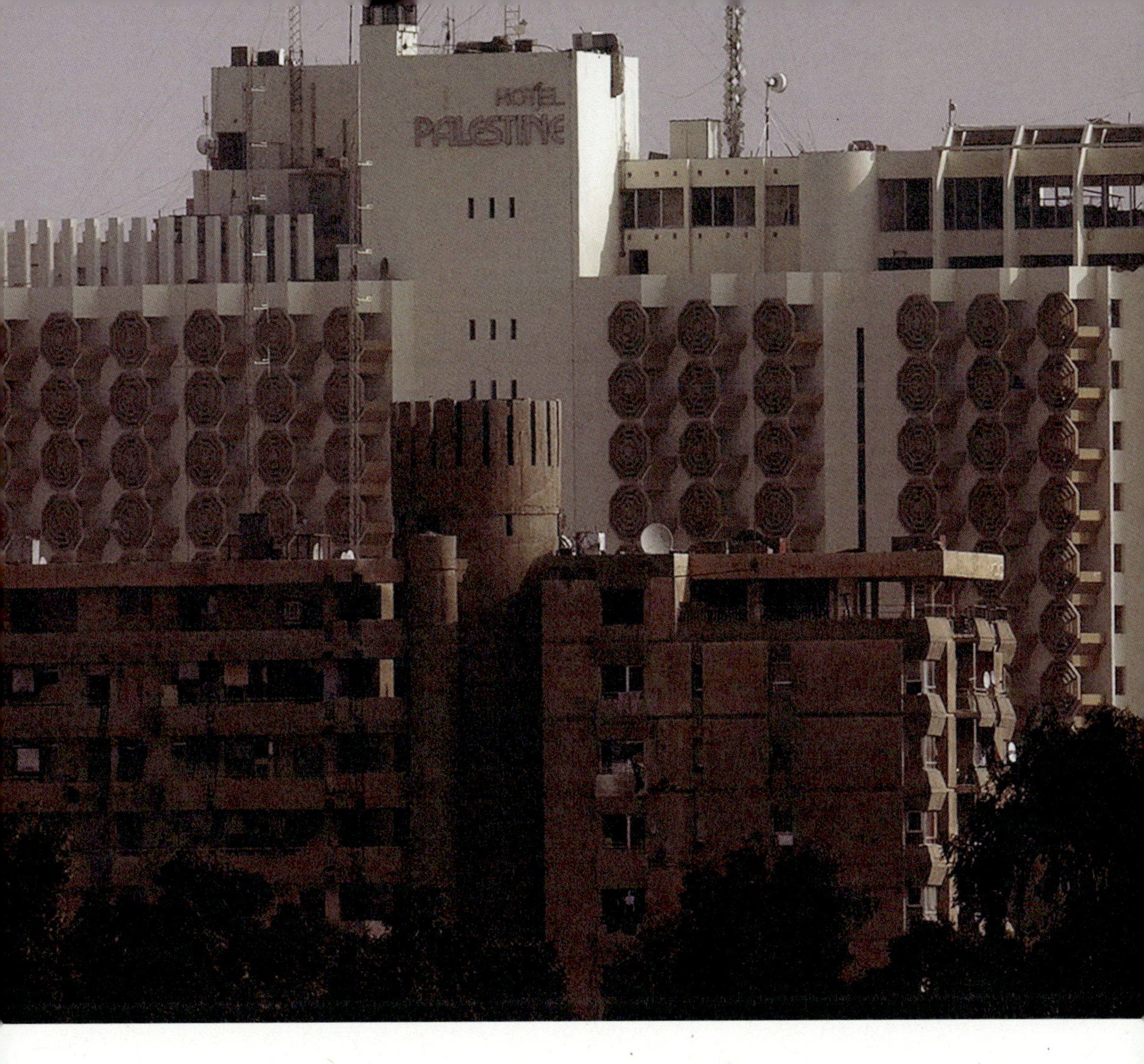

38' 00"

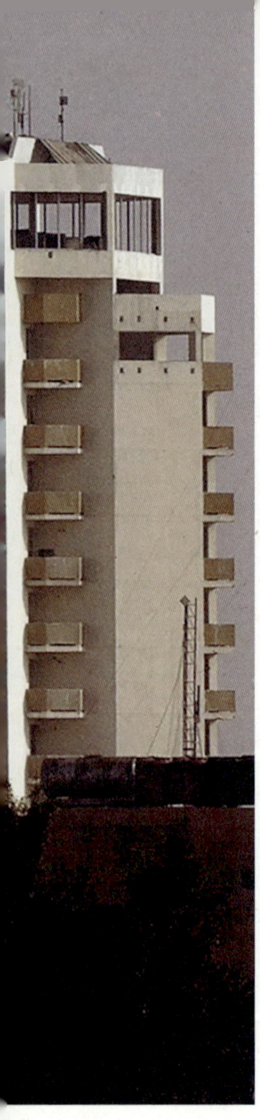

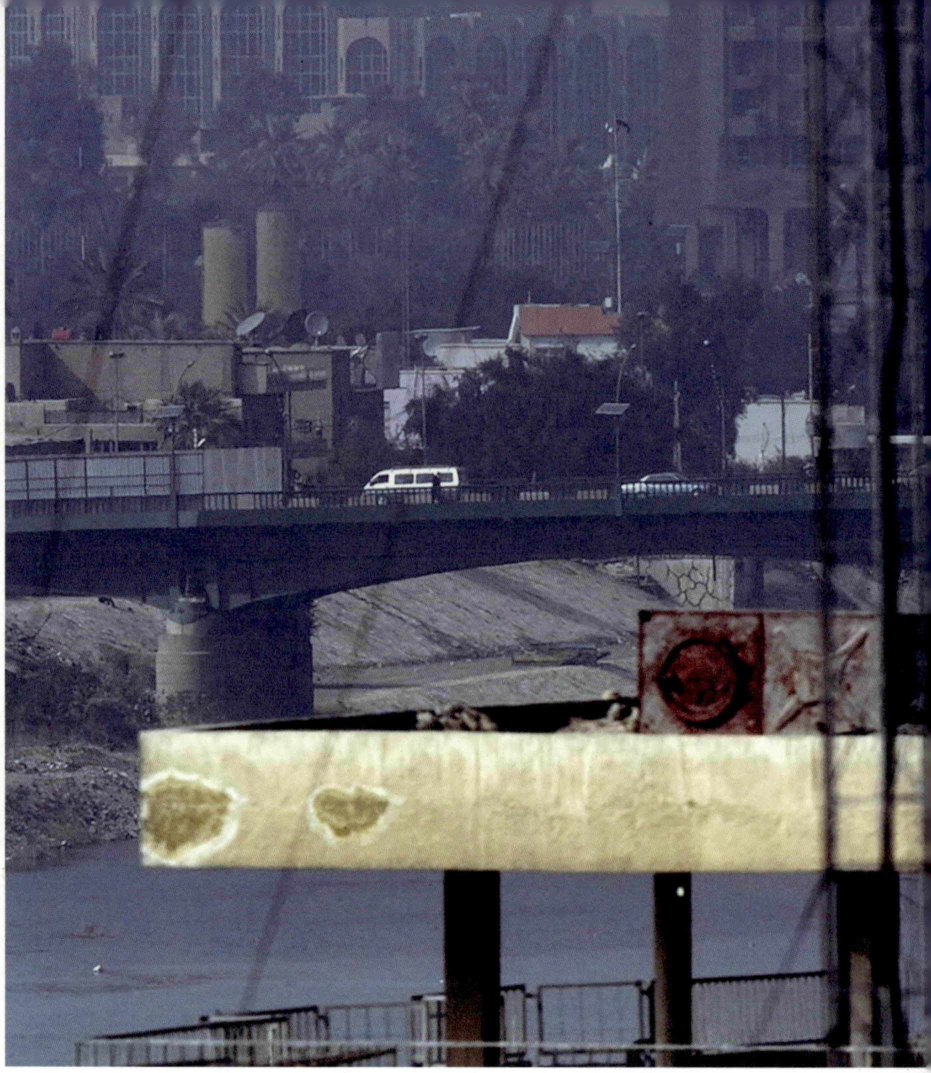

They are, after all, the way they looked at each other, right before the defining moment.

00' 00"

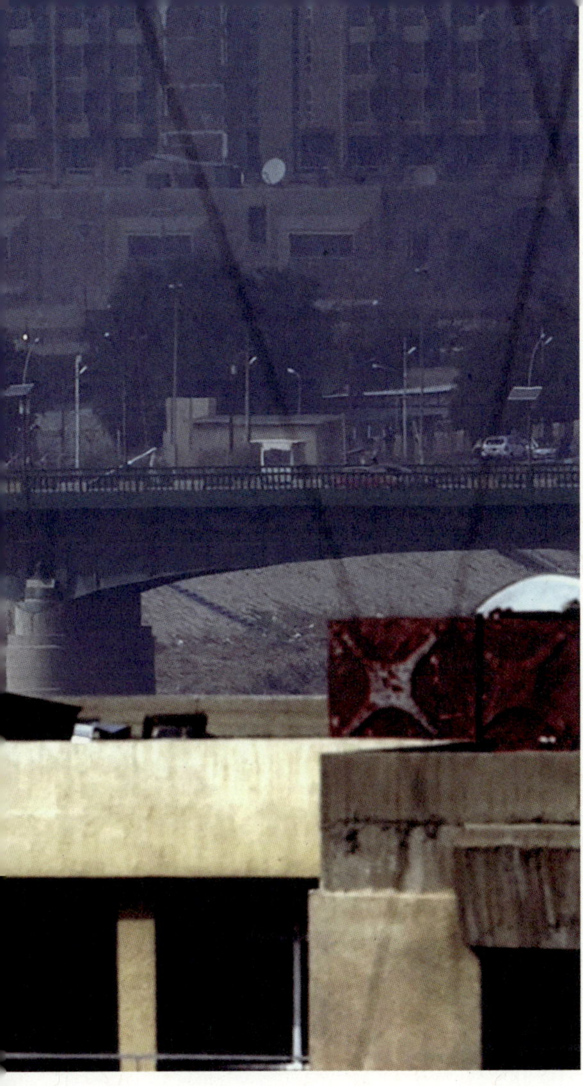

38' 00"

Daniel Garza-Usabiaga

Undoing the Archive: Notes on *Sounds Like Isolation to Me*

A strange feeling of comfort but also uneasiness transcends the physical space of *Sounds Like Isolation to Me*. As one approaches the work, there is something attractive yet unlocalizable inside what Mario García Torres calls a "museographic essay." There are recognizable, mostly high-pitched percussion notes, but they are not rhythmic; nor do they offer any kind of melody, as one would expect with this kind of sound. Only later in the experience of the work does one realize that they are sounds that Conlon Nancarrow recorded in the early 1950s but never used, which were later rearranged by the Berlin-based composer Nils Frahm for the installation. The contradictory yet harmonious nature of the piece could encapsulate a number of arguments in García Torres's piece, in which seemingly conflictive lines of thought meet and complement each other.

García Torres has described his practice as a "way of making history"; he articulates narratives that "function as complements" to established and better-known accounts.[1] *Sounds Like Isolation to Me* could be seen in relation to this premise. It presents a study, as a museographic essay, of the American avant-garde composer Conlon Nancarrow (1912–1997), who spent the latter part of his life in exile in Mexico. García Torres focuses on certain aspects that are often overlooked by Nancarrow scholars, most of them specialists in music, like the architecture of his studio and the community of international political exiles in Mexico. He also speculates about actual and possible connections between the composer and other avant-garde artists as well as

---

1   Mario García Torres, quoted in Montse Badia, "The Structures of Art. An Interview with Mario García Torres," *A*Desk*, http://www.a-desk.org/spip/spip.php?article1589.

about issues related to plastic and conceptual concerns drawn from twentieth-century art. Although García Torres articulates different perspectives on the composer, his reflections remain open-ended; the project does not aspire to a totalizing narrative, and although informed by history, it does not aspire to be factual in all aspects.

García Torres's presentation relies on putting into evidence the problematic implications of traditional forms of display found in museums. After working in the composer's archives housed at the Paul Sacher Foundation in Basel, García Torres produced reproductions of specific original materials from the archive, gathered various documents, historical objects, and artworks from other artists, and produced modest objects of his own, which all found their way into the various vitrines that make up the piece. These objects and documents offer different perspectives on Nancarrow's history and work. *Sounds Like Isolation to Me*, at first glance, resembles the kind of exhibition that one would expect to find in a traditional historical museum. García Torres's project, however, calls into question the value of truth associated with this kind of institution. There are no explanatory texts accompanying the objects displayed in the vitrines; they are simply accompanied by short descriptive labels. Each collection of things is open to a field of connections and relationships to the other objects that make up the project.

Although the vitrines gather historical and recently produced documents and objects, all the materials seem to belong to the same temporal register, as if they all came directly from Nancarrow's archive. One experiences a sort of temporal disorientation when seeing the information that identifies and dates them. Thus each vitrine becomes a play of different fragments that together conjure multiple temporalities as well as a set of actual and speculative relations between Nancarrow and certain of his contemporaries, to artistic disciplines and spheres of creativity, and to García Torres's own production. This potential sequence of relations expresses the artist's intention to draw a "cosmology of synchronicity and chance within the realm of invention."[2] This aim somehow echoes what he identifies as the "temporal dissonance" present in Nancarrow's work. This posture goes against the most traditional forms of historiography, which privilege an understanding of history based in temporal continuity and attempt to control the dynamics of time in order to present coherent narra-

---

2   Mario García Torres, "Sounds Like Isolation to Me." Wall text in the exhibition, written by the artist, 2016.

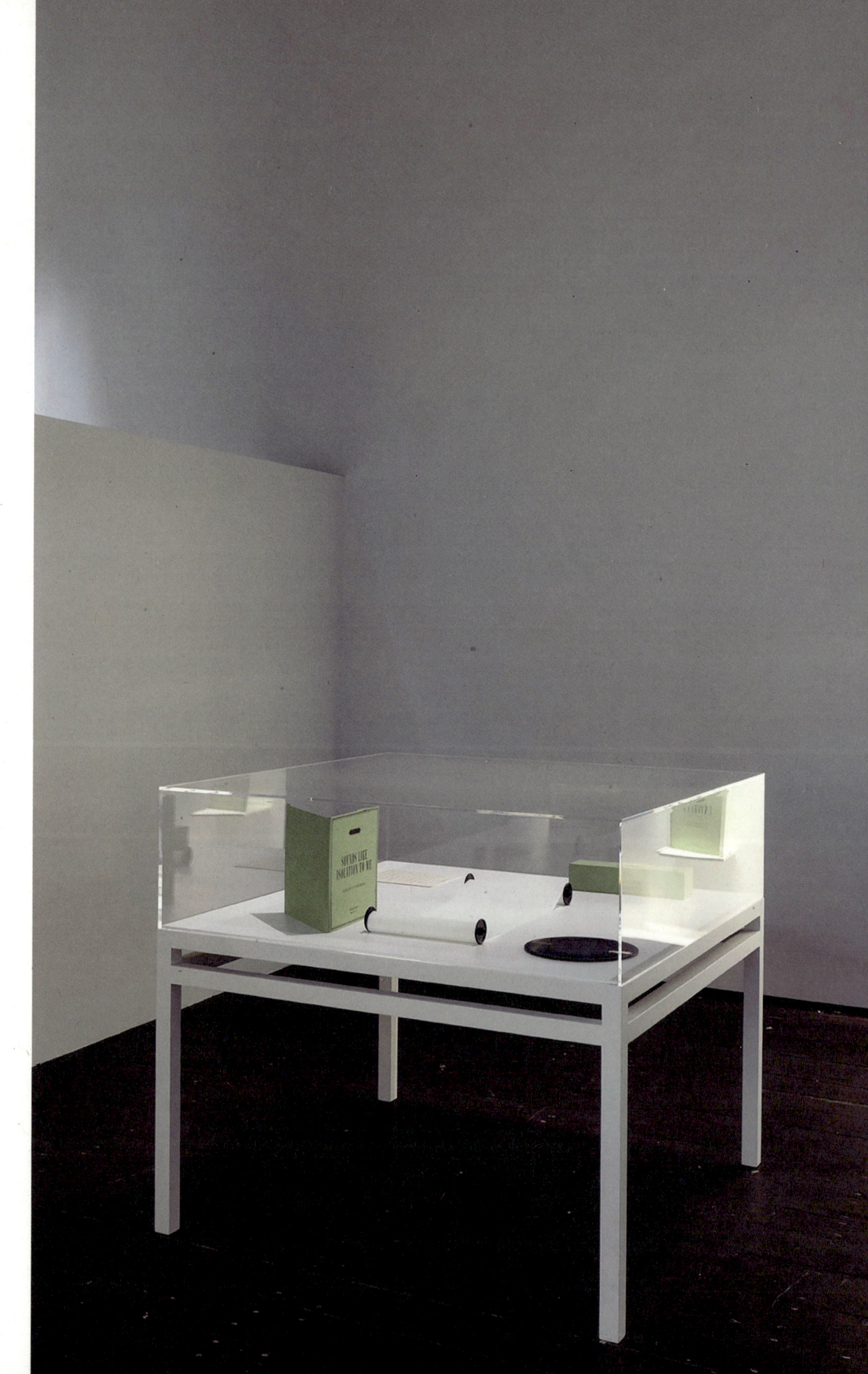

Sounds Like Isolation to Me
n.d., acetate, cardboard, ink, linen, magnetic tape, oil, paper,
sheet metal, sound, video, wire, wood, dimensions variable
Thyssen-Bornemisza Art Contemporary Collection, Vienna

tives. Here instead the artist offers and emphasizes breaks, unsynchronized moments, disjunctions, and multiple temporal dimensions, while historical speculation opens alternative directions, including connections between past and present experiences.

From this perspective *Sounds Like Isolation to Me* mimics a certain feeling experienced when conducting archival research, which arises when documents are seen as fragments. Although archives are often perceived as complete entities, capable of allowing us to decipher the totality of an individual's complex production, in reality they tend to evade definitive closure. Archival documents are open to an array of different relations; they communicate not only within the archive but also with other archives and sources of information. They can even demand the articulation of new archives that dialogue with and complement their contents. The informed imagination of a particular scholar, for example, is crucial to establishing the kind of connections that can open new perspectives or change established conceptions on a particular issue. As Dalibor Vesely writes, it demands a particular capacity "to establish similarities between different objects, and as a consequence the capacity to reveal on a deeper level what is common to them."[3] García Torres's project echoes this perspective on historical research. In a coherent artistic experience, he brings together different documents, objects, and artworks as a means to articulate relations between distant realities that might not have obvious connections. In this way, Nancarrow and his work can be appreciated in a new light. In *Sounds Like Isolation to Me*, for instance, García Torres constantly revisits and ponders the actual and potential connections between the composer and certain practices within the legacy of the artistic avant-garde of the twentieth century.

153

3   Dalibor Vesely, "The Rehabilitation of Fragment," in *Architecture in the Age of Divided Representation: The Question of Creativity under the Shadow of Production* (Cambridge, MA: MIT Press, 2005), 338.

Conlon Nancarrow is remembered as a sort of hermetic individual
who produced most of his work in isolation in his studio in Mexico City.
He did not perform his compositions in public for several decades.
For García Torres, Nancarrow encapsulates a sort of struggle "between the
avant-garde's worldly consciousness and the romantic notion of isolation
as a space of creativity."[4] His museographic essay gives visibility to such
struggles by introducing works and gestures that signal either toward
Nancarrow's originality and inventiveness or toward his strong inclination
for seclusion, in the same way that Nils Frahm's composition for the installation creates a space in which concrete poetry meets aboriginal-related
sounds. Nancarrow was more than an outstanding musician; he was an
early version of a gifted programmer who designed mechanical percussion
instruments and made his own drums and manipulated player pianos. But
for decades his production never went beyond the boundaries of his studio,
and few people experienced it there.

Nancarrow moved to Mexico in 1940 (becoming a citizen in 1956) as
one of the many American Cold War exiles who found a sort of safe haven
from the quasi-totalitarian policies of McCarthyism in the United States.[5]
He had joined the Communist Party in 1935, when he was twenty-three
years old, and soon after that participated in the International Brigades,
which fought on the side of the Republican Army during the Spanish Civil
War. Nancarrow began to be harassed by the American government soon
after his return from Europe in 1939 and left his country for good one year
later. Prior to the 1980s he went back only once, in 1947, when he traveled
to New York to acquire a custom-built manual punching machine, which
he needed to make the work for which he is recognized today: his compositions for player piano. Nancarrow's interest in this sort of outmoded
instrument was based in part on the fact that he wouldn't need to interact
with a musician to play his compositions. He also valued the instrument's
capacity to perform music at a speed that a musician could not accomplish
and to present many different rhythms simultaneously.[6] As an early form of

4   García Torres, "Sounds Like Isolation to Me." Wall text in the exhibition,
     written by the artist, 2016.
5   García Torres showed *Sounds Like Isolation to Me* at La Tallera in Cuernavaca, Mexico in 2015.
     For this installment of the project, he included a vitrine dedicated to Cuernavaca, where
     Nancarrow lived for a few years, as an important urban center for various communities
     of exiles in Mexico.
6   Kyle Gann, *La música de Conlon Nancarrow*, ed. Julio Estrada (Mexico City: Escuela Nacional
     de Música, UNAM, 2008), 41–57. Originally published as *The Music of Conlon Nancarrow*
     (Cambridge: Cambridge University Press, 1995).

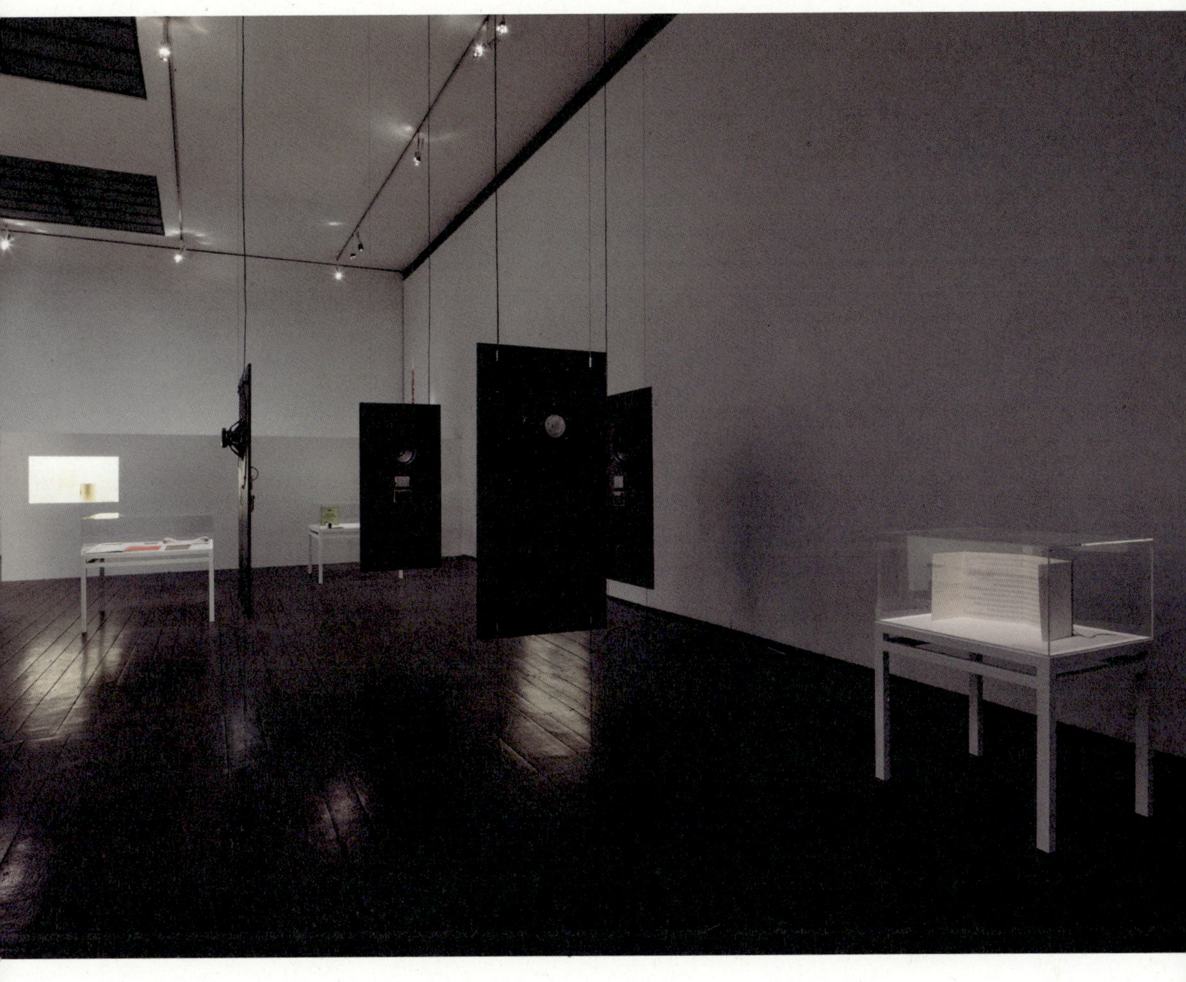

programmed music, his work reflects his interest in performing machines
as an alternative to collaborating with fallible human musicians.
He manipulated his player pianos to increase their speed and get a more
aggressive sound.[7] These changes turned the piano hammers into percussion
devices of sorts.

Nancarrow composed the music for his player pianos manually,
perforating the roll of paper using a process that involved intuition and
mathematical precision. The shape of each circular hole on the paper is the
result of hand punching. It took Nancarrow around six months to compose
and punch by hand a piece that lasted around five minutes. This mundane,
mechanical, and repetitive action, as well as its mark or perforation, is
revisited by García Torres in this project, in which the process is compared
to practices within the domain of visual arts. Among the materials that the
artist assembled is a copy of the 1968 album *Studies for Player Piano*. The
album cover features the image of the instrument overlaid with the imprint
of an LP disc—a circle, like the basic unit of Nancarrow's compositions.
García Torres produced several photographs of Nancarrow that feature
perforations that, just like those in the composer's player-piano rolls, operate
as significant marks. The circle reappears in another object, a wooden frame
with cane mesh, which is evocative of the local context and time period
in which Nancarrow lived most of his life. Mexican artisans would weave
this natural material for chairs and other pieces of furniture following such
designs. This object also points toward the manual labor involved in Nancarrow's work. Other pieces in *Sounds Like Isolation to Me* attempt to establish
a similar geographic link. A case in point is *Not All Rhythms Run the Same
Times*, a work in which the artist rearranged the keys of a wooden marimba
one after the other, as if in a line. Hung from the ceiling, this piece could be
seen in relation to an unfolded paper piano roll. The work simultaneously
echoes Nancarrow's interest in percussion and reflects the design sensibility
common in Mexico at the time. The linear solution of this work also brings
to mind the production of other artists and composers who are revisited in
this project, such as John Cage and La Monte Young.

---

7   This issue of acceleration is addressed by García Torres in the video *An Act the Outcome of
     Which Is Unknown*, which is part of this project. This work documents the artist's review of
     Nancarrow's archive through microfilm at the Paul Sacher Foundation. He moves the film
     at different speeds, with several sudden stops. In the meantime, using subtitles, he recounts
     the different times when Nancarrow, during his lifetime, changed the speed at which his
     compositions for player piano were played. When he stops the movement of the machine,
     a particular document elicits attention: what is heard is the noise of the roll of film moving
     through the microfilm reader.

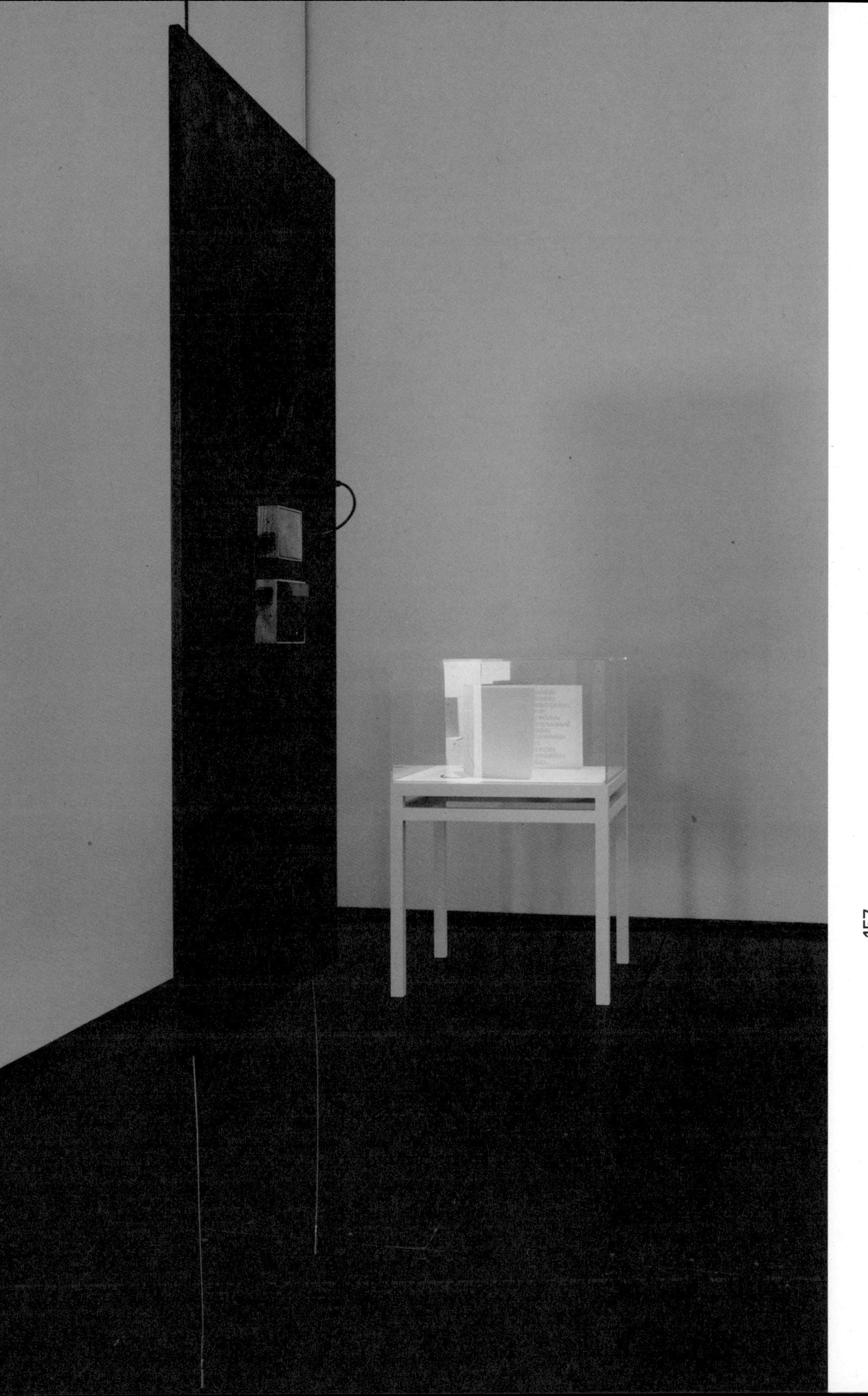

In another moment of revision of the piano player, the artist produced an artwork that suggests a common ground between Nancarrow's perforated rolls and the practice of concrete or visual poetry. *In Solo for Typewriter*, García Torres typed the word *solo* on a piece of white paper, creating, through its repetition in lines of different lengths, a diagonal form. If we consider the sound of the typewriter, which operates as a sort of percussion instrument, García Torres's work can be regarded as a nontraditional form of notation. With this, he brings Nancarrow closer to the domain of the visual arts while giving a practice such as visual poetry an aural dimension. The artist also made a percussion instrument, echoing Nancarrow's interest in producing musical devices and inventions. *Maraclave; or, From Bullet to Hole, There Is a Tube Drawn (An Instrument for Conlon Nancarrow)* presents two cylinders that, as the title suggests, resemble a pair of circles connected by lines. Like the marimba, this instrument brings to mind certain geographic contexts while, simultaneously, touching on Nancarrow's interest in percussion. The maraclave contains metal pellets, and if it is moved and played by hitting one element with the other, the pellets inside it leave marks and imprints on the wood.

At another point in the project, García Torres revisited the work of the artists Lucio Fontana, Mathias Goeritz, and Dieter Roth. He presents works and archival materials that evidence their common interest in perforation as a plastic gesture. These objects are placed at the same level as a photograph in which Nancarrow is operating his manual punching machine. This image could easily relate to another photograph in which it is possible to appreciate Fontana's hand, holding a nail and making holes in a canvas. García Torres also decided to show a copy of the periodical *Il Gesto* with its cover punctured by Fontana. This piece of cardboard cover could easily relate to one of Nancarrow's notations. Fontana used punctures in his work to represent "energy itself in space," its flow and dynamism.[8] It is possible to speculate that Nancarrow's perforated rolls performed exactly this function, in terms of sound, when played in the player piano. Like Fontana, Goeritz also produced several works perforated by hand. These constitute a series known as *Messages*, which was endowed with certain spiritual undertones. Unlike Fontana's works, Goeritz's always had metallic surfaces, and the punctures usually occupied the totality of the surface, even in large-scale, mural-size works. It is possible to draw a line connecting Goeritz's repetitive

---

8   Germano Celant, *The Italian Metamorphosis, 1943–1968* (New York: Guggenheim Museum, 1994), 708–9.

action with the composer's work using the punching machine. By linking Nancarrow, Goeritz, and Fontana and their works, these objects articulate another common ground, one that outlines a shared sensibility cutting across geographies. García Torres's strategy of establishing these connections shows how there are latent worlds "that are always present, waiting for articulation."[9] The artist realizes a sort of "restorative mapping" in which the composer gets situated as part of the artistic neo-avant-garde of the post–World War II years.

A revision of the legacy of the avant-garde continues at other points in *Sounds Like Isolation to Me*. García Torres also speculates, for example, on the possible connections between Nancarrow and Marcel Duchamp. He used as the starting point of this inquiry a note found in the composer's archive, handwritten by Cage and informing Nancarrow about Duchamp's visit to Mexico. Cage's note, as a single thing coming out of an archive, shows how any document, as a fragment, acts as an "incomplete project that aims for completion."[10] García Torres speculates about whether this document led to the meeting of Duchamp and Nancarrow. Certain objects are brought into relation with this document, which is reproduced by the artist. One of these is the 1976 album *The Entire Musical Work of Marcel Duchamp*, which contains the artist's 1913 aleatory composition *Erratum Musical*, coincidentally also recorded on player-piano rolls. Along with these objects, García Torres constructed a small machine, a work that recalls Nancarrow's, and also Duchamp's, inventiveness. *Speed Can Make a Hole Become a Circle* is an instrument that creates an optical effect through the rapid rotation of a black circular surface with a tiny white circle on it. With this work the artist reconciles the mechanical and retinal concerns of Duchamp's rotary machines of 1925 and his *Rotoreliefs* of 1935 with Nancarrow's perforations and his fascination with velocity and speed. History appears here not as it was but as it could have been.

The presence of John Cage and his work deserves special mention; his production permeates this project. During his trip to New York in 1947 Nancarrow attended Cage's presentation of *Sonatas and Interludes*, and the aleatory nature of the piece had an eye-opening impact on Nancarrow's work. Cage, for his part, was introduced to Nancarrow's work in the early 1960s by John Edmunds, a composer and at the time the curator at the Music Division of the New York Public Library, who had previously requested

9   Vesely, "The Rehabilitation of Fragment," 338.
10   Ibid., 331–32.

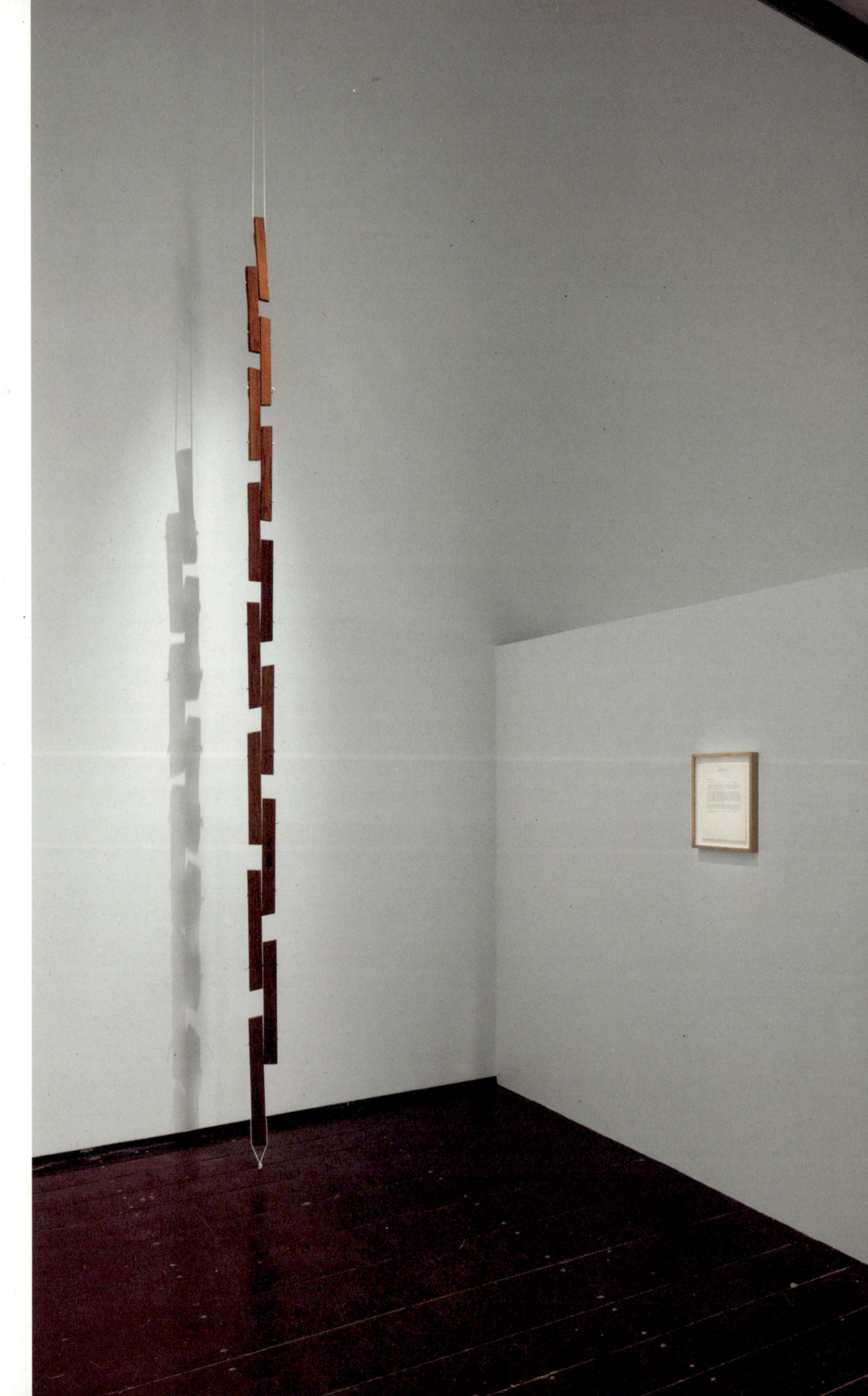

recordings from Nancarrow to be filed at the library. Surprised at such compositions, Cage further introduced Merce Cunningham to the music, and Cunningham would later tour the world with a dance piece using a Nancarrow composition. Cage thus became one of the first promoters of Nancarrow's music even before meeting him. Later Cage would travel to Mexico City to meet him in his studio,[11] and they would meet on several subsequent occasions, either in Mexico City or abroad.

Several objects in García Torres's work testify to this friendship. One of the first documents that is found in the installation is a letter written by Nancarrow to Cage in which he reaffirms his state of living in isolation. Some critics have defined both these artists as antipodes in many ways, even though they coincide in representing the most notable experimental tendencies in American postwar music.[12] García Torres speculates on potential similarities and connections between these two individuals. He does this through the theme of silence, for example, assembling a collection of objects comprising, among other things, *A Long Letter* (1977), a visual poem written by Cage and dedicated to Nancarrow, and Cage's sheet music for *4'33"* (1952). This work is related to two other works presented by García Torres. One is an unperforated roll of player-piano paper found in Nancarrow's studio. The other is a tape: *Blank Player Piano Roll*. The roll was played and recorded by the artist. The tape is presented here with the other objects; its sound, of the paper rolling through the player piano, remains mute. This collection of objects, displayed in a vitrine, attests to how these systems of things operate. García Torres shows how a collection of objects of this kind accomplishes a sort of completeness—"an attempt to overcome the wholly irrational character of the object's mere presence at hand through its integration into a new, expressly devised system."[13] Through these elements he establishes connections that bring closer the figures of Cage and Nancarrow. A piece like *Blank Player Piano Roll* seems to reconcile the production of both.

García Torres's interest in Nancarrow became more acute after he visited the former studio of the musician in Mexico City for the first time. He dedicated a section of *Sounds Like Isolation to Me* to this space, which he revisits in order to speak of Nancarrow's predilection for confinement and

11 Conversation between Conlon Nancarrow and John Cage, moderated by Charles Amirkhanian (1989), http://johncagetrust.blogspot.mx/2015/06/cage-and-nancarrow-1989.html.

12 Julio Estrada, "Prólogo a la primera edición en español," in Gann, *Música de Conlon Nancarrow*, XXIII.

13 Walter Benjamin, "H [The Collector]," in *The Arcades Project*, trans. Howard Eiland and Kevin McLaughlin (Cambridge, MA: Belknap Press, 1999), 205.

solitude. In 1947 Nancarrow married an American artist living in Mexico, Annette Margolis, and commissioned his friend Juan O'Gorman to build a studio and a small house next to his new wife's residence. O'Gorman, also a strong believer in the ideals of communism, designed functionalist solutions for these structures, inspired by the idea of the minimum dwelling. He also produced several outdoor murals in stone in his realist style, designed to complement the architecture.[14] Nancarrow's seclusion is evident in the fact that these buildings are not at all well known, even by O'Gorman scholars. So in this vitrine García Torres also gives visibility to the work of the architect and muralist. At the same time he shows how archives sometimes demand the production of new documents and thus of new archives that can enter into dialogue with and expand the study of existing materials. One object that he produced is a kind of frottage (*Conlon Nancarrow's Studio West Wall*) made from the walls of studio, a document of sorts that shows O'Gorman's treatment of the wall surfaces, designed perhaps with acoustic considerations in mind. García Torres also included three blueprints of the studio based on photographs that he took of the present state of the space. In these images the space appears simultaneously as empty and inhabited. The presence of some objects, like a player piano in the middle of an otherwise empty study, carries the original memory of the presence of the composer. For *Conlon Nancarrow's Studio Perimeter*, García Torres strung a cotton cord around the perimeter of the studio and then placed the cord within a small box, a material metaphor for the composer's acutely hermetic disposition. The artist also presents a work as a set of instructions, *Sharing While Caring*, which consists of inviting a technician to tune a piano as a sort of live act or concert. The work can recall, in part, Cage's score for 4'33". García Torres did exactly this with Nancarrow's piano found at his studio and recorded the aleatoric composition. The recording produced from these instructions—*Untitled (Sharing While Caring), for Piano and Tuning Wrench*, which was executed by Valentín Yáñez—lies as an object, unheard. It has never been played. With this gesture the artist draws a bridge between Nancarrow's reclusive production and his own practice—that is to say, between the past and the present.

   Sounds Like Isolation to Me revisits different themes around the figure of Nancarrow besides actual and possible connections with the legacy of

---

14   Antonio Luna Arroyo, *Juan O'Gorman: Autobiografía, antología, juicios críticos y documentación exhaustiva sobre su obra* (Mexico City: Cuadernos Populares de Pintura Mexicana Moderna, 1973), 146.

the artistic avant-garde of the twentieth century. The theme of sound, for example, runs through the installation, even though most of the instruments, tapes, and recordings produced for it remain unheard and mute, except for *Music for Diary by Nils Frahm*. This piece consists of Nancarrow's previously unheard stock percussion recordings, which were rescued from his studio to be rearranged by Frahm. Frahm's work presents a nine-week-long composition that functioned as the sound track of the exhibition.[15] The sound was not only heard throughout the installation but transcended its limits, serving as an aural backdrop to this otherwise still and silent collection of documents, artworks, and other objects. García Torres produced a specific installation for playing Frahm's composition, consisting of four panels, each holding a speaker in an almost architectural manner. These panels, with the speakers facing the interior, articulate a sort of semienclosed structure with four walls, which might recall the space of the studio and Nancarrow's disposition to confine his production to its interior. The sound of the original tapes also highlights his interest in percussion and could bring to mind the musician's original plan for a percussion orchestration machine.

If special attention has been given here to the connections established by García Torres between Nancarrow and figures such Cage, Fontana, Goeritz, and O'Gorman, it is because they move the understanding of the former's work toward a different field of knowledge, a displacement of ideas executed by the artist that provokes a radical reevaluation. The revision of the production of the composer departs from the domain of the history and theory of music, which is where it is usually situated. García Torres's work brings together different individuals, temporalities, and geographies and establishes between them connections and a sort of reconciliation. Through this strategy Nancarrow's production can be appreciated from a new perspective; historical speculation, in this way, can be productive in outlining unseen potentialities.

15   *Sounds Like Isolation to Me* was first shown in 2014 during the 8th Berlin Biennale, at the Museen Dahlem. The sound of these original recordings, played from four speakers, invaded the adjacent galleries of the museum. This made palpable, in aural terms, Nancarrow's interest in and study of non-Western music. The Cold War historian Rebecca M. Schreiber recounts how in the early 1950s another American exile in Mexico, the Hollywood producer Julian Zimet, brought Nancarrow a collection of more than fifty records of African and Asian music sent by someone at the Musée de l'Homme in Paris, when Claude Lévi-Strauss was serving as its interim director. See Schreiber, *Cold War Exiles in Mexico: U.S. Dissidents and the Culture of Critical Resistance* (Minneapolis: University of Minnesota Press, 2008), 11.

Sounds Like Isolation to Me

n.d., acetate, cardboard, ink, linen, magnetic tape, oil, paper,
sheet metal, sound, video, wire, wood, dimensions variable
Thyssen-Bornemisza Art Contemporary Collection, Vienna

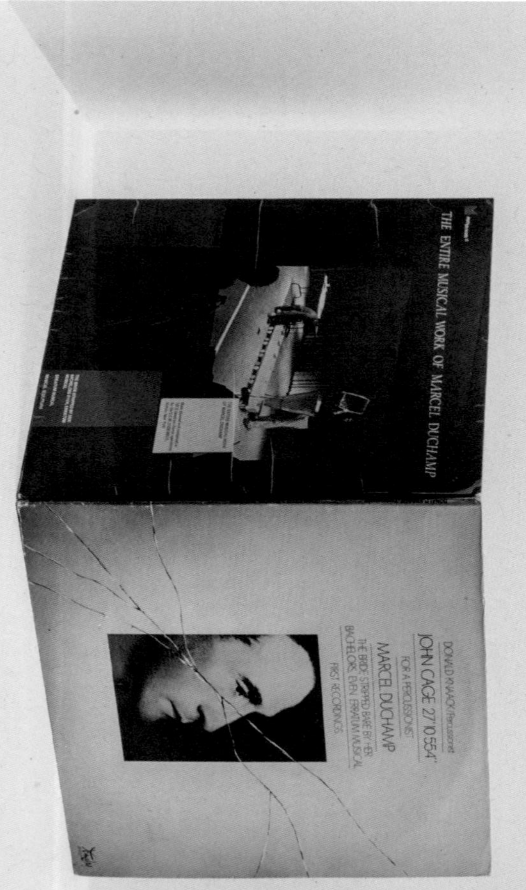

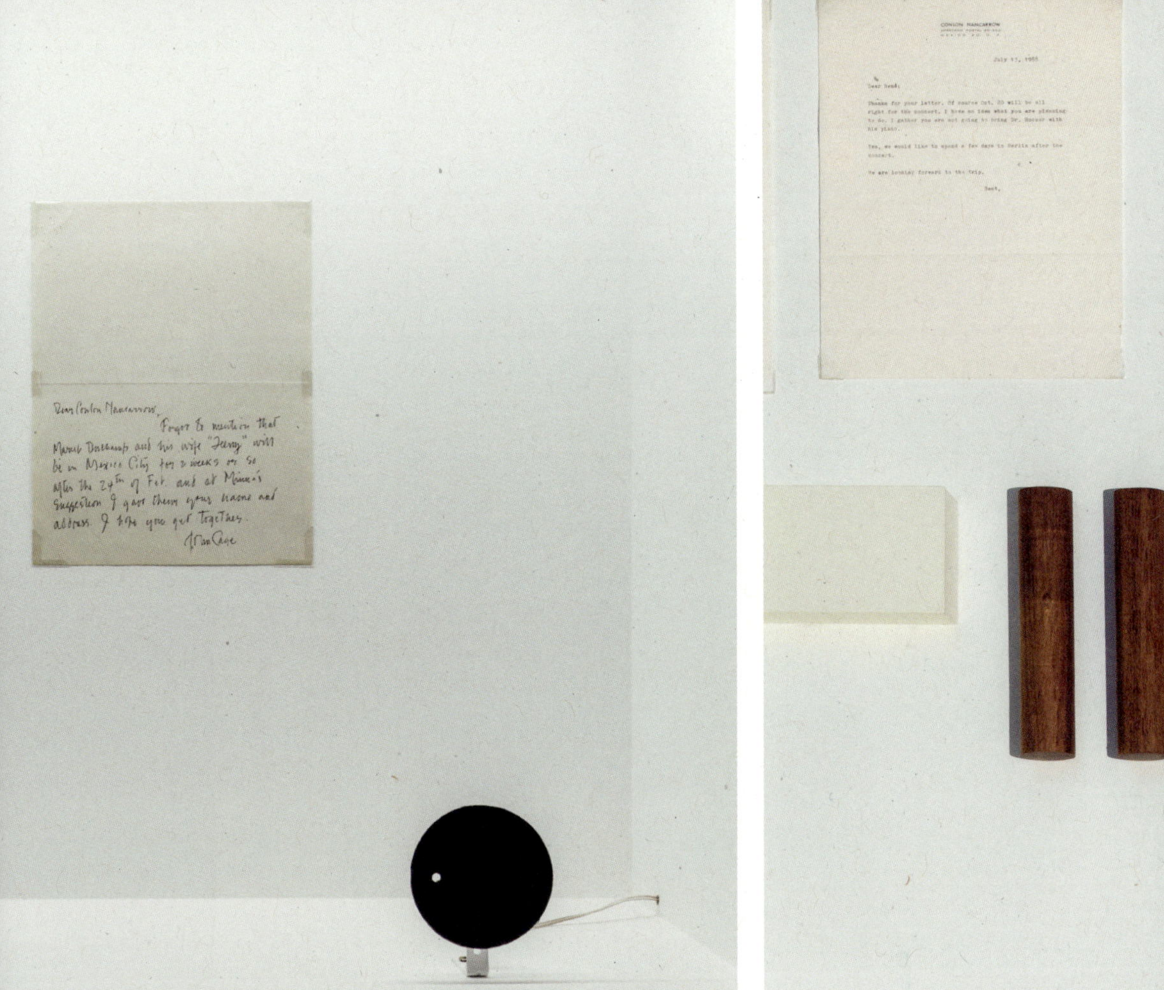

Dear Conlon Nancarrow,
        Forgot to mention that
Marcel Duchamp and his wife "Teeny" will
be in Mexico City for 2 weeks or so
after the 24th of Feb. and at Minna's
suggestion I gave them your name and
address. I hope you get together.
                        John Cage

CONLON NANCARROW
Apartado Postal 20-332
Mexico 20, D.F.

July 11, 1966

Dear Dent:

Thanks for your letter. Of course Oct. 20 will be all
right for the concert. I have no idea what you are planning
to do. I gather you are not going to bring Dr. Hoover with
his piano.

Yes, we would like to spend a few days in Berlin after the
concert.

We are looking forward to the trip.

                        Dent.

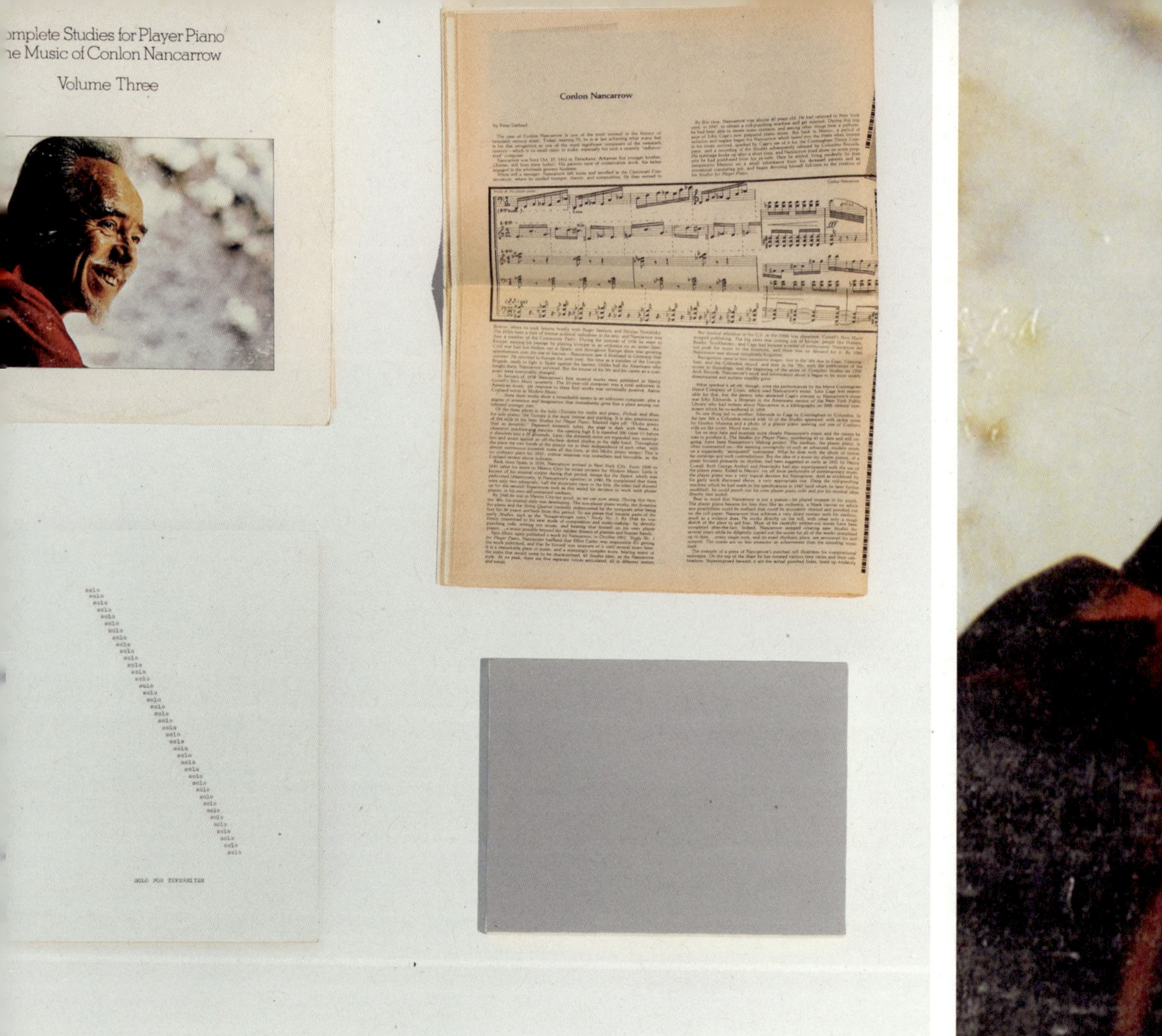
omplete Studies for Player Piano
ne Music of Conlon Nancarrow
Volume Three
Conlon Nancarrow
by Peter Garland
solo
solo
solo
solo
solo
solo
solo
solo
solo
solo
solo
solo
solo
solo
solo
solo
solo
solo
solo
solo
solo
solo
solo
solo
solo
solo
solo
solo
solo
solo
solo
solo
SOLO FOR TYPEWRITER

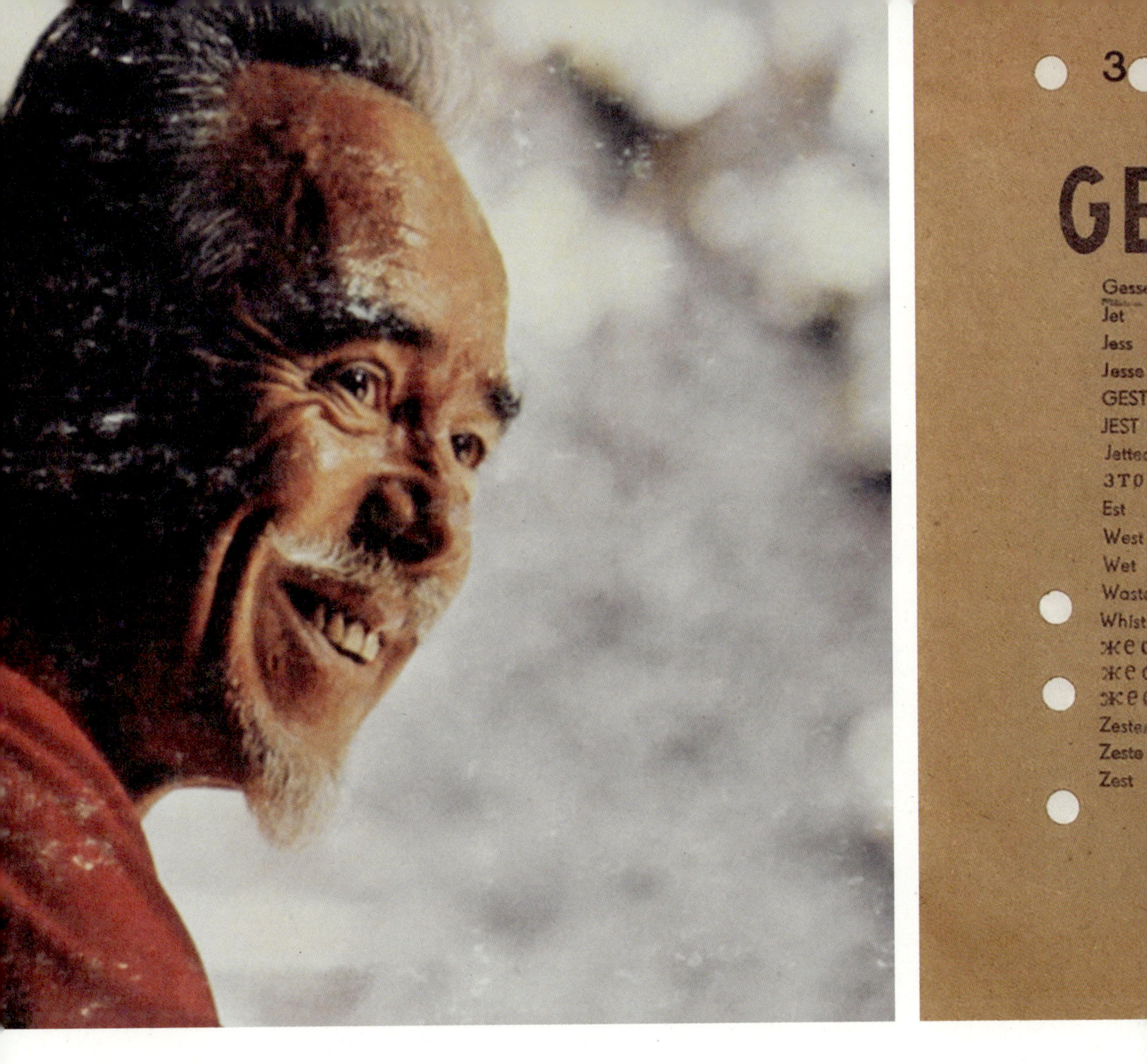

3
GE
Gesse
Jet
Jess
Jesse
GEST
JEST
Jettec
ЭТО
Est
West
Wet
Wast
Whist
же с
же с
же с
Zester
Zeste
Zest

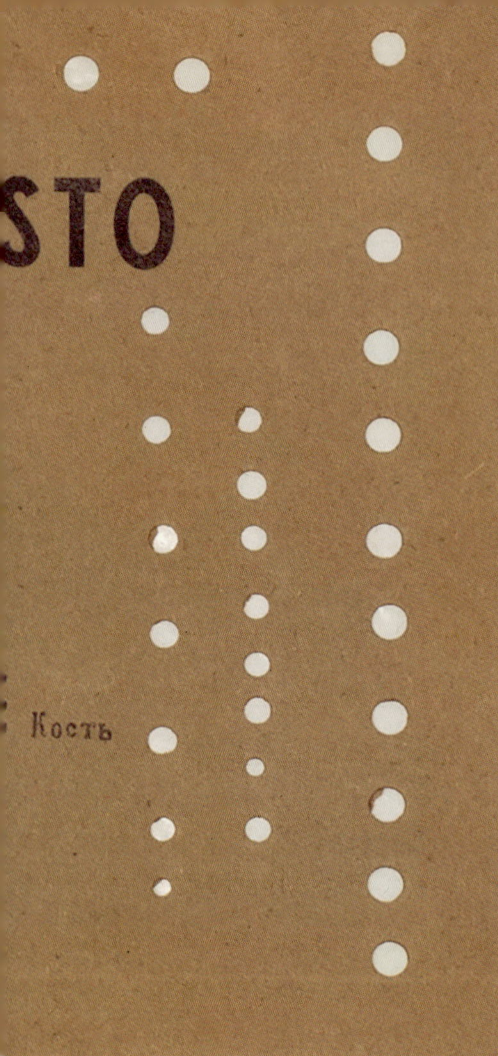

STO
Кость

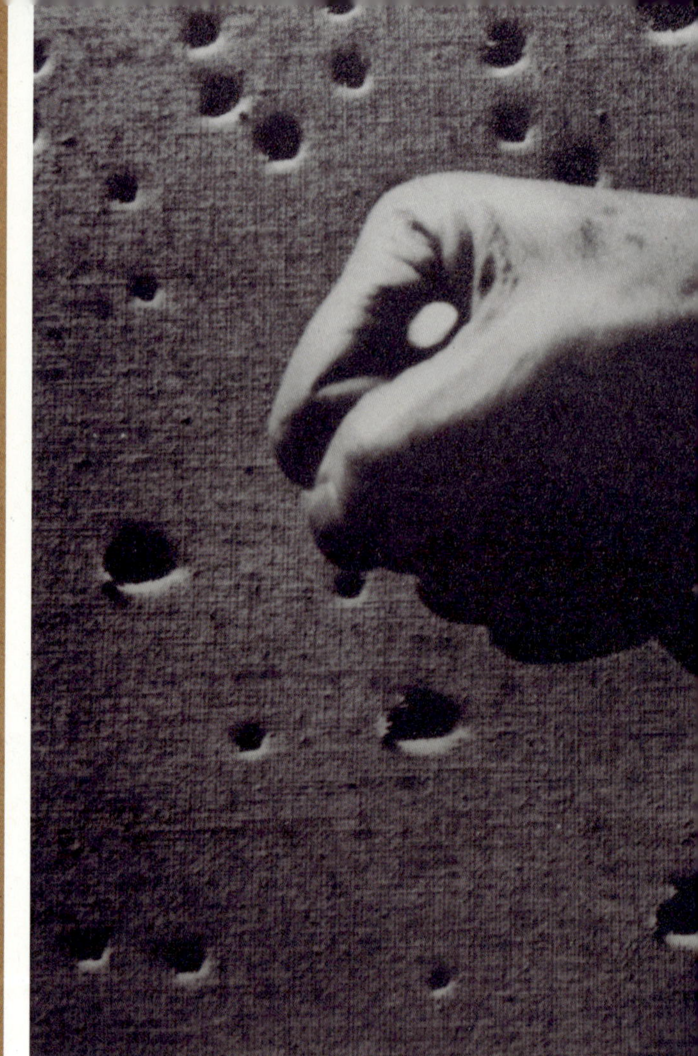

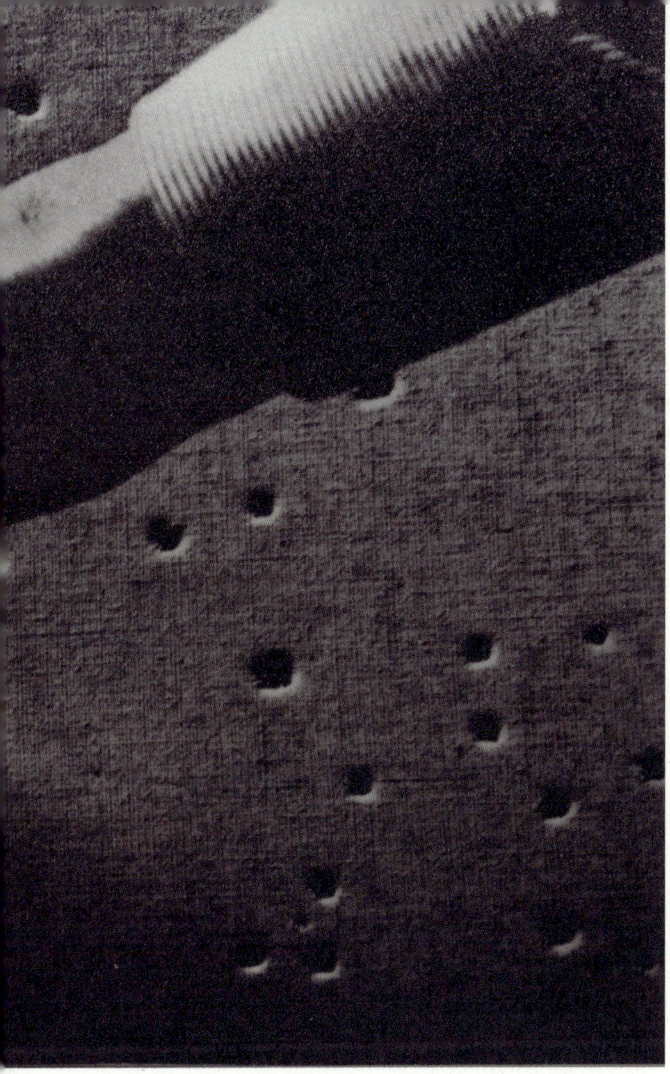

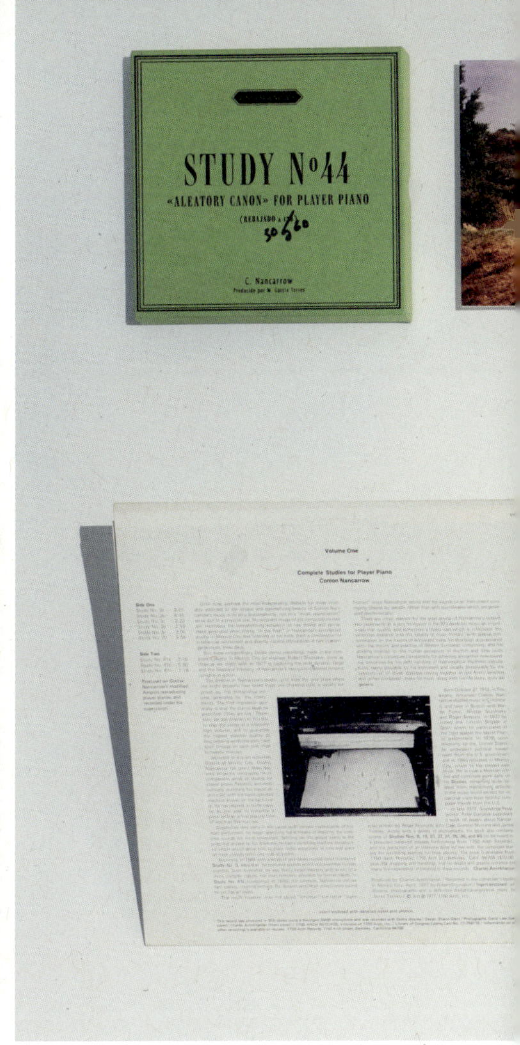

STUDY Nº44
«ALEATORY CANON» FOR PLAYER PIANO
(REALIZADO A
C. Nancarrow

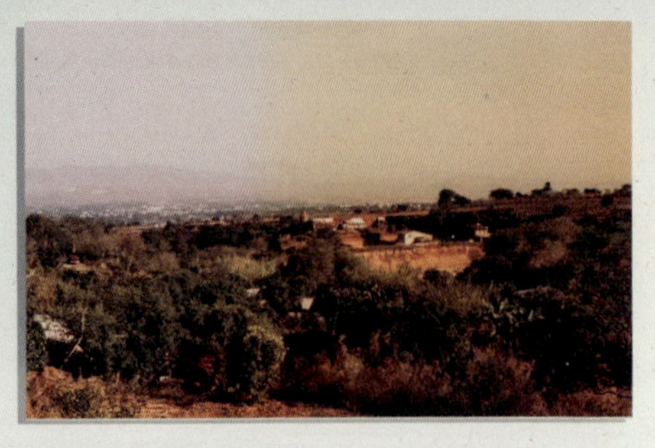

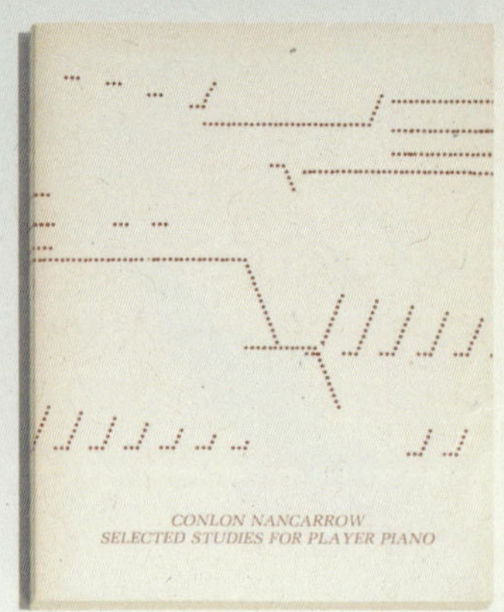
CONLON NANCARROW
SELECTED STUDIES FOR PLAYER PIANO

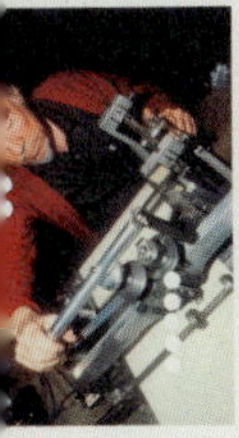
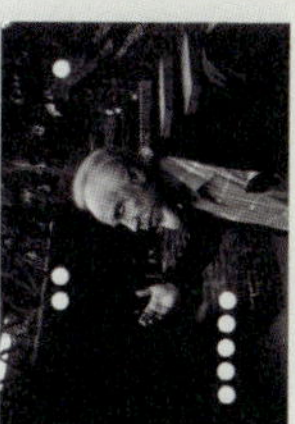
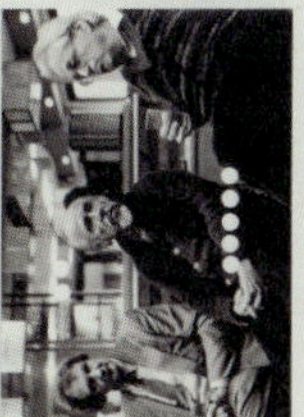
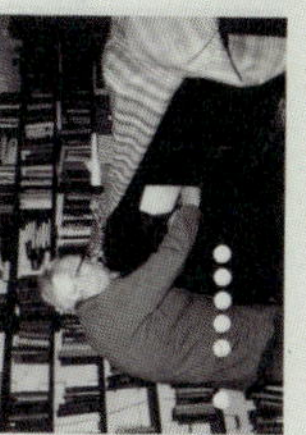

TABLE OF PREPARATIONS

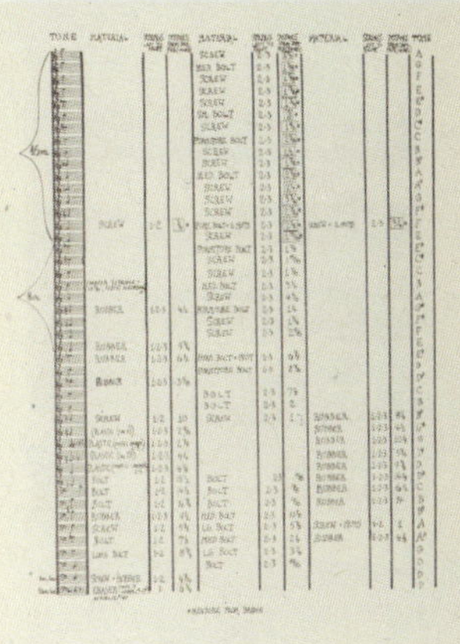

[MUTES OF VARIOUS MATERIALS ARE PLACED BETWEEN THE
STRINGS OF THE KEYS USED, THUS EFFECTING
TRANSFORMATIONS OF THE PIANO SOUNDS WITH
RESPECT TO ALL OF THEIR CHARACTERISTICS]

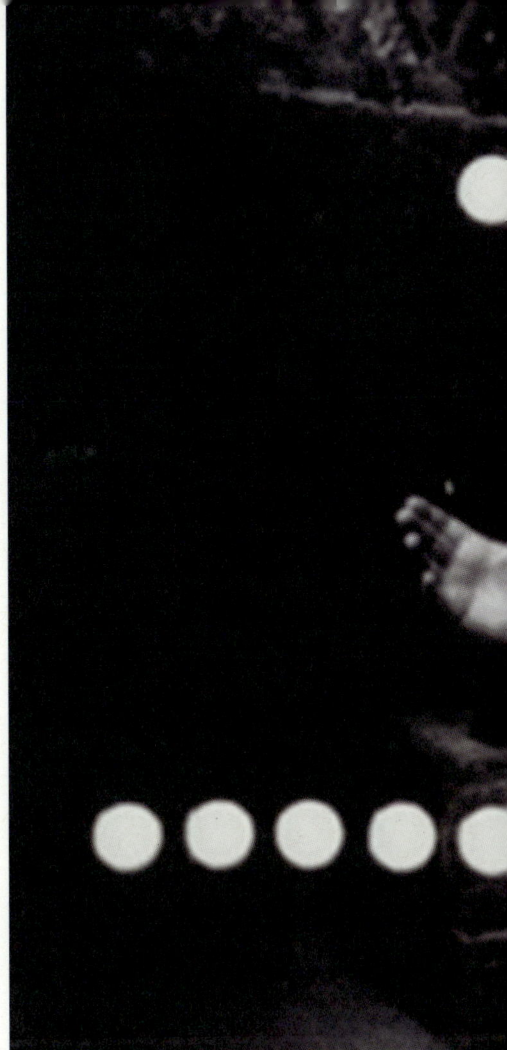

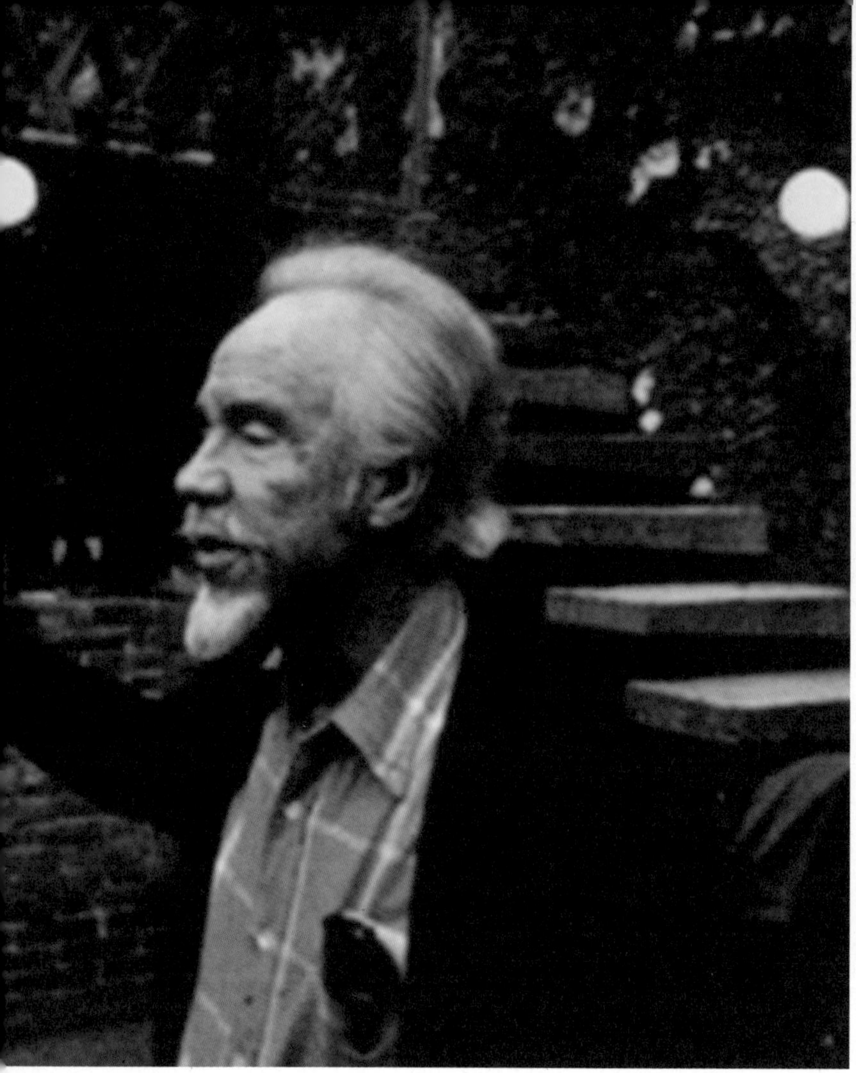

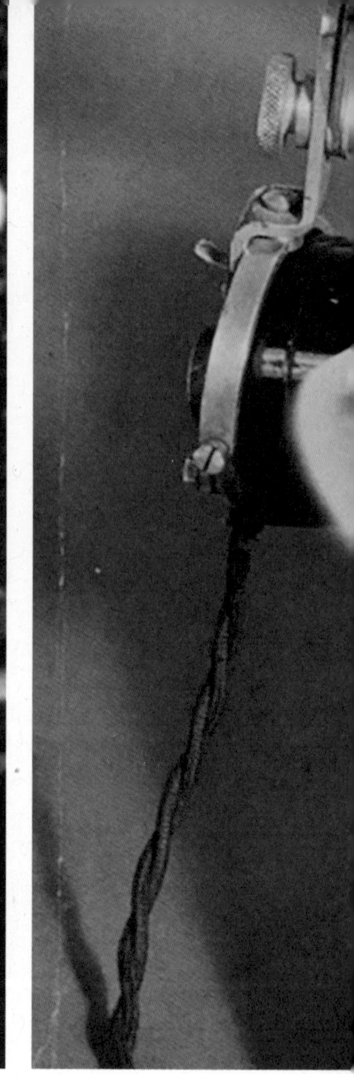

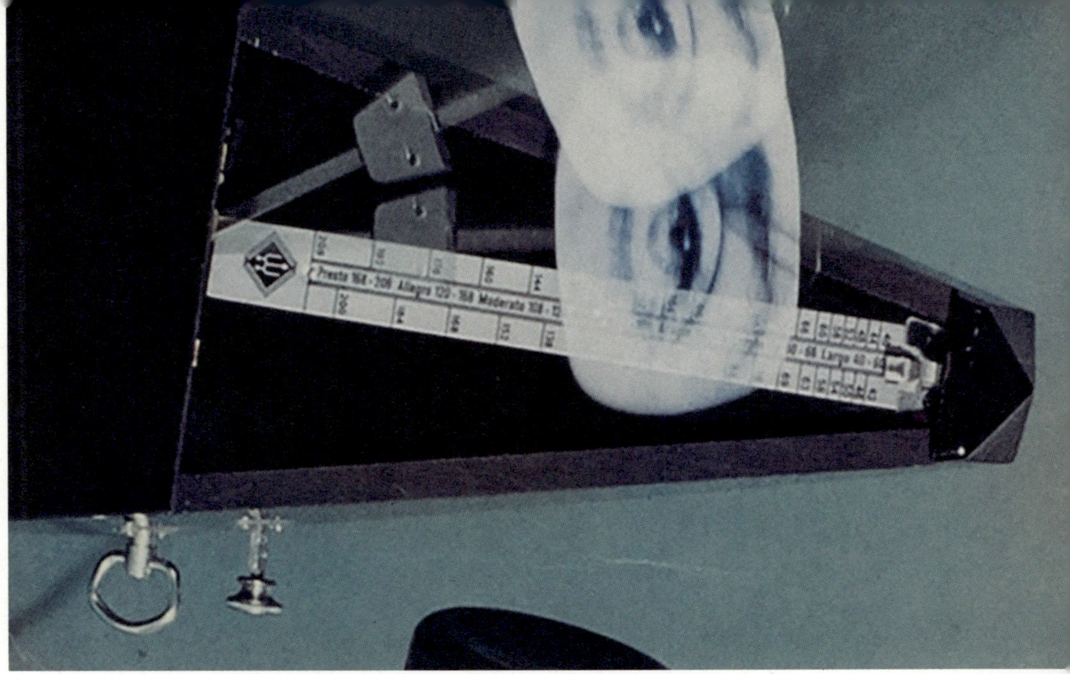

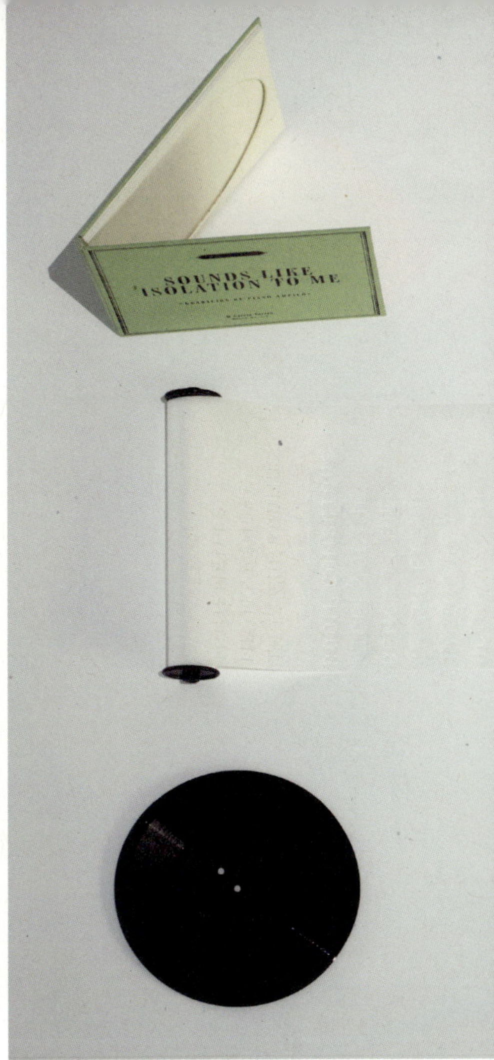
SOUNDS LIKE
'ISOLATION' TO ME

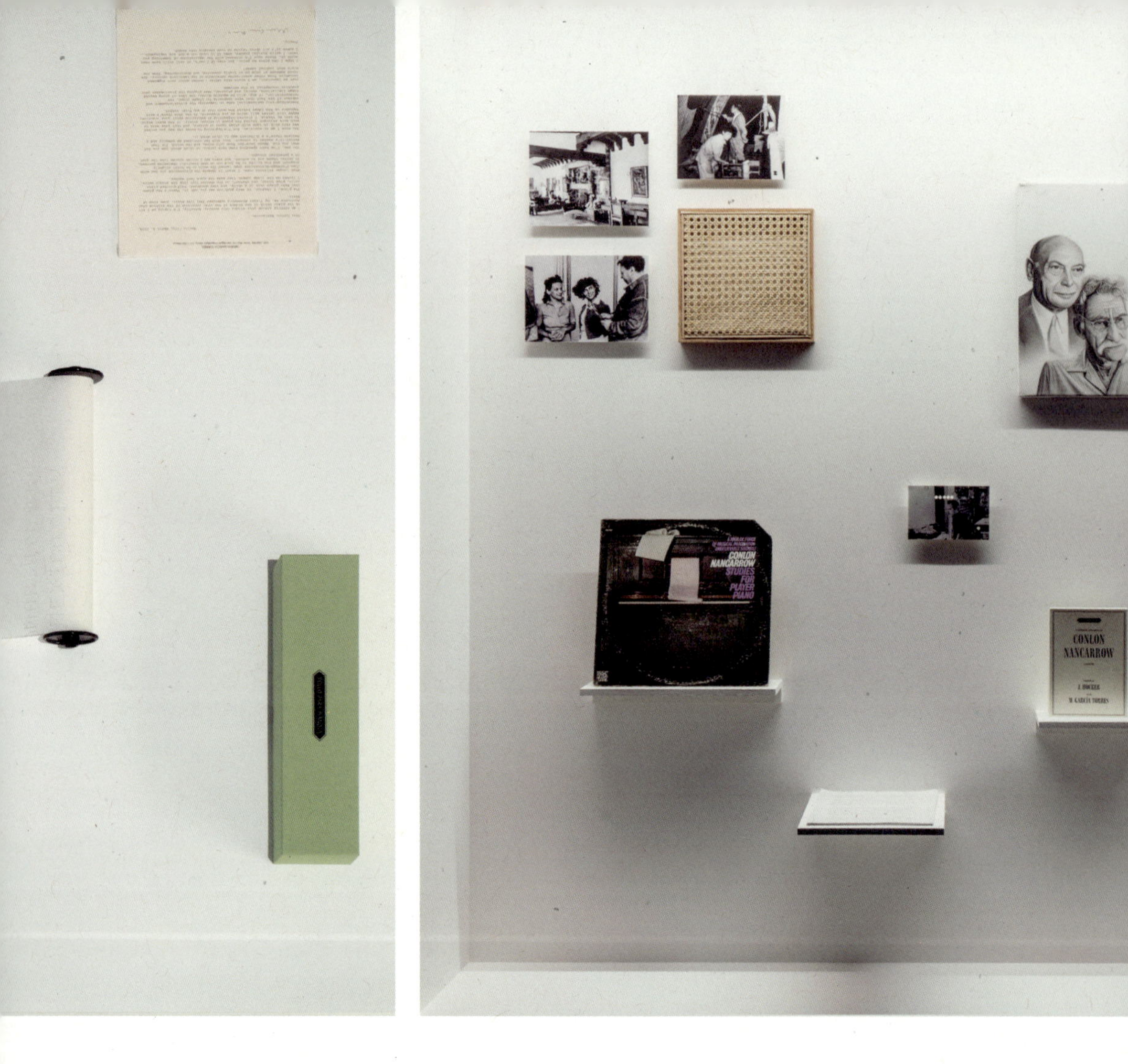

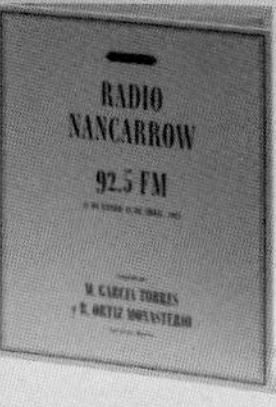

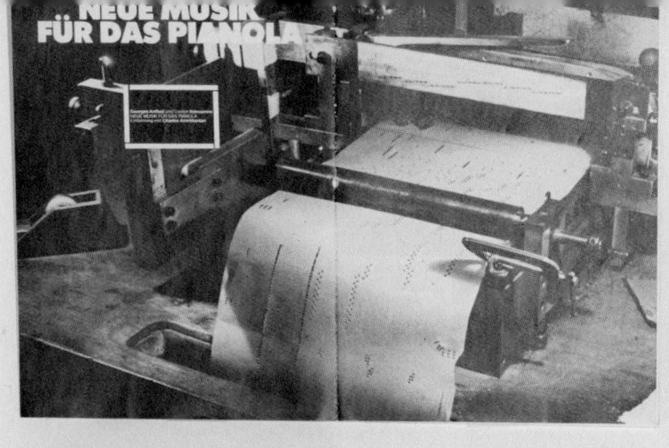

NEUE MUSIK
FÜR DAS PIANOLA

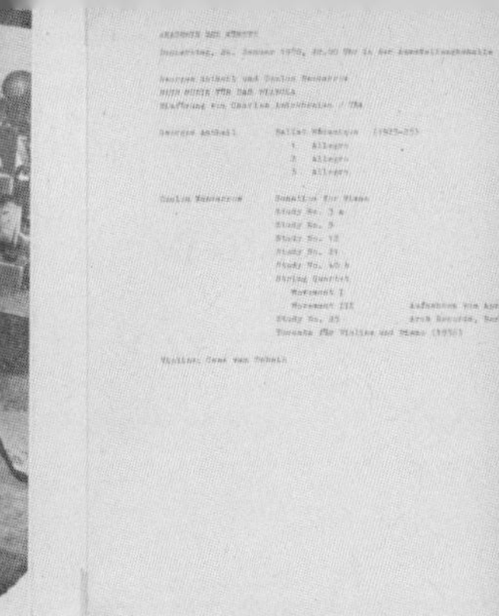

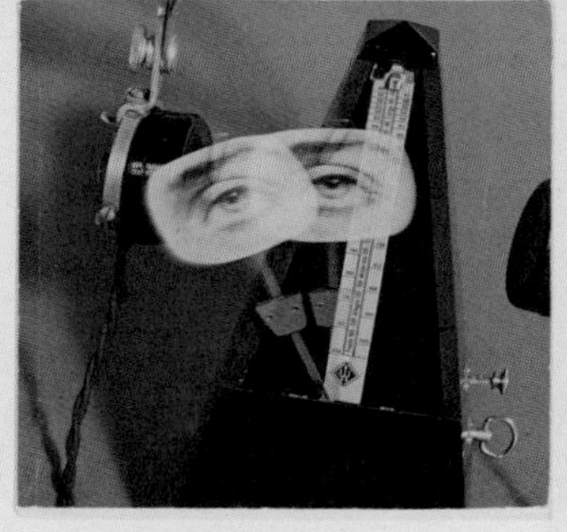

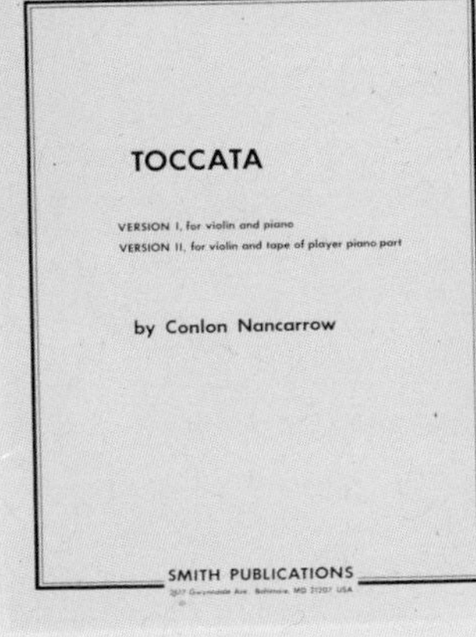

TOCCATA

VERSION I, for violin and piano
VERSION II, for violin and tape of player piano part

by Conlon Nancarrow

SMITH PUBLICATIONS

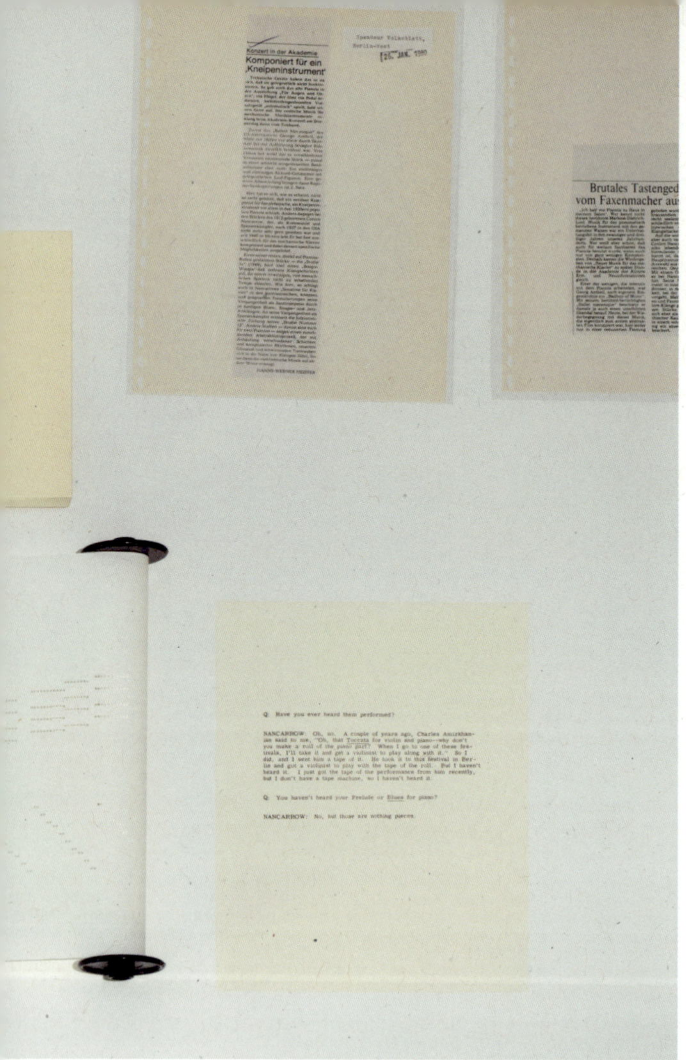

Q: Have you ever heard them performed?

NANCARROW: Oh, no. A couple of years ago, Charles Amirkhanian said to me, "Oh, that Toccata for violin and piano—why don't
you make a roll of the piano part?" When I go to one of these fes-
tivals, I'll take it and get a violinist to play along with it." So I
did, and I sent him a tape of it. He took it to that festival in Berlin and got a violinist to play with the tape of the roll. But I haven't
heard it. I just got the tape of the performance from him recently,
but I don't have a tape machine, so I haven't heard it.

Q: You haven't heard your Prelude or Blues for piano?

NANCARROW: No, but those are nothing pieces.

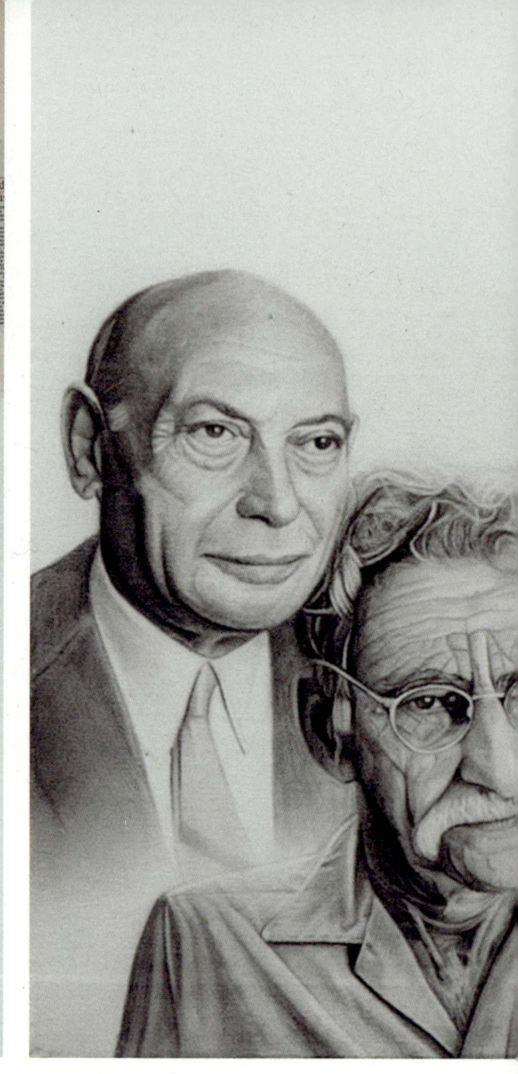

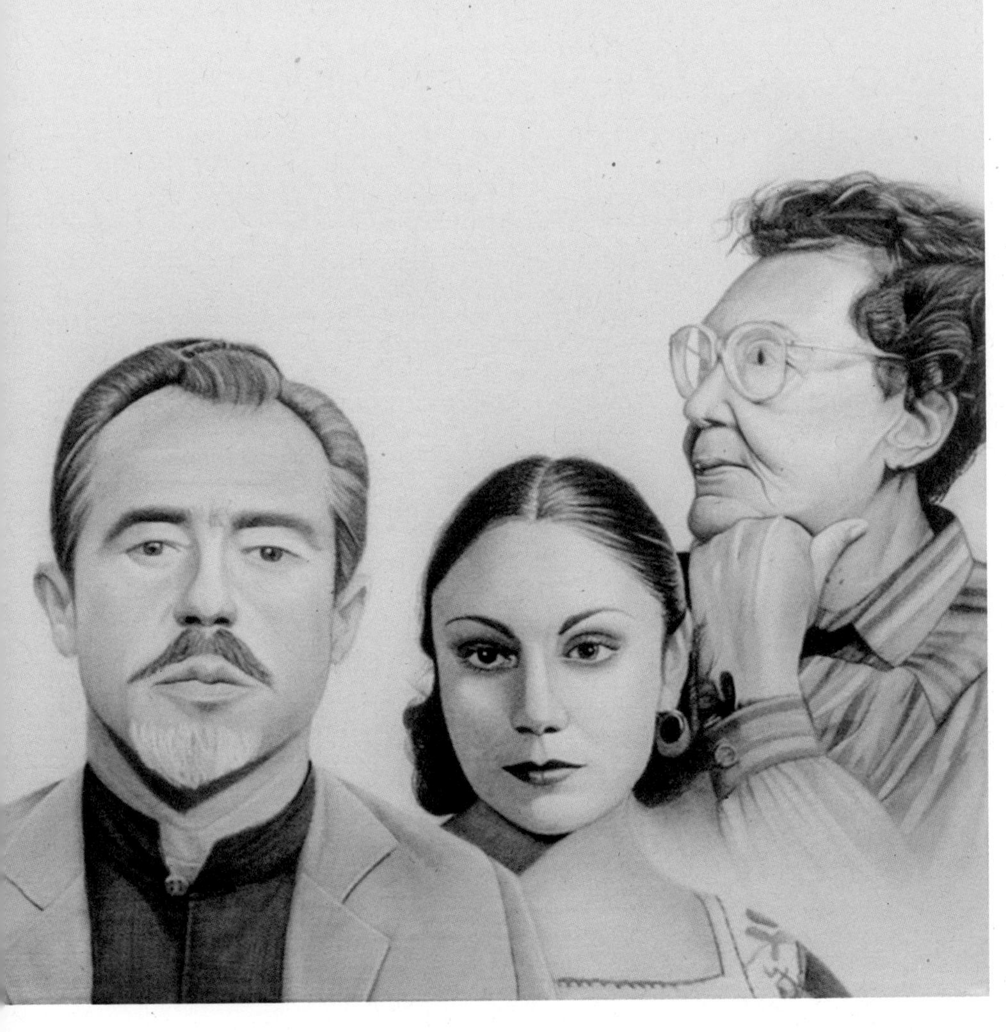

Daniela Zyman

On Mistakes, Failure, Unfinitude

Nov 18, 2001

Dear Alighiero: I keep comparing photos. Sometimes I think any building could have been the One Hotel's and then I think precisely the opposite. Yesterday I didn't walk as much. I just went to get a haircut, by the park. On my way back I stared for a long time at some kids playing stickball. More later, M

Mario García Torres, *Shar-e-Naw Wanderings (A Film Treatment)*

This nonchalant message, apparently composed in quite some haste, opens the line of correspondence between Mario García Torres and the Italian artist Alighiero Boetti, which would last from November 18 to December 16, 2001. Written as a kind of diary, it traces the author's stay in Kabul, Afghanistan, searching for the remnants of the One Hotel, used by Boetti as his Afghan headquarters between 1971 and 1979. Conceived as, or rather pretending to be, a film treatment, the work describes various forms of failure: García Torres's failure to find the hotel, the failure to make a film, and the failure to make sense of the political situation in Afghanistan. These seemingly unfortunate incongruities and a somewhat disturbing sense of open-endedness emanating from this epistolary exchange are further complicated by a series of factual entanglements. Dated 2001, the work was, however, made in 2006, and Boetti died in 1994. Furthermore, García Torres did not visit Kabul until 2011 and thus based this work entirely on research and hearsay. The notes as such take the form of nineteen prints on thermal fax paper, a material known to be unstable, to bleach out and become unreadable over time. And lastly, the roughly one-month period of García Torres's supposed research in Kabul also coincided with the first military operations leading up to war and the ensuing destabilization of Afghanistan. (The Taliban abandoned Kabul on November 12, ahead of the US-backed Northern Alliance forces, which took over the city a few days later. The military operation known as the Battle of Tora Bora started on December 6 and ended with the US failure to capture the Al Qaeda leader Osama bin Laden.)

Shar-e Naw Wanderings (A Film Treatment) opens the exhibition *An Arrival Tale* at TBA21 and introduces themes and mediums, set directly or indirectly in dialogue with one another, paradigmatic of the uncertain, interstitial, and speculative moments that concern the artist. Over the past few years García Torres has developed a practice that has mined (hi)stories of art, interrogating and resuscitating the life and work of various deceased personalities, and posed some intriguing questions about the nature of contemporaneity. His works have mixed fiction with fact through aesthetic gestures such as the confusion of chronology (he refuses to date artworks), the positing of dubious evidence, and the introduction of fake objects and mistakes. In short, he privileges a certain prevalence of doubt, failure, and speculation.

> *Alighiero: Things tend to get lost—disappearing between movements and changes. Maybe that is the case of the hotel building. In 2004, an Ariana plane will disappear from the local airport radar for a few days. It will then be found having crashed in the mountains, almost covered by snow. There will be no survivors.*
>
> Mario García Torres, *Shar-e-Naw Wanderings (A Film Treatment)*

While the five works on display in the exhibition were made at different times, deal with different subjects, and employ various mediums, they present a register of tentative arguments and "small" gestures that collectively argue, perhaps, for the relevance and possibility of unfinitude as an aesthetic position. Unfinitude in García Torres's world is a diachronous operation allowing for movement through time and space while inserting thoughts, events, and writings into narratives that otherwise are historically closed and concluded. Through these gestures the artist seems to keep a dissonant and transgressive calendar that sensibly registers things that are suspended, that happened or not, before or after an allegedly real and "objective" event, opening small wedges in space-time in which we contemporaries can intervene.

The "tale of arrival" thus hinges on parallel realities full of questions, derailments, and disjunctions to account for times and moments outside of "history" and its telos and leading to the emergence of events that are both immediate (in the present) and past, disruptive, and paradoxical.

While the informal exchange with Boetti set out in *Shar-e Naw Wanderings* was suspended in 2001/06 by García Torres's alleged departure from Kabul and the aborting of the planned film project, the ambition to find the One Hotel was rekindled in 2011. After he was invited to participate in documenta 13, García Torres embarked on several extended visits to Afghanistan to finally take possession, if only for one short year, of the coveted site. Not unexpectedly, the house had fallen into disrepair. Pretending to have been invited to Kabul, he accepted the invitation and decided, along with a team of collaborators, to have it cleaned up. In the course of his late arrival, he would make the feature-length essay-film *Tea*.

On the Impossible Images

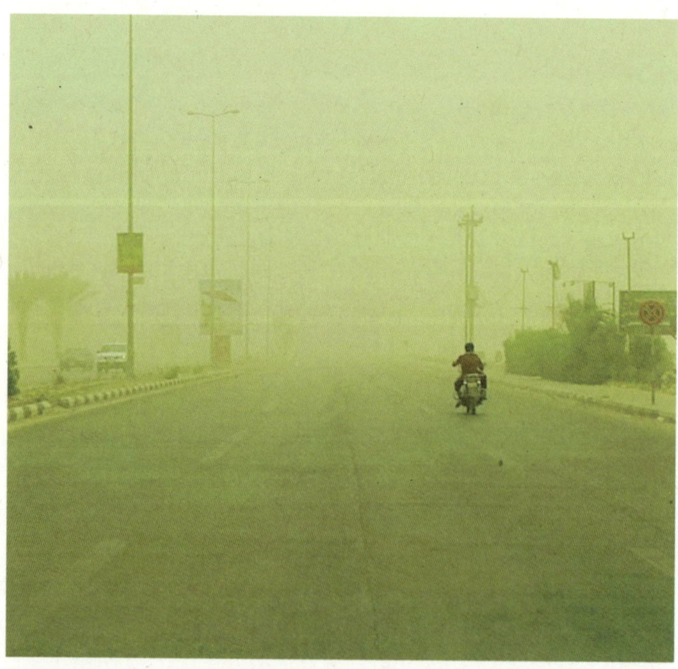

Photo: Jamal Penjweny, 2016

I keep looking at the photograph of a sandstorm.
Yellowish gray dust and dirt limit visibility. In the foreground a single motorcyclist is heading into the diffused, misty space. Billboards, lampposts,

a street sign, two cars in the opposite lane are the only other recognizable features in this blurry photograph. It is an "impossible" picture, at best sentimental, as its referent is concealed by atmospheric clouding. García Torres has been waiting for this image for weeks. He had commissioned it from an Iraqi photographer, who wishes to be called Jamal. Maybe not *it* exactly. Jamal, along with a few other photographers, has tried for several weeks to capture two images that would conclude the most recent filmic work, temporarily suspended for the purpose of public exhibition on June 16, 2016, called *The Way They Looked at Each Other*.

Two specific photographs: one taken from Baghdad's Al Jumhuriya Bridge toward the Palestine Hotel and overlooking the Tigris's eastern bank and one shot near the Palestine focusing on the center of the bridge. These *missing* photographs were meant to complete the archive of images assembled over the past months and to connect the fluid filmic narrative of times and spaces, vaguely meandering along the years 2003, 2011, and 2016; the cities of Vienna, Budapest, Monclova, and Baghdad; and the mighty Danube, Tigris, and Amazon Rivers, as well as the invisible Consulado River in Mexico City.

With the increasing impossibility of these two photographs being captured in Baghdad and the approaching deadline of the exhibition's opening, the image of the sandstorm, delivered by Jamal via WhatsApp a fortnight before the event, started to embody a ghostly place, a no-man's-land, an enclosed military zone, disconnected from the photographic gaze.

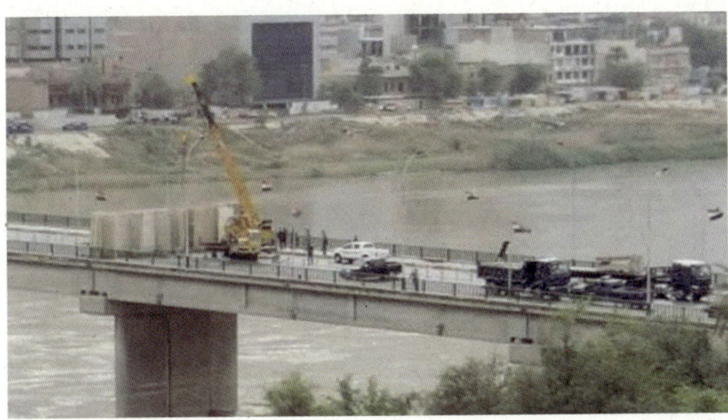

Photo: Jamal Penjweny, 2016

A place obscured by clouds of dust and airborne particles. And yet it was very much possible to follow events in Baghdad through images circulating in the media. In the last weeks of May, the Al Jumhuriya Bridge had been besieged by some of the many militias struggling for power in Iraq. Protests and killings had been taking place on its pavement, and pictures—other pictures, including one Jamal had sent, of flames and barricades, of acts of violence on the bridge—were only a Google search away.

"When I hold images from somewhere else in my hands, I like to analyze them, to look at them closely. Who took the picture? From where? What kind of lens was she or he using?" asks the first-person narrator in *The Way They Looked at Each Other*. Indeed, the two indices from Baghdad set in motion an inquiry into how the situation on the ground in Baghdad connected to the story of "looking at each other" and about the unfitting possibility to seam together past and present.

Photographs, for the American artist Allan Sekula, are always "fragmentary and incomplete utterances,"[1] threatened by the loss of specificity and depending on the matrix of conditions in which they are embedded or from which they are derived to form their readability. Is being fragmentary and incomplete a defect or a surplus of possibilities? And which matrix of conditions? Is it the story behind the images, the facts rescued or extracted from a series of interrelated events and their unraveling? Or is it the repeated gesture of "returning the gaze," of "shooting back" (used here in filmic terms), of analyzing the reciprocal space between the camera and its subjects? Or the fact that we are latecomers to the events depicted, divorced from them through time and space? So what does a photographic image convey beyond the objects it represents, *despite* the powerful impression of reality it seemingly translates without loss?

On April 8, 2003, a US M1A1 Abrams tank positioned on the Al Jumhuriya Bridge fired a series of shells onto the balconies of the Palestine Hotel, killing two journalists and wounding others. As the shell struck a fifteenth-floor balcony of the hotel, fatally wounding veteran Reuters cameraman Taras Protsyuk and Spanish cameraman José Couso of Telecinco, the camera was rolling, directed at the nearby bridge. We know that; we can even find the footage online. We know quite exactly what Protsyuk *saw* from his position on the hotel's balconies; we even know what he perceived the moment he was struck.

At the same time we can only assume what the troops assigned to the 3rd Infantry Division's 4th Battalion 64th Armor Regiment under the command of Captain Philip Wolford would have seen from their tank,

---

1   Allan Sekula, *Photography against the Grain: Essays and Photo Works, 1973–1983* (Halifax: Press of Nova Scotia College of Art and Design, 1984), 4.

what kind of enemy action was registered, how elaborate their telescopic viewing apparatus was in 2003, in what ways they were using "aided" forms of perception to enhance the visual information on which they based the military operation, and how information analysis was processed at the time. In their report the US military alleged that "combat actions" had occurred at the Palestine Hotel and that "initial reports indicate that the [Iraqi] coalition forces operating near the hotel took fire from the lobby of the hotel and returned fire."[2] The disturbing semantic correspondence of "returning the gaze" and "returning fire" resonates in Captain Wolford's statement. "Me, I return fire," Wolford was quoted as saying. "Without hesitation, that's the rule."[3]

This asymmetrical gaze exchanged between the journalists and the tank commander, only imagined, beyond the available images and classified information, is a gaze beyond justice, outside of any classical power relationship, of an encounter that should have never taken place as such. We can certainly support assumptions by research, by an analysis of the media deployed at that moment and in these circumstances. The *media* would include the tank, the communication channels, the visual resolutions, the reports and investigations around the case, independent journalistic investigation into the case—in short, the channels, instruments, and technologies through which actions were propagated and registered.

To unravel the series of images that have so far been collected around the Palestine incident, how might it matter to set the political and sociocultural milieu in which they were embedded, such as the contested election of US president George W. Bush in 2000, the historical fracture known as 9/11, and the ensuing campaign against the "axis of evil," resulting in the "war on terror" and leading to the invasion of Iraq on March 20 and the "fall of Baghdad" only three weeks later, on April 9, 2003. Is this ideological setting contained in the *way* they looked at each other? And how is it shifting today, a dozen years later, in the aftermath of the election of the forty-fifth US president and the daunting xenophobic and Islamophobic statements issued by the new president-elect? Can we look at any of these images and cancel out the epistemological violence inscribed in them?

In what ways are the *images* (the existing ones and the ones construed from context) from the 2003 incident similar or comparable or in relation to the images reshot in 2011 by the forensic commission working with the

183

---

2   Joel Campagna and Rhonda Roumani, "Permission to Fire," *Committee to Protect Journalists*, May 27, 2003, https://cpj.org/reports/2003/05/palestine-hotel.php.

3   Ibid.

Spanish judge Santiago Pedraz or the ones captured by the judge himself? Pedraz took the case to Spain's National Court and subsequently appealed in the Supreme Court, which has jurisdiction over universal justice cases and issued arrest orders on three separate occasions against the three US troops who allegedly carried out the attack. The case was aborted, seemingly for political reasons, in 2012. To argue their case, the commission, using the logic of forensic connoisseurship, tried to demonstrate through expertise in optics and physics the visibility across the relatively short distance of about one kilometer from the tank's position on the bridge and the reporters' position on the balcony of the Palestine Hotel.

But more importantly, somewhat contradicting the forensic validity of evidence, Judge Pedraz made two inconspicuous photographs of the site, taken with a commercial camera. These images, rescued and rehabilitated by García Torres, use a different logic, a poetic and aesthetic sensibility perhaps, one severely out of focus as concerns its main motif, the Al Jumhuriya Bridge. Personal pictures, souvenirs at best, delegitimizing the epistemological superiority of the state's powers to claim, through this gesture, that even to the naked and untrained eye, to the bare gaze of the beholder, the relation of visibility between the two positions (those of the victims and the perpetrators in Pedraz's view) is casually evident. In his demonstration of personal resistance, if these images can be read this way, they *were* looking at each other. These two *conceptual* images were, however, not taken *out of context* but placed within a different context, in a possible inversion of the judicial process, one that the architect and scholar Eyal Weizman calls the forensis, the political forum.[4] By turning the gaze against the state, or at least obliquely away from it and its apparatuses of investigation and truth finding, Pedraz addresses with his images the collective body, the general public, the common logic. "Forensis," writes Weizman, "is here employed as the operative concept of a critical practice, one that is committed to investigating the actions of states and corporations and also to critical reflection on the terms by which contemporary forensic investigations—on the scales of bodies, buildings, territories, and their digital representation—are currently undertaken." Moreover: "The aim here is to bring new material and aesthetic sensibilities to bear upon the legal and political implications of state violence, armed conflict, and climate change."[5]

4   See Eyal Weizman, "Introduction: Forensis," in *Forensis: The Architecture of Public Truth* (Berlin: Sternberg, 2014), 9–32.

5   Ibid., 9.

The archive of images collected and staged by García Torres creates a lateral network of impressions, of viewpoints and vistas, that talk about looking from, looking at, seeing, gazing, recognizing, and overthrowing the strictly demonstrative and explanatory logic of facts. This lateral archive produces and dissolves correspondences and connections between documentary material and fictional production; it allows travel between the images—historically and inquisitively but also literally, inside the space of the photograph. With each image, through each movement, new layers of significance open up to make a critical claim on contemporaneity.

> *When I stare long enough at a picture of a river, I forget what I was looking for, and sometimes I feel like it turns into a moving image. The water starts to actually drift making a sound, and boats start to disappear in bends. It starts to become a fiction, a film.*
>
> Mario García Torres, *The Way They Looked at Each Other*

Speculation on the Archive

While the relationship between the photograph and the archive has been extensively researched and brought to bear in García Torres's most recent work, the question of the archive is even more directly posed in *Sounds Like Isolation to Me* (n.d.), a large-scale installation presented in the second space of the exhibition. Hal Foster, who has analyzed what he calls the "archival impulse" of artists, describes the initial objective of such strategies. "In the first instance archival artists seek to make historical information, often lost or displaced, physically present. To this end they elaborate on the found image, object, and text, and favor the installation format as they do so. (Frequently they use its nonhierarchical spatiality to advantage—which is rather rare in contemporary art.)"[6]

In this multifaceted installation, García Torres arranges a complex museographic display—indeed an exhibition within the exhibition—around the life and work of the American-born composer Conlon Nancarrow, who spent most of his career in Mexico. Vitrines and display cases are carefully composed around themes such as Nancarrow's studio; his instrument of choice, the player piano; the contemporary cultural history of perforation in mid-twentieth-century artistic practice; the critical reception

→ P. 134

---

6   Hal Foster, "An Archival Impulse," *October*, no. 110 (Fall 2004): 4.

of Nancarrow's music; his relationship with contemporaries such as John Cage and Marcel Duchamp.

Within these vitrines, objects are placed in careful compositions, each object unfolding multiple readings and correspondences to the neighboring historic records. Each vitrine thus reframes with acuity certain moments or sets of relationships and sensibilities. However, what seems like a precise and diligent composition of historic material is in fact a total re-creation. Each item, each photograph, each letter on display is either a facsimile of an object discovered among Nancarrow's effects or an object (or work of art) that could have existed but was made or interpolated by García Torres. Some objects (or historical records) have factual relevance but are not directly related to the musician, other than through an interpretative gesture made in hindsight. The constant fluctuation between fact, facsimile, fake, and montage gives the work the character of an essay, an open (literary) form that has expanded to other mediums beyond writing (film and photography).

In this museographic essay, the artist's maneuvers are so complex that it becomes nearly impossible to unravel them in their totality, and it is possibly also irrelevant to try to do so. Perhaps what García Torres attempts is to reimagine the space and circumstances of Nancarrow's life and practice, pushing it to its ultimate logic, but also, at the same time, assuming the position of the historian vis-à-vis the object of his research, both rather contradictory impulses further complicated by the methodological freedom and free fall of an artistic production. García Torres ungrounds and detemporalizes his essay on Nancarrow, removing it from the factual temporal/historic axis, placing it in a free-floating circulation of experience and practice. "Every work of art comes into the world not in order to replace something that already exists but to foreshadow, anticipate, and rehearse possibilities that are yet to be," wrote the Indian artists' group Raqs Media Collective, accomplished specialists in the question of untimeliness.

In the same way, perhaps, the painstaking acts of reproduction that have led to the creation of the material by the artist in the first place—for example, the analysis of paper, typewriters, and ink ribbons but also the simulation of writing patterns of letters—are not intended to replace something that already exists but are intended to express new relationships and possibilities and to anticipate new futures. Thus, for García Torres, "Rescuing tapes, tuning a piano, and writing and rewriting letters are among a number of other contemporary gestures, which act as narrative joints that advance the missing links in this museographic essay."

Like *Shar-e Naw Wanderings (A Film Treatment)*, García Torres's *Carta Abierta a Dr. Atl (Open Letter to Dr. Atl)* takes the form of an intimate epistolary conversation with a dead artist, in this case with the Mexican painter Gerardo Murillo, known as Dr. Atl. An exceptional revolutionary character, Dr. Atl is asked to reflect on the consequences of the establishment of a branch of the Guggenheim Museum in Guadalajara. In this long-coveted plan mobilizing former Guggenheim director Thomas Krens's grand vision of a truly global museum empire, the Barranca de Oblatos, outside of Guadalajara, was to become the site for the first realization of the franchise venture in 2008.

The little video essay, like the other works in *An Arrival Tale*, are what can be called *fractal objects*, full of cracks, waves, movements, and possibilities, creating and projecting ever new thoughts and speculations but also keeping a certain silent distance from any form of resolution or veracity. By understanding art as unfinished and fractalized and by navigating the practical and theoretical limits of what can or cannot be thought, García Torres's works not only "revisit" the past but unfold the past as a form of becoming, an unfinished experience of thought. Time is inhabited by an unfinished, spectral logic, perhaps, in which past agencies enter the stage, only to be dismissed again. But unfinitude is also a time when the future becomes operational in the present (or, conversely, the past resurfaces in the future) to create a "speculative temporality" that both destabilizes and activates notions of contemporaneity. If events in time are not causal, if they don't form a static string of occurrences but are created retroactively, then any form of historicity can live in the present and be altered, recounted, and rearranged. Consequently, the definition of what a work of art means, constitutes, and represents—its status as a self-contained "thing," or its thingness—remains forever incomplete, never fixed but nested in an unfolding, emerging, and transient space of future interventions, images, gestures, constellations, and words, a space of possible invention and dialogue.

Endings and Rewinds;
or, The Other Way Around

A conversation between
Cory Scozzari and Mario García Torres

This conversation was conducted in July 2016 on the occasion of the exhibition Mario García Torres: An Arrival Tale.

CORY SCOZZARI

I am interested in exploring the interconnectedness of your ideas and finding out more about your methodologies. I would like to discuss various artworks, both those featured in *An Arrival Tale* and other pieces that informed those works. All the while through this process hopefully we can uncover and crystalize some of the thematic tendencies spanning your multifaceted practice. First, could you discuss the formation and backstory of *Shar-e Naw Wanderings (A Film Treatment)*?

MARIO GARCÍA TORRES

I was living in the United States when the war in Afghanistan and Bush's "war on terror" were raging. It was a difficult situation because there was no space to voice any disagreements about the war at that time. While I knew about Alighiero Boetti's One Hotel in Kabul and the story had always intrigued me, I was looking first at the current political situation in Afghanistan and then started to think about how these ideas coincided at this particular moment. It seemed interesting to talk about Boetti's story from that point of view, even though the contexts were totally different.

CS

You dated the letters 2001, and the work was made in 2006. Was this because you wanted to talk specifically about 9/11 and that political context?

Yes, I wanted to talk about the beginning of the war in Afghanistan, and that is why I set up *Shar-e Naw* in the year 2001. Somehow the abundance of information from that specific period was more interesting to keep weaving into my story as the narrative was not about the war per se. At the time the United States and the Allied forces were looking for Osama bin Laden, and many speculative reports about his whereabouts were in circulation. He had apparently just escaped and disappeared, and us intelligence realized that he was gone and had been for a number of years. People were starting to think that he was already dead. His disappearance brought up a lot of questions, some that I pose through the piece, like "What are they doing there anyway if the guy is dead?" Eventually the us forces got to the caves of Tora Bora, where they thought Bin Laden had been hiding, and claimed the coffee was still hot and created all these stories, regardless of whether or not they were true. I was interested in these threads. The narrative on the faxes follows stories of disappearance: Osama bin Laden, the Boetti hotel, and then the arguments for the war.

CS

I am interested in the presentation method and material choices: you chose thermal fax paper, this really nonarchival material that deteriorates quickly, and yet you present the papers in these hyperarchival vitrines.

MGT

I had started using the fax paper because I knew that the writing was going to fade away. As the work ages, I keep telling the registrars: "Come on, you need to expose these faxes to the sun!" I like the angled sheets of paper in the vitrines because you can see the fragility of the paper; at the same time they look like they are flying. The artistic statement becomes very fragile and could just blow away and disappear, like the myth of the One Hotel.

CS

In many of your works, in *An Arrival Tale* and beyond, you focus on the stories of artists. How did you come to make a work about a particular artist?

MGT

I really like most of the artists whom I quote or relate to, but at the same time I am not in agreement with everything they did; nor am I obsessed with them. Yes, I think Boetti was a great artist, but it is the stories that I am interested in rather than the characters or artists themselves. See, when

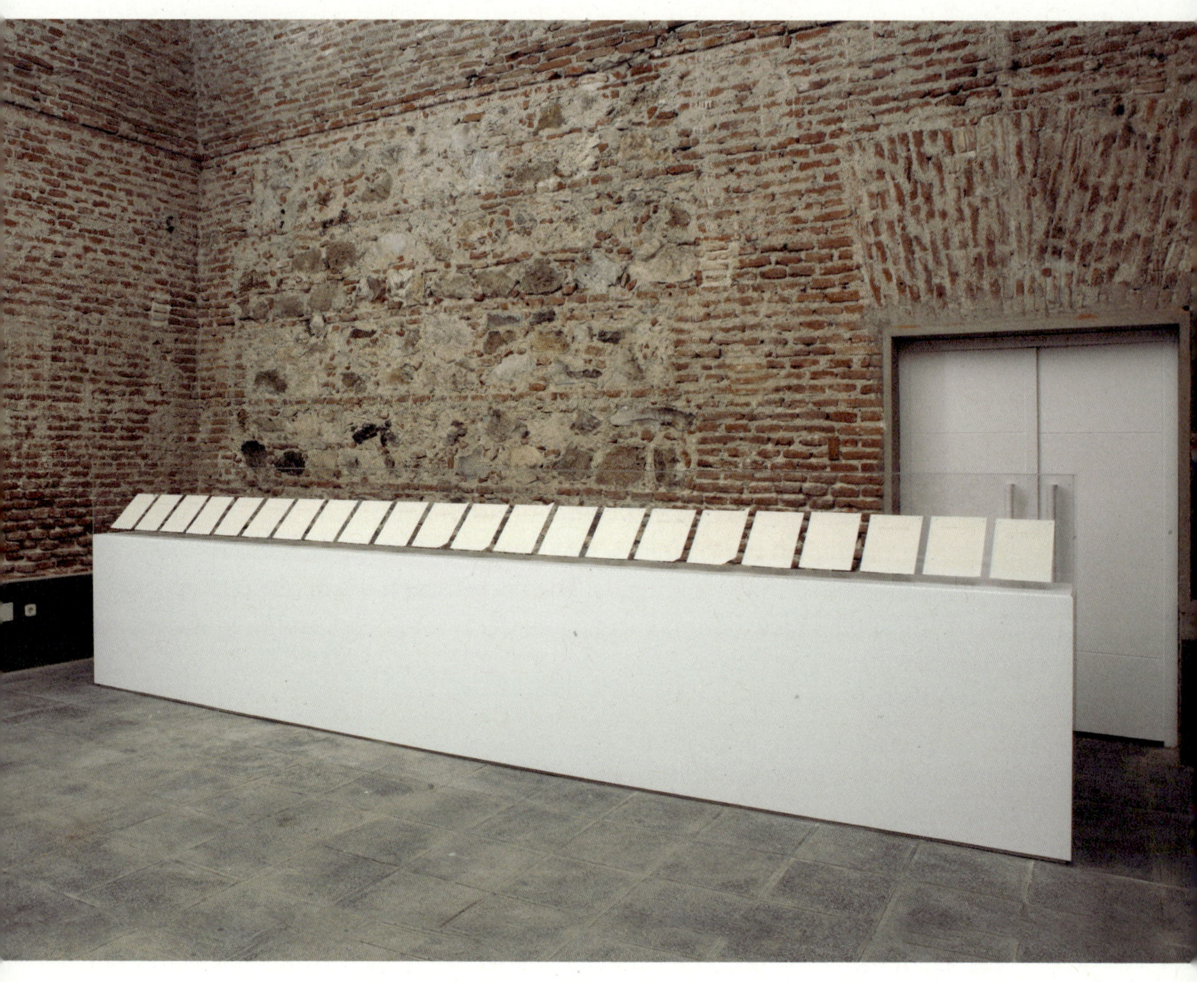

→ P. 34

Shar-e Naw Wanderings (A Film Treatment)
2010, installation at the Museo Nacional
Centro de Arte Reina Sofía, Madrid

I go to Italy, people want to talk to me about Boetti and share their own memories, because they think that I know absolutely everything—but I don't! I know the story about Afghanistan because I researched it. Today there is way more information available on Boetti's time in Kabul, but only a few years ago you would find the same five lines in every book. It would always say, "Boetti had a hotel with his partner Gholam Dastaghir. It was on Chicken Street." It was never clear what the hotel was, how many rooms it had, etc. There were very few pictures, mainly one black-and-white photograph of the outside of the building, which was very misleading. I think what really made me curious is how Boetti created this fantastic myth. Every artist I address through my work has to do with specific moments and specific questions. Dr. Atl is the same.

CS

How so? Can you walk us through the process for the work that features Dr. Atl, *Carta Abierta a Dr. Atl (Open Letter to Dr. Atl)*?

MGT

When I made *Carta Abierta*, it had a specific urgency; there were plans in place to build a Guggenheim Museum in Guadalajara, Mexico. I was living in Los Angeles at that time, so I flew to Guadalajara with the intention to produce a documentary about something that didn't exist but was going to be built. That was what we all believed at the time. What intrigued me was that the work could take us back into this space before the museum's existence. I meant to interview a number of people involved, but once I was there, I realized that nobody I met in Guadalajara was at all critical of the project. They were all so happy and saying how great it was that they were finally going to be a world city. They didn't see the implications I saw. So I ended up thinking that I couldn't use any of those conversations. Also at the time I was thinking specifically about different formats for documentaries and the way a personal narrative could get interwoven. When I came back

191

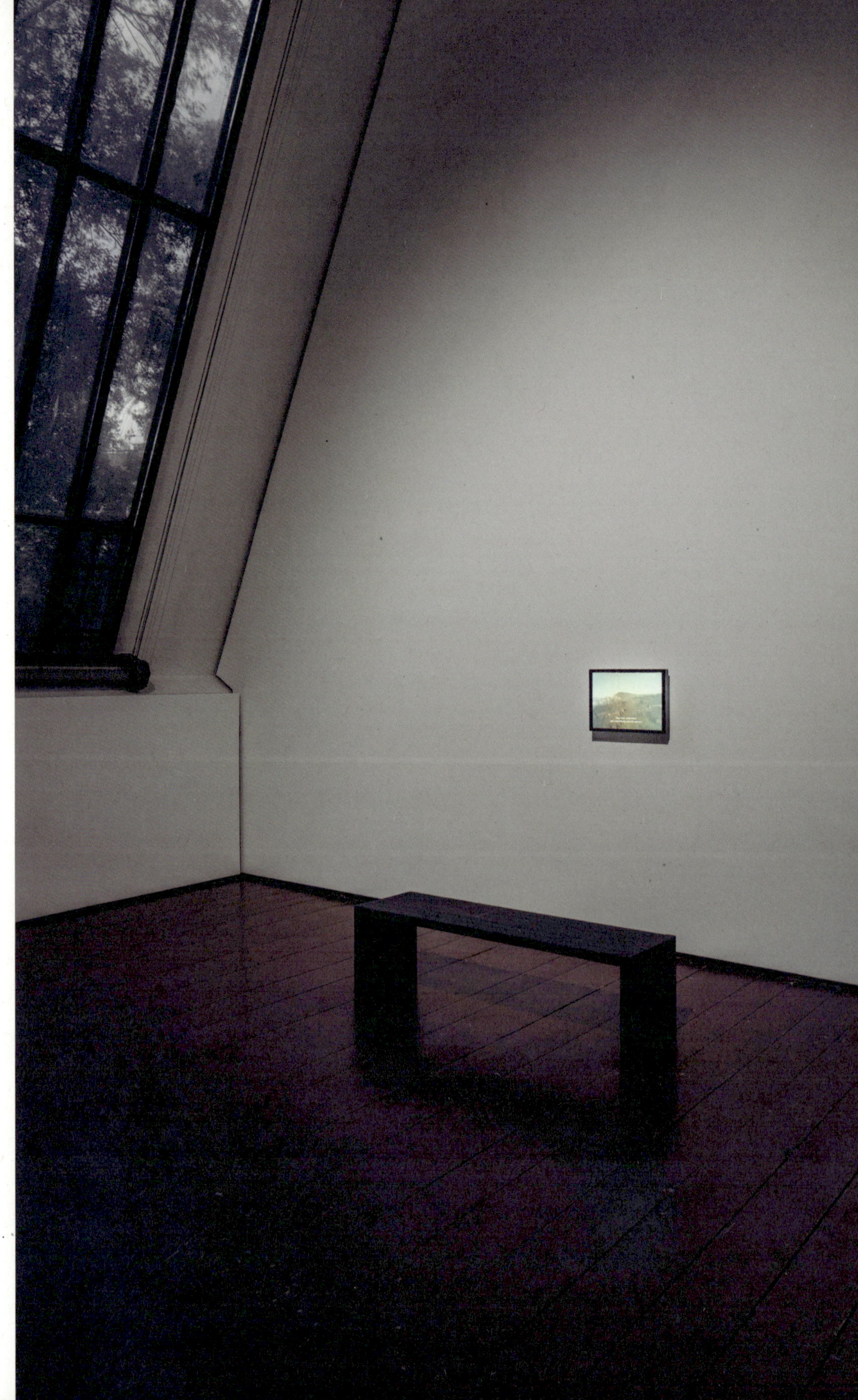

→ P. 16

to L.A., I realized that I needed to have a conversation with somebody else. So I ended up writing this letter to a long-deceased artist.

CS

So then you posed the questions instead to Dr. Atl, who as an artist was very close to this landscape?

MGT

Dr. Atl was from Jalisco, and he actually had painted that landscape three times. I wanted to update him and tell him, "This is happening with your landscape." Actually I don't know if it is a myth, but I heard the museum was going to be built on one of his favorite spots; it is even called Dr. Atl Park. It is a kind of overlook where you can come and see the landscape. In the end the Guggenheim didn't materialize there. I think they needed money both from the city and the federation. And politically this was not a moment when these forces could coincide. In Mexico it is always like that, and looking back, it could have just been some kind of PR stunt.

CS

Moving back to Boetti, you made a number of works related to his story and Afghanistan, *Shar-e Naw*, which you mentioned, and *Tea*, which we will touch on later. Were there others aside from these?

MGT

Yes, I did a metal sculpture in 2006 called *The Kabul Golf Club: Opened in 1967, Relocated in 1973, Closed in 1978, Reopened around 1993, Closed Again in 1996 and Reopened in 2004*. It is related to the Golf Club in Kabul, which is quite telling—nothing to do with Boetti—but it tells the story of Afghanistan through the changing history of a golf club. It was hidden for years, following the communist coup in 1978 and again in 1996, when the Taliban banned sports. It is kind of strange and revealing of how politics move in Afghanistan. Then I showed a work called *Have You Ever Seen the Snow?* at documenta 13, which was really important and crystalized some of the other ideas. That work is a slide show, with a similar rhetoric to *The Way They Looked at Each Other*, explaining my research when I was looking for information and images and trying to imagine the first fiction.

CS

Because you were already thinking about making the film?

MGT

Well, *Shar-e Naw Wanderings (A Film Treatment)* is a film treatment (hence the full title). I had this dream of making a film, but eventually I thought that it would be nice to leave it as a treatment and encourage people to imagine it. But while making the faxes, I kept writing and looking for images to try to picture the place, and because of the war, more and more images started to come up. I was able to map the neighborhood where the hotel supposedly was located and figured out that it was not possible for it to be on Chicken Street. So this other piece, *Have You Ever Seen the Snow Fall?*, realized in 2010, is a slide show analyzing many images, following the discovery of the hotel's location. When Carolyn Christov-Bakargiev came to visit me while she was organizing documenta, I was working on that piece, and I read a version of my script looking at the images. Carolyn is very close to the Arte Povera movement, and I guess she was really taken with my story, because the next morning she said that we should go to Afghanistan to see the place, since it really existed. That is how the whole documenta Kabul thing began.

CS

And this was a research trip?

MGT

Yes. In the beginning it was only a trip to go see what is happening there with the hotel and to assess if something could happen there. We were very doubtful. But once we realized that it was interesting to try to bring

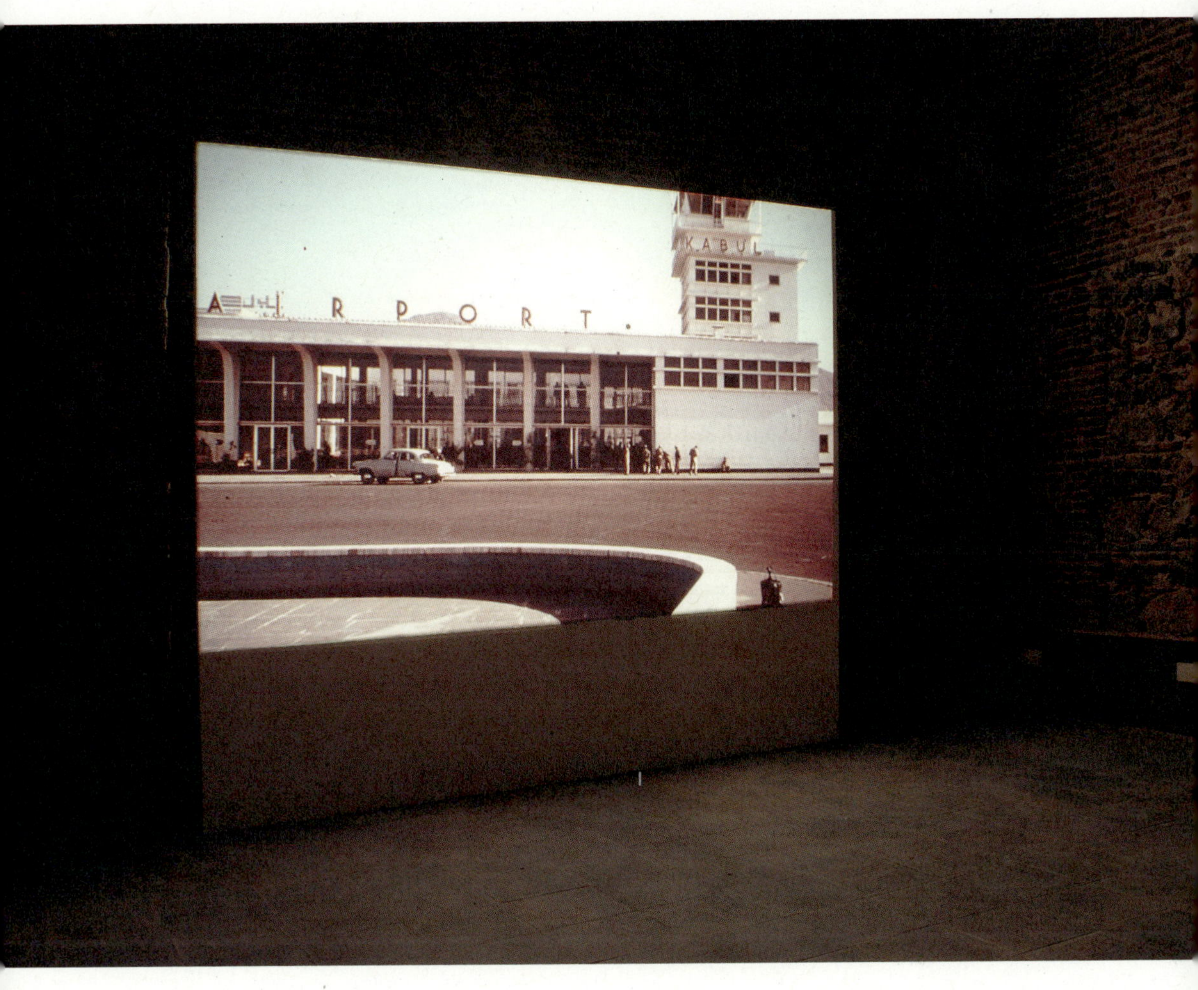
AIRPORT.
KABUL

→ P. 82

Tea
1391, single-channel 35mm film transferred to HD,
color, sound, English with Dari subtitles, 64' 00"
Thyssen-Bornemisza Art Contemporary Collection, Vienna

documenta to Kabul, in some part, we decided to rent the former One Hotel. So I said, "Let's close this deal!" I didn't really know what I was going to do with it, but I insisted that we should take it over, which was quite expensive. We rented it basically for a year and signed a contract that lasted until the last day of documenta. When we got possession of the building, they told us about the construction problems, so *Tea* came to be about taking care of the space. I wanted to recognize the personal importance that the building had for me, without freezing it in time or separating it from history, but also avoid the "Oh, this is where Boetti was!" attitude. I just wanted to keep it for a year and invite people to come and have tea and explain the importance of that building for me.

CS
How did this process pan out? Were you there often?

MGT
I made four trips to Kabul in the end. When we started filming, we started the process of reconstruction and remaking the garden, so different people were in charge of different aspects. We also left a camera there, and one of the photographers recorded what was happening. Some of the footage made it into the final film. Also, I was very clear that I wanted time to pass seasonally, summer to winter. I was very conscious about that, because we always think of Afghanistan as the desert, but actually it has a very cold winter that can be dangerous because a lot of people don't have money to keep warm. I felt it was very important to acknowledge this seasonal aspect.

CS
Those are some of the most visceral parts of *Tea*, the parts with the snow!

MGT
Yes, so that was very specific, and I wanted to make sure it was included. It was a very long process with a lot of footage we had collected. The second

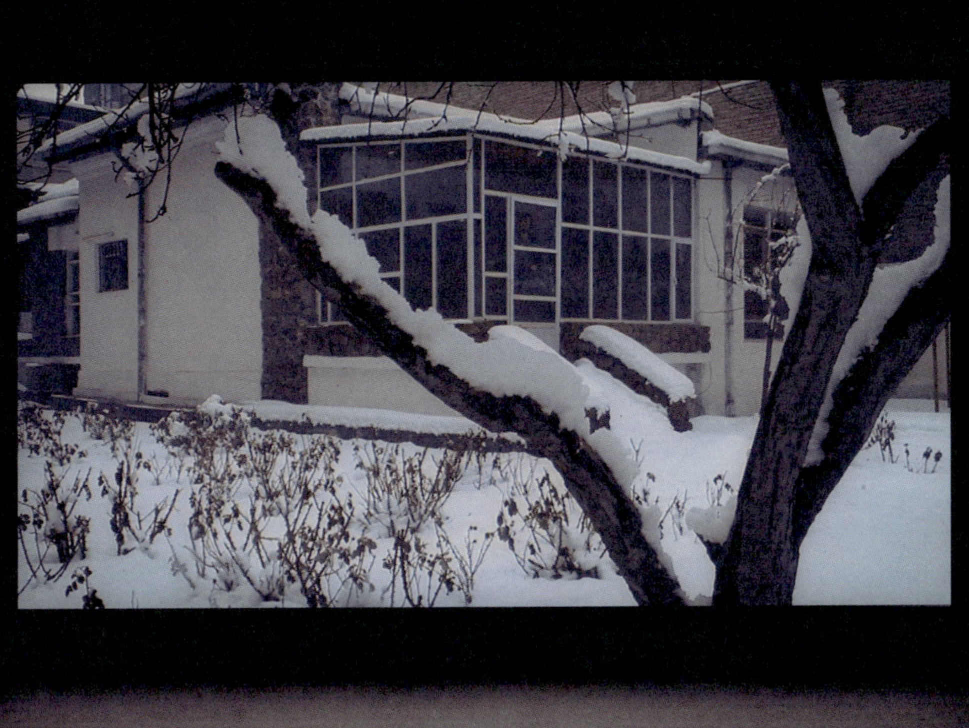

time I went, I started shooting, and I didn't know what I was going to do or
what the outcome was going to be. I knew that we needed to document this
process of taking care of the building, and there and then I decided that
I was going to be in it, because we needed somebody to move the narrative.

    CS

But you had already inserted yourself into this story partially through
Shar-e Naw anyway?

    MGT

Yes, it took me a long time though to accept that I was going to be in my
own film and also that I would read the script myself. We tried a professional recording, but at some point it was just very clear that the recording
didn't match my physiognomy and my image. And it was too trained and too
professional. I needed to go back and do it in a more intimate way.

    CS

Can you discuss *Sounds Like Isolation to Me*? How did this work come about?
Why Conlon Nancarrow?

    MGT

Again, I think the most important thing for me was to tap into intriguing
stories and the ways in which they coincide with things I wanted to talk
about. It's not that I look for artists; it is more the issues that bring the thing
or person. Conlon Nancarrow is a character that I knew I was going to have
to introduce. Even though a lot of people in Europe know of him, he is a
much more esoteric figure than Dr. Atl (even in a Mexican context) or Boetti.
Initially a friend of mine, Rodrigo Ortiz Monasterio, asked me to contribute
to a magazine he was making, and the first issue was going to be about the
relationship between Nancarrow and Juan O'Gorman, the architect who
designed Nancarrow's sound studio in Mexico City in the early 1950s.
I immediately wanted access to the studio, and it was really incredible, like
a museum. When Nancarrow died, most of his archive had been already sold
to the Paul Sacher Foundation in Basel, so his studio stayed exactly as he left
it. Simultaneously, as I was trying to figure out my proposal for the 8th Berlin
Biennale, I thought about re-creating this atmosphere. There was a certain
aura there, something that I thought could be transmitted into another aura
somewhere else. The first idea was to do it through music because I couldn't
bring the space to Berlin. So I thought about inviting different pianists to
come, compose, and record a song in the studio in order to then transport

that music to Berlin. Nancarrow was a sort of proto-electronic musician, very mathematical and mechanical. Then I realized that Berlin was also very important for his artistic recognition: he went there a couple of times, and an early piece was first released in Berlin, many years after it was conceived. The music idea didn't come about because there were a lot of copyright issues and complications, but the sound element of the installation came from that research. I talked to Nils Frahm from the beginning, and although he couldn't visit the studio, he was excited to work with Nancarrow's tapes, originals that we had rescued from the studio. This was how the sound aspect of the piece came alive.

CS

How did the archival material come about, beyond what you brought from Mexico? And what about the facsimiles? Are any of the objects originals?

MGT

I wanted the installation to look like an archival exhibition with the slight difference of using facsimiles instead of original things. The closest thing we got from the original archive material is a piece of player-piano roll that was left in the studio and displayed in the square vitrine. It is actually punched, but we don't know what piece it is. Also some aspects are partially real: for example, the paper on which the first letter to John Cage is printed is indeed on Nancarrow's original letterhead. What intrigued me was the question of what remains of somebody's signature and subjectivity through an interpreter or copyist and how that figures especially in musical performances and interpretations, which are always passed from one to the other, and how each musician works with material very differently. That is how I came to bring in new objects that were not in the archive.

CS

Could you discuss the research for *The Way They Looked at Each Other*, including the text you wrote for *frieze*? How did that lead into the production of a new film with the same title?

MGT

My article "The Way They Looked at Each Other" was published in *frieze* magazine in January 2012, about six months before documenta opened. The text developed at the same time as the script for *Tea*. I was thinking a lot about the way that war had happened, how it was unfolding, and how images circulated. I became caught up in a case that I was following for a long time, but I didn't know what to do with it. (For a few years the war in Iraq took the newspapers' attention off the one in Afghanistan.) I actually proposed the article to *frieze*. It talks about a lot of the same themes as *Tea*—about returning to a place, being too late, and so on. But here it was somebody else, not an artist returning to a place but a judge. It became a depository for the larger spectrum of the ideas that I was going to present in documenta, and when I saw it published, I immediately had the desire to turn it into a work.

CS

So since then you have been holding onto it?

MGT

Yes, but then I couldn't resolve it for a long time. I really pushed toward it when we started talking about *An Arrival Tale*. I thought about the many Iraqis in the refugee camps today, and then I thought this work could address that.

CS

Do you work that way a lot, where you hold ideas for long periods of time?

MGT

Yes, I think so! I mean not always, but some ideas are in these drawers, and they take time to mature. In a way I felt that this text was very important for me, for the development of my ideas, and I realized that magazines fade really fast, and I felt these themes had the potential to do something more powerful. So I went back to the text several times through those years, hoping I could do something with it, trying to get back into the problems to be solved, specifically how to deal with those war images and how to get around them.

CS

It is interesting because there is this really sensitive line that I think you are toeing. You were not necessarily trying to talk about the war directly but more in the way that the images sit or move around it.

MGT

From the beginning it was very much a piece about photojournalism and about understanding that there was this gesture that could and should be read in the symbolic realm instead of the technical realm—the gesture performed by the judge Santiago Pedraz, that is. In a way this thinking comes from a number of works that I had made before, older works that look into coincidences between how artists and journalists treat images. This genealogy is rooted in conceptual art's investigation of these overlaps. I did a piece in 2004 called *Abandoned and Forgotten Land Works That Are Not Necessarily Meant to Be Seen as Art*, in which I started to locate photographs of landing strips in the United States. These are mostly in the middle of nowhere, in the desert, and they were used during World War II for planes to land and for doing tests. Many had been abandoned now for twenty or thirty years. What I was interested in is how they look like land art, like Robert Morris or Walter De Maria works, and they were photographed in exactly the same way. The piece is very simple, a slide show of these low-quality images I found online. This also feels like background for *The Way They Looked at Each Other*. But that was somehow more sophisticated because with Pedraz it was not a photojournalist doing something like art but a judge making a symbolic artistic gesture. He did this of his own accord, and it is really futile to do something like that if you want to prove something in precise terms: you don't go to a place with your little camera and take pictures. I think he was using artistic terms to bring up an argument, disclose, and circulate it. This time, when I went back to the text, I realized yet another war in Iraq was still taking place, so I meant to acknowledge that without making a piece about it directly.

CS

What is the distinction between this content for you? Do you feel that it can be removed somehow from the war context?

MGT

No, it cannot. That is why I created a larger context for it, which was the text and all those images of rivers and trying to set the narrative in a more poetic space—a way of looking from one side of the river to the other, for example— to give it a larger interaction. I wanted to prepare people with a stream of romantic images that are saying something interesting simultaneously about the war but also about landscapes, water, and personal relationships.

CS

When did you decide you wanted someone to actually rephotograph the site and to repeat Pedraz's gesture?

The Way They Looked At Each Other
n.d., HD video, color, sound, English with Arabic subtitles,
38' 00", commissioned by TBA21, Thyssen-Bornemisza
Art Contemporary Collection, Vienna

MGT

I finished the text, and I knew that this could be an ending, but it failed at
getting to the point, so I realized that I needed to go back to the space that I
created in the introduction to close the text. The introduction highlighted the
human side of the story, but the end fell too short, too fast. I started thinking
that if I could transmit more care for the image, and if I could ask somebody
to take the photographs with a certain story or certain humor in mind, then
this act could shift from politics to people really looking at each other.
I think the original text was more aggressive toward the military personnel,
and then I felt like those military guys were also in a difficult moment.
So I wanted to bring that in at some point and erase the military armor and
the context by saying that the people who shot were actually human beings
too. I am not trying to say that they were evenly armed or even less to justify
their actions but somehow to bring it back to a human relationship by the way
that they look at each other and relativize the overwhelming image of the tank
and the gunfire. I am still in contact with photographers in Baghdad, and they
keep promising that they will send the images.

CS

Where does it sit now? Do you feel that the work is unfinished?

MGT

I think the piece should be finished. I have a couple of versions of how the
film could end, but it all depends. I still hope that they will come up with
the photos and that we can close it the way that we had imagined it before.
Alternatively, I can take it to closure with the image of the recent sandstorm
(which a photographer just sent), which is also very common in Afghanistan.
There are a couple of other ways of it fading out.

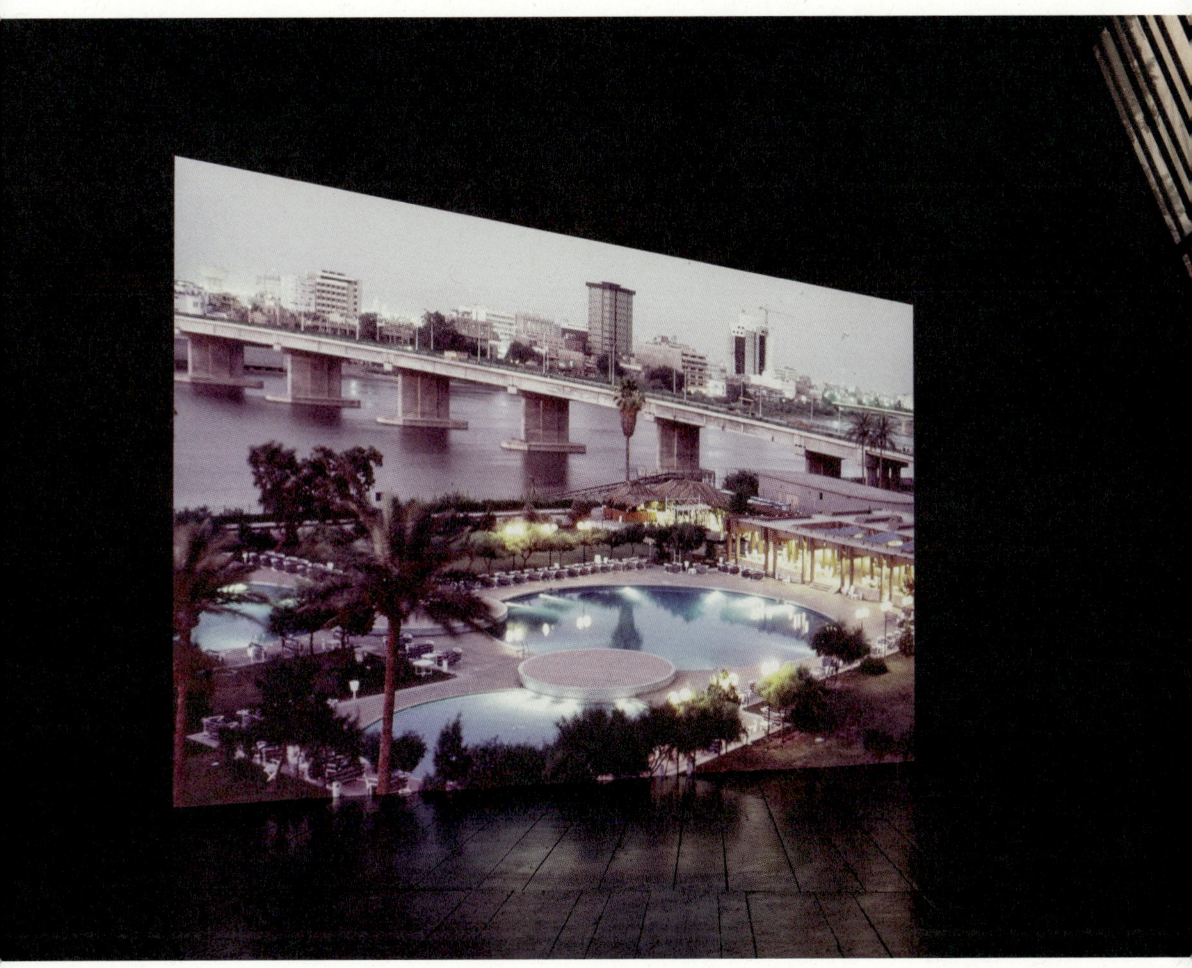

CS

It is convenient then that you don't date the work. Can you talk a little bit about that moment when you decided to stop dating your works and why?

MGT

Precisely. I think this relates to these ideas that are sitting in the drawer and that don't get realized until later, when they always reappear at the right moment. There are a number of connections between works that span time. I want to keep those relationships among works in a more horizontal connection, and that is why I stopped dating them.

CS

So it has more to do with the way the works interact with one another?

MGT

Dating, I use it in different ways. For example, *Tea* is dated 1391 because it uses the Iranian calendar. I meant to use that little space of the work's caption to say something, to argue that the piece was made for Afghanistan and for an Afghan public. Every decision is carefully considered, and that little place is also one where you can say something.

CS

You mean within the ephemera of the artwork, the label?

MGT

Yes, just thinking about the label, when you see 1391 and think, what is that? I have done works that consist only of captions, for example. This idea of using captions also has to do with negotiations with an institution. I am testing how to deal with these things, when institutions are pushing back against them, saying that a caption must provide an objective form of information to orient visitors—in a way it is a very small revolution space that an artist can occupy. The caption is still mine, even if the institution claims it. Usually people and institutions don't like it. Even now that I have been doing this for two or three years, they keep trying to challenge that gesture, of having the work dated in another calendar.

CS

And now no works are dated? What was the moment when that shifted, not in terms of time per se but in terms of your thought process, your ideas? Do you feel that saying "not dated" takes a position?

MGT

It is a clearer position. It is the same when you say a work is untitled. It is
a very clear statement. Also, one thing that was very influential was a piece
that happened a while back, which was a performance about Alan Smithee,
called *I Am Not a Flopper*. It talks about artists creating works that are not
chronological. I don't know how I came to this decision; there wasn't really
an epiphany, just a shift to being more explicit about these aspects that had
mattered to me for a while.

CS

Do you situate this choice, or align it, with a critique of progress, this idea—
especially present in the West—that everything is constantly getting better
and better?

MGT

Not only that but I am also in a way breaking with the idea that I cannot
have a conversation with Dr. Atl and make it possible even though he is
dead. Same with Boetti. I can break away from these time frames and travel
through temporalities, and in a way I was doing that!

CS

(A)historically?

MGT

Yes! And I believe in (a)historicity. I am always trying to provoke some kind
of conversation, even though sometimes there are things that are technically
not easy to resolve, but it requires a kind of trust.

CS

It seems like you are interested in pushing and playing with these ideas
of control. Do you think not dating is a refusal?

MGT

Yes, I think there is some kind of political position, really against capitalism,
which makes us think about progress and wants us to push the future
and pushes these linear things onto us all the time. I am saying that I don't
want to be pushed by a larger structure. I want to be able to navigate these
things myself.

CS

How do you think about this in relation to modernism or the art historical idea that the avant-garde was always about this new position, always about pushing past something else, etc.?

MGT

This question connects also with Nancarrow. When I really started to think about Nancarrow, I asked myself, why do we keep thinking that the avant-garde is like this? Why have we so radically separated the avant-garde thinking and the previous more romantic notion of art? At the same time, I feel like there are many things in my works that I keep discovering sometimes and questioning myself other times. This was one aspect. Why can we not be romantics, bohemians, and avant-garde at the same time? I am just always trying from a low-point position to keep questioning and breaking these preconceptions of how the world is structured and how we explain the world to ourselves.

CS

Which you also do within the work! Probably in all of them but really directly with *Sounds Like Isolation to Me* through your relationship to material, this idea of copying, and the insertion of new materials. There are parts of the work that are real or are not real, in which you are providing or observing different possible leads. For example, the pencil drawing of the group with Nancarrow and Diego Rivera that you had made specifically for the work. We can imagine that this could have happened, but the fact that it didn't is also very interesting because it is opening space—which I think the not dating action also does, a space that doesn't authoritatively say it is all real, which allows for a fictionalized or speculative relationship to history. Still somehow we believe in this drawing, even though we know it is only drawing. Of course photography has a closer relationship to the production of truth, but I think at some point drawing also creates this dichotomy. Was this conscious?

MGT

What you say is really important, and I try to push that in the new piece by making an argument about what an image is. The photograph is one thing, but by the time it fades, what is that image then? I suggest that photographs are actually made of many layers, because we are not always looking at all these things, at all the details. We are all looking at different details of every

photograph, so in a way it creates a multiplicity of that image. I wanted to
make a large installation, a large projection to highlight this, sort of implying
that there are many more things to see that way. Normally we see images
on the scale of inches, and it is more framed and digestible, so we don't
pay so much attention, but when we see it this way, enlarged into cinema
size and slowed down by the narrative, we give in to the layers. It becomes
clearer that each image in truth is many, and more so if it's different each
time to each one of us.

List of Works

Carta Abierta a Dr. Atl
(Open Letter to Dr. Atl)

2005, single-channel Super 8 transferred to video,
color, silent, 06' 26" looped, Thyssen-Bornemisza
Art Contemporary Collection, Vienna
→ P. 16

Shar-e Naw Wanderings
(A Film Treatment)

2006, nineteen sheets of thermal paper, dimensions variable
Thyssen-Bornemisza Art Contemporary Collection, Vienna
→ P. 34

Tea

1391, single-channel 35mm film transferred to HD,
color, sound, English with Dari subtitles, 64' 00"
Thyssen-Bornemisza Art Contemporary Collection, Vienna
→ P. 82

The Way They Looked at Each Other

n.d., HD video, color, sound, English with Arabic subtitles,
38' 00", commissioned by TBA21, Thyssen-Bornemisza
Art Contemporary Collection, Vienna
→ P. 134

Sounds Like Isolation to Me

n.d., acetate, cardboard, ink, linen, magnetic tape, oil, paper,
sheet metal, sound, video, wire, wood, dimensions variable
Thyssen-Bornemisza Art Contemporary Collection, Vienna
→ P. 164

Biographies

Mario García Torres was born in 1975 in Monclova, Mexico, and currently lives and works in Mexico City. He received his BFA from the Universidad de Monterrey in 1998 and his MFA from the California Institute of the Arts, Valencia, in 2005. García Torres's work responds to and complicates the legacies of conceptual art and institutional critique, using film, photography, slide projection, sound, text, and video to debunk modernist myths, deconstruct art-world icons, and reveal the contingent nature of supposedly universal truths. He often deploys storytelling, reenactment, and reportage as strategies to uncover (hidden) histories and narratives embedded in archives, sites, and places, thereby highlighting the limitations of factual evidence and the agency of historical records and objects. Solo exhibitions of his work have taken place at TBA21, Vienna (2016); Museo Rufino Tamayo, Mexico City (2016); Museum of Modern Art, Fort Worth, Texas (2015); Pérez Art Museum Miami (2015); Hammer Museum, Los Angeles (2014); Museo Nacional Centro de Arte Reina Sofía, Madrid (2010); Kunsthalle Zürich (2008); and Stedelijk Museum, Amsterdam (2007). He has also participated in such international exhibitions as Manifesta 11, Zurich (2016); the Berlin Biennale (2014); the Mercosul Biennial, Porto Alegre (2013); documenta 13, Kassel Germany (2012); the 29th São Paulo Bienal (2010); and the 52nd Venice Biennale (2007).

Armen Avanessian studied philosophy and political science in Vienna and Paris. After completing his dissertation in literature, he worked at the Freie Universität Berlin from 2007 to 2014. He was previously a visiting fellow in the German departments at Columbia University and Yale University and a visiting professor at various art academies in Europe and the United States. He is editor-at-large at Merve Verlag, Berlin. In 2012 he founded the bilingual research platform Speculative Poetics, including a series of events, translations, and publications: www.spekulative-poetik.de. Recent monographs include *Irony and the Logic of Modernity* (Berlin: De Gruyter, 2015); *Speculative Drawing* (with Andreas Töpfer; Berlin: Sternberg, 2014); *Present Tense: A Poetics* (with Anke Hennig; London: Bloomsbury, 2015); *Metanoia: Ontologie der Sprache* (with Anke Hennig; Berlin: Merve, 2014; English forthcoming from Bloomsbury, 2017); *Überschreiben: Ethik des Wissens–Poetik der Existenz* (Berlin: Merve, 2015; English forthcoming from Sternberg, 2017); and *Miamification* (forthcoming).

Daniel Garza-Usabiaga is an independent curator and the artistic director of Zona Maco, Mexico City. Previously he was a curator at the Museo de Arte Moderno and head curator at the Museo Universitario del Chopo, both Mexico City. He is the author of *Mathias Goeritz and Emotional Architecture: A Critical Review (1952–1968)* (Mexico City: Vanilla Planifolia, 2012) and the founder of NIXON, a nonprofit exhibition space in Mexico City. He earned his master's and doctorate in art history and theory at the University of Essex, and later he did a postdoc at the Instituto de Investigaciones Estéticas, UNAM, Mexico City.

Carl Michael von Hausswolff is a sound artist, photographer, and curator who lives and works in Stockholm. Since the end of the 1970s Hausswolff has worked as a composer, using the tape recorder as his main instrument, and as a conceptual visual artist working with performance art, light and sound installations, and photography. He is also a conductor and the curator of the sound installation collective Freq_Out.

Anke Hennig is a theorist of 21ˢᵗ century
literature and visual culture. Currently she is
visiting professor for media theory at University
of the Arts, Berlin, and she teaches at Central
Saint Martins, University of the Arts, London.
She chairs the international research group
Retro-Formalism (www.retroformalism.net) and
in cooperation with Armen Avanessian concep-
tualized the transnational research platform
Speculative Poetics (www.spekulative-poetik.de).
She holds a PhD from the Peter Szondi Institute
of Comparative Literature at the Freie Universität
Berlin and has been a Fulbright Fellow at New
York University. She is the author of *Sowjetische
Kinodramaturgie: Konfliktlinien zwischen Literatur
und Film in der Sowjetunion der 1930er Jahre*
(Berlin: Vorwerk 8, 2010) and, with Armen
Avanessian, is coauthor of *Present Tense: A Poetics*
(London: Bloomsbury, 2015) and *Metanoia:
Ontologie der Sprache* (Berlin: Merve, 2014;
English forthcoming from Bloomsbury, 2017).

Chus Martínez is the head of the Art Institute
of the FHNW Academy of Art and Design in
Basel. She has been the chief curator at
El Museo del Barrio, New York; head of depart-
ment for documenta 13; and a member of Core
Agent Group. She was previously chief curator
at Museu d'Art Contemporani de Barcelona;
director of the Frankfurter Kunstverein; and
artistic director of Sala Rekalde, Bilbao (2002–5).
Martínez curated a film installation by Albert
Serra for the Catalan Pavilion at the 56ᵗʰ Venice
Biennale (2015) and curated the National Pavilion
of Cyprus for the 51ˢᵗ edition. She served as a
curatorial adviser for the Carnegie International
(2008) and the 29ᵗʰ Bienal de São Paulo (2010).
Most recently, she curated *The Metabolic Age*
(2015) at the Museo de Arte Latinoamericano
de Buenos Aires; *Undisturbed Solitude* (2016) at
Kunsthaus Hamburg; and *Idiosyncrasy: Anchovies
Dream of an Olive Mausoleum* (2017) at the Centro
de Ártes Visuales Fundación Helga de Alvear,
Caceres, Spain. She is currently preparing a
project for the Stiftung Skulpturenpark, Cologne,
and an exhibition for Castello di Rivoli, Turin.
She is the author of *Club Univers* (Berlin: Sternberg,
2016), a selection of texts on total inclusion.

Cory Scozzari is a curator and artist. He is an
assistant curator at Thyssen-Bornemisza Art
Contemporary. He was a founding member and
codirector of Jupiter Woods, London/Vienna,
from 2014 to 2016 and is the founding director
of Cordova, Vienna. He received his BFA in
photography from Savannah College of Art
and Design in Savannah, Georgia, in 2010 and
an MFA in curating at Goldsmiths, University
of London, in 2015. His recent projects as an
independent curator include *Carlos Reyes: Fashion
Café* and *Emily Jones: News from Nowhere* at
Cordova, Vienna.

Eva Wilson is a writer and curator based in
Berlin and London and is currently working on
a doctoral thesis at Freie Universität Berlin and
the Warburg Institute, London, researching the
concept of virtuality and the virtual image in the
nineteenth century. She was an assistant curator
at TBA21, director of the Schinkel Pavillon,
Berlin, and is currently an editor for documenta
14. Exhibitions include *A pudding that endless
screw agglomerates* (with works by Tomek Baran,
Pauline Beaudemont, and Nicolas Deshayes)
and the group show *That Time* in Kópavogur
and Reykjavík, Iceland, as part of Cycle Music
and Art Festival, both 2016. She has contributed
to numerous magazines and anthologies and
has edited several books and other publications,
among them *Ragnar Kjartansson: The Visitors*
(The Vinyl Factory, 2016). With Adam Gibbons
she coedited the forthcoming series " "
(quotationmarkquotationmark) featuring conversations with artists (including Becky Beasley,
Paul Chan and Badlands Unlimited, James Hoff,
and Olaf Nicolai).

Daniela Zyman is chief curator at Thyssen-
Bornemisza Art Contemporary in Vienna.
Between 1995 and 2001 she served as curator
and chief curator at the MAK—Austrian Museum
of Applied Arts / Contemporary Art in Vienna
and was a founding member of the MAK Center
for Art and Architecture at the Schindler House
in Los Angeles, which she directed for several
years. Between 2000 and 2003 she was artistic
director of Künstlerhaus, Vienna, and A9 forum
transeuropa at Museumsquartier, Vienna.
She has read critical theory at the University
of Applied Arts for several years, has written
and edited numerous books, and contributed
essays to catalogues and international journals.

About Thyssen-Bornemisza Art Contemporary

Founded in 2002 by Francesca von Habsburg in Vienna, Thyssen-Bornemisza Art Contemporary (TBA21) represents the fourth generation of the Thyssen family's commitments to the arts. After more than fifteen years of collecting, commissioning projects, and engaged exhibition practice, TBA21 has established a highly respected collection of more than seven hundred contemporary artworks in the field of new media, including film, video, light, sound and mixed-media installations, sculpture, painting, photography, and performance. TBA21's unique collection is the result of its ongoing commitment to commissioning and disseminating numerous art projects, including multimedia installations, sound compositions, endurance performances and contemporary architecture. This has led to its pioneering reputation in the art world. The foundation sustains a far-reaching regional and international orientation through a number of collaborations with other cultural partners around the world, and explores modes of presentation that are intended to provoke and broaden the way viewers perceive and experience art. In 2015 Francesca von Habsburg decided to dedicate the foundation's ongoing program to becoming an agent of change by focusing on the complexities and urgencies of the age of the Anthropocene, as well as today's pressing challenges caused by climate change, with a special focus on marine ecosystems.

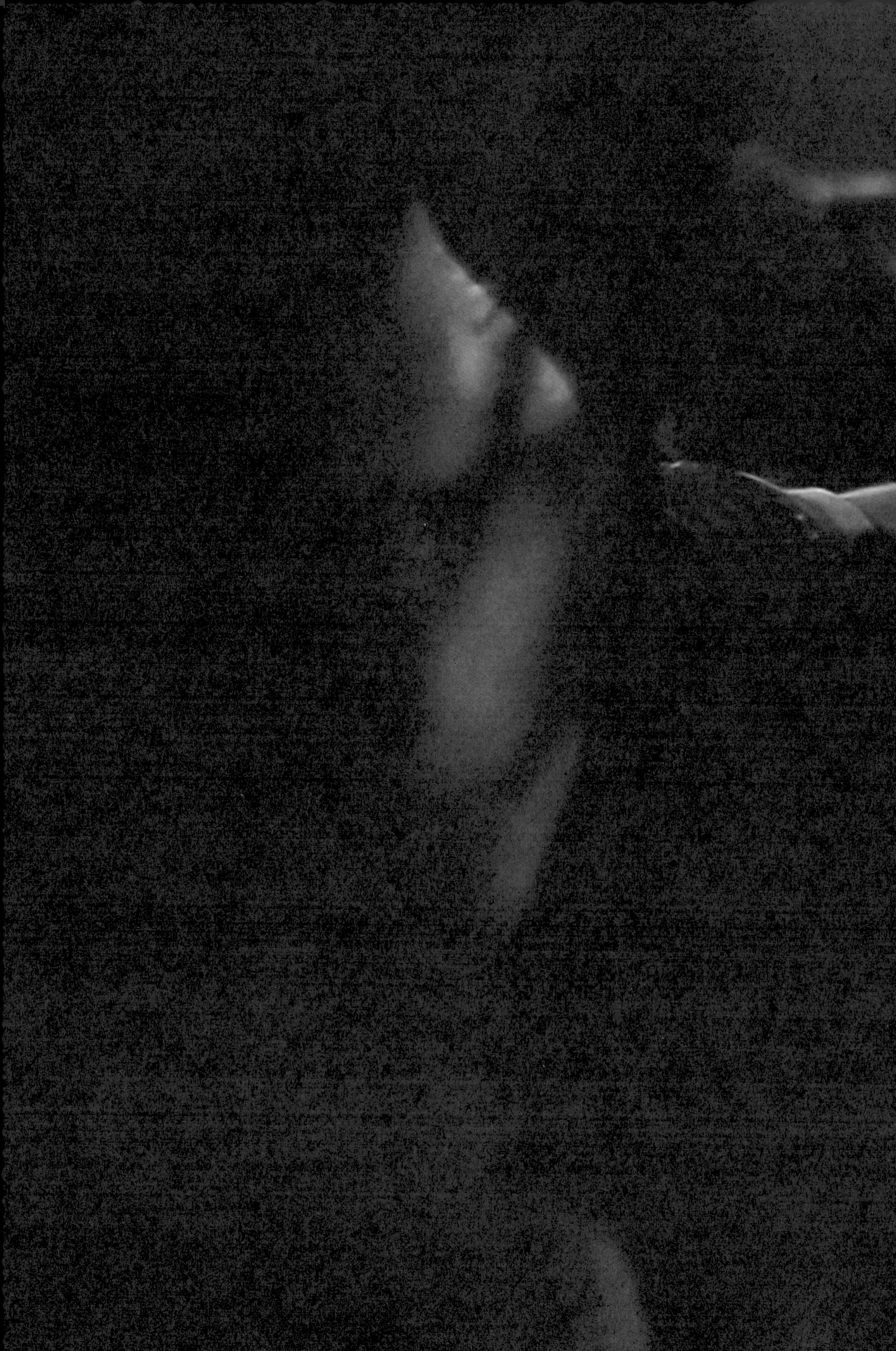

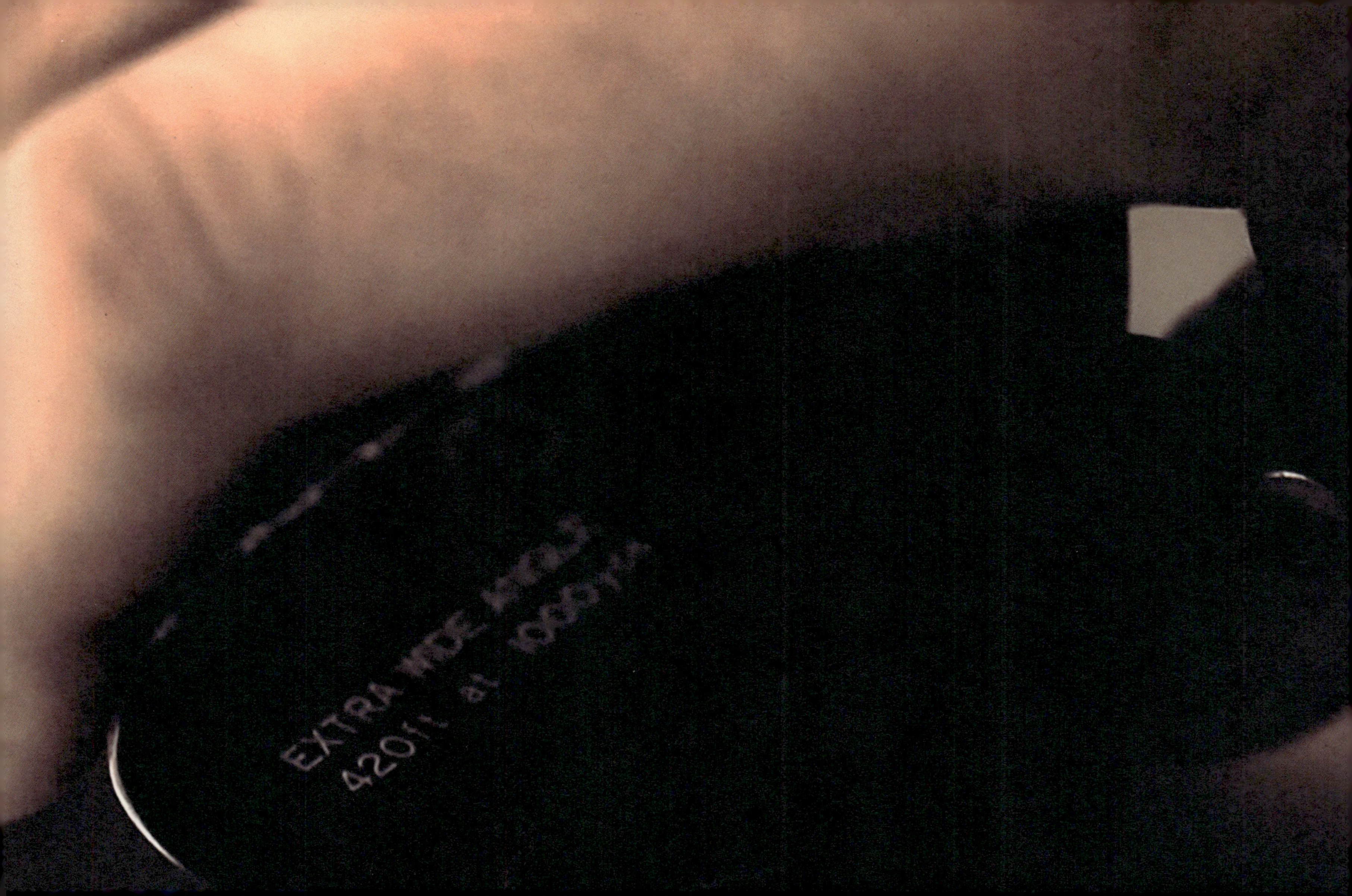

EXTRA WIDE WORLD
4201

Mario García Torres
An Arrival Tale
June 17–November 20, 2016
Thyssen-Bornemisza
Art Contemporary—Augarten

Chairwoman
Francesca von Habsburg

Curator
Daniela Zyman

Assistant Curator
Cory Scozzari

Collection Management
Simone Sentall, Andrea Hofinger,
Elizabeth Stevens

Project Architect
Philipp Krummel

Audio & Video
Markus Taxacher

Video Translation
Rafaat Alhashimy, Ghifar Al Darkazanly,
Ibrahim Al Bayati, Tawab Baran, Milad
Wasil, Milad Amiry, Akbar Muratov,
Tahajud Alghrabi

Exhibition and Visitor Service
Markus Schlüter, Philipp Bauer,
Philipp Kolla, Clemens Rettenbacher
(Educational Program), Ziva Drvaric,
Christina Gruber, Anna Schmoll,
Lisa Slawitz, Nadia Brandstätter,
David Weidinger

Art Handling, Technicians
Valentin Aigner, Stephan Kobatsch,
Clemens Leuschner, Bianca Pedrina,
Stephan Riedel, Stephen Zepke, Wolfgang
Prohaska, Robert Siwiec, Herbert Fürst

Conservation
Alexandra Grausam, Melanie Nief,
Almut Schilling

Administration
Karin Berger, Azra Demir-Ramovic,
Barbara Hörhan, Susanne Janetzki,
Claudia Naue, Paulina Sosna,
Florence Wehinger

Curator ephemeropteræ
Boris Ondreička

Head of Publications
Eva Ebersberger

Media and Communication
Sophie Bayerlein, Gérard Rabara,
Mariana Yanez Rodriguez, Manufaktur
für neue Medien – Istvan Szilagyi & Rocío
Burchard, Ana Berlin Communications,
Pickles PR – Juan Sanchez

Catering
Die AU Café / Restaurant

TBA21—Academy
Markus Reymann, Georg Eder,
Stefanie Hessler, Jens Radke

Mario García Torres's Studio
Gerardo Villar, Arturo R. Jiménez

**Mario García Torres and
Thyssen-Bornemisza Art Contemporary
would like to thank:**
Jan Mot, Brussels, neugerriemschneider,
Berlin; joségarcía ,mx, Mexico City; Taka
Ishii, Tokyo; the Green light Team; Afghan
Translation Service. And for contributing
with the photographs taken in Baghdad:
Ayman al-Amiri; Jamal Penjweny;
Furat al Jamil, Iraq Office Director, Ruya
Foundation for Contemporary Culture in
Iraq; Tamara Chalabi, Ruya Foundation.

**Thyssen-Bornemisza Art Contemporary
wishes to extend special thanks to its
generous sponsor.**
As one of the leading insurance groups
in Central and Eastern Europe, the Vienna
Insurance Group and its main share holder
Wiener Städtische Versicherungsverein
clearly perceive its social responsibilities
and have been reliable sponsoring
partners for Thyssen-Bornemisza Art
Contemporary and other cultural projects
for many years. Numerous museums and
galleries have insured their collections
with Vienna Insurance Group. The main
objective for cooperating with cultural
institutions is to promote the international
exchange in the field of arts and culture.

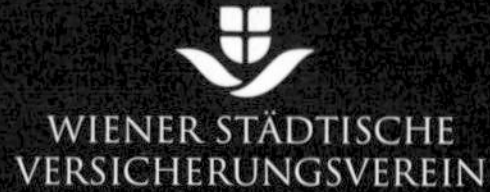
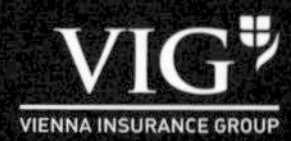